MILE HIGH MADNESS

MILE HIGH MADNESS

A Year with
the
Colorado Rockies

BOB KRAVITZ

Foreword by DON BAYLOR

TIMES 𝕋 BOOKS

RANDOM HOUSE

Library of Congress Cataloging-in-Publication Data
Kravitz, Bob
Mile high madness : a year with the Colorado Rockies / Bob
Kravitz : foreword by Don Baylor.
            p.   cm.
Published simultaneously in Canada.
Includes bibliographical references and index.
ISBN 0-8129-6359-8
1. Colorado Rockies (Baseball team)   I. Title.
GV875.C78K73   1994
796.357'64'0978883—dc20   94-2423

Manufactured in the United States of America

9   8   7   6   5   4   3   2

First Edition

This is for my beautiful wife, Cathy,
who wouldn't let me quit. Ever.

FOREWORD
by Don Baylor

AFTER I BECAME the rookie manager of a rookie team, I kept hearing people talk about the size of the Rocky Mountain region and how the entire region would be Rockies fans. But I didn't really know what they were talking about until I was in Salt Lake City in January 1993 on our first preseason publicity "caravan."

I was at the Delta Center watching the Lakers play Utah. With me were Rockies PR director Mike Swanson and two of our new players, David Nied and Eric Wedge. As we were walking out of the stands at the end of the game, a man turned to his wife and said, "There's the manager of our baseball team." That stopped me cold. I said, "What? Where am I?" I had never been in Salt Lake City before in my life. Salt Lake is quite a distance away from Denver, but the word about the Rockies had spread.

Maybe I shouldn't have been surprised. Every day brought a new example of how eagerly people followed developments with the Rockies. The day after I was named manager, Mike Swanson wanted to take a picture of me with the Continental Divide at my back. We drive up to Boulder, up to the top of a mountain, and there's snow all around us. I'm standing on this cliff in my baseball uniform, posing for the photographer. People are driving from the mountains in their four-wheel-drive Jeeps, and when they make this turn, they see this big black guy standing on a mountain in a Rockies uniform. It can only be one person because the announcement was the day before, and here I am standing with the Continental Divide at my back. People are stopping their cars to pose with me and take pictures.

It was all very strange and unusual, but that was only the beginning. The entire 1993 season turned out to be unusual, but in the most wonderful way. When four and a half million fans go to one ballpark in one season, you know it's different. They talk about Rocky Mountain fever for sports, but no thermometer could have recorded the temperature of the Rockies fans!

On draft day they had 20,000 people at Currigan Hall watching the draft unfold, televised from New York. We flew Andres Galarraga and David Nied to Denver, so the two of them were there at Currigan and they had no idea what to expect. When they said the Rockies had won the coin flip and selected David Nied and David walked out there, the place just went crazy. Galarraga got a standing ovation, too. "Cat" and David told me later that nothing like that had ever happened to them.

During spring training, so many people came in from Colorado, you would not believe it. The city of Tucson rolled out the red carpet for us. The first day I went out with the pitchers and catchers and ran into twenty or more TV cameras! *For pitchers and catchers*—that never happens.

When we went to New York to start the season, we got off the bus and walked into the lobby of our hotel. Ninety-five percent of our front office was there, including all of our owners, and everybody was at the escalator cheering as we were coming in. Very seldom are you cheered in the lobby of the Grand Hyatt.

Unfortunately, we lost the first two games, but that didn't change anything in Denver. We didn't have a chance to relax like other teams do. Whereas they might have to go to a luncheon, we had a parade through town with more than 20,000 people there. Then we had a luncheon, and 3,000 people were *there*. It was unbelievable! It was mayhem. They didn't care that we were 0-2. We went to a workout right after that and had about 5,000 fans at Mile High Stadium—for a workout!

The people just wanted to be a part of something that they

had wanted for a long time. There were people who left major cities and moved to Denver and said, "What, no big-league baseball?" I ran into people from Baltimore, Chicago, St. Louis and a lot of other cities that had teams. They had been in Denver 10, 12 years and had no baseball. I got letters from fathers, from mothers, saying now we can finally take our kids to a major-league baseball game.

When you have crowds that continue to come out and support you after being drummed 18–1 and 17–2, you have to love it. But whatever we did, they came and it was exciting. It was exciting when we put on a squeeze bunt. They loved that. The first month of the season I probably did it four or five times, and the fans thought it was one of the greatest things they had ever seen. We were their team.

Before we got to Denver, I didn't know how the players would respond. I told them in spring training what they would be in for: more autographs than they'd ever signed in their lives; doing lots of off-the-field things. You're brand-new in town, I said. We're not in competition with the Broncos, but we have to make a good showing.

I guess we did things right because the fans stayed with us all year, from 80,227 for our first game at home to 70,069 for the last. People wrote us letters congratulating us and saying they couldn't wait until next year. Two days after the season was over, we had a "Sports Spectacular" in which the Broncos, the Nuggets and the Rockies signed autographs. Our line went completely out the door and around the corner, and the Broncos and the Nuggets were probably saying, "There's a new team in town now." Before, they had gotten all the play. One man said, "Well, it's 162 days to spring training." These are fans who appreciated what they saw and wanted to come back.

They're in for the long haul, but they expect a lot more now. We want to give it to them. As a manager, I want to improve and continue to improve. And I know the dedicated employees of the Rockies' organization and the 4,483,350 fans will help me do that. I accept the challenge.

ACKNOWLEDGMENTS

MY DEEPEST APPRECIATION and love to my wife, Cathy; to my oldest daughter, Michelle, whose 18-month-old typing hand is responsible for any and all typos; and to our newest and littlest Rockies fan, Dana Marie, who was born about the same time as this book. Heartfelt thanks and love to my folks, Dick and Edith, who still can't get over the fact that Colorado got a team and Tampa–St. Pete didn't; my brother, Gary, whose Cubbies just may win a Series before the Rockies—but don't count on it—and his wife, Ellen; to my grandparents, Murray and Rose, the two best people on the face of the planet; to my in-laws, Dick and Betsy, whose Mets will definitely win 60 games this year, and to my brothers- and sisters-in-law (Doug, Steve, P.J., Dick, Sue and Bizy), whose addled rendition of "Silent Night" will not have me converting anytime soon.

Many thanks to Matt Bialer, who got the ball rolling; to Paul Golob, for his deft and steady editing hand and his unflagging support; to all the good people at Times Books; and to Gary Williams, for his great help in preparing this book (welcome to parenthood . . . sucker).

Thanks to Barry Forbis, who supported and pushed the idea from the very beginning and gave me the freedom necessary to complete the project; to Kevin "Moose" Huhn, a wonderful guy with a bad life; and to Tracy Ringolsby and Jack Etkin, the two hardest-working men in journalism. Thanks to the guys who kept me company and indulged my moods and late-night beer runs: Mike Klis (head of the Jeremy Roenick Fan Club), Barney Hutchinson, Jim Armstrong, Jerry Crasnick and Woody Paige, who is not mentioned again in this book. Thanks to the electronic-media types: golfmate Wayne Hagin (not to be confused with Walter Hagen), Jeff Kingery, Mark Goldsmith, Rob Menschel, Ingrid Serra, Duane Kuiper, Charlie Jones, Ron Zappolo, John Keating (we'll always have Tucson) and a good friend, Les Shapiro. Thanks to the staff of the *Rocky Mountain News* for giving me the help and time to complete this book, and especially Mark Wolf, who often had to change his schedule to accommodate mine, and always did so with unfailing grace and professionalism. Thanks also to Tom Kelsey, for organizing the photographs. Thanks to Sue Warner, travel agent extraordinaire, who made sure I didn't end up in Zagreb; and to Chip Verrill, who made me understand the difference between a hard drive and a megabyte.

Thanks to the Rockies' public-relations department, specifically Mike Swanson, Coley Brannon (ranked as the 18th most likely to succeed by the high school class of 1988) and Karin Bearnarth.

And a special thanks to the Rockies' front office, support staff, players and coaches who were unfailingly helpful and accommodating despite the steady diet of losses early in the season. In particular, thanks to Don Baylor for his help and guidance through the long year.

Finally, a note of gratitude to the fans of Colorado and the entire Rocky Mountain region, who came by the millions and gave me something very special to write about. This is about you as much as it is about the team.

CONTENTS

MILE HIGH MADNESS

1

Three Men and a Baby

THE OLD MAN came early, as had been his habit for so many years. Bob Howsam, Sr., was one of those baseball people who could derive as much joy and information from infield practice as most folks could from a twi-night doubleheader. He sat in the fifth row of stands, thinking private thoughts, gazing down at the manicured diamond of Tucson's Hi Corbett Field.

It was 9:25 on the morning of February 19, 1993, and a strangely chilly Arizona spring was finally giving in to the demands of baseball. The skies were clearing. The sun was making a cameo, as if on cue.

"It's almost here," Howsam told a friend, glancing at his watch. He smiled. "Almost."

Five minutes until the Colorado Rockies, an expansion team, *his* expansion team, took the field for the very first time. Five minutes and the frustration, longing and waiting would be over. Five minutes and a crazy dream would be realized.

Howsam, who had become a kind of consultant emeritus to the ownership group, shifted in his seat, checking his watch every few seconds. He brushed his hand through his wavy, white hair, his stevedore arms still apparent some fifty years after he'd served as a navy test pilot during World War II.

Five minutes was taking forever.

And then, at 9:30—right on time—Howsam's face brightened. He looked down at the Rockies' dugout and saw what he had been waiting to see for more than 30 years—Colorado's major-league baseball team. First there was veteran pitcher Bryn Smith. Then there was young lefty pitcher Butch Henry. And manager Don Baylor. In all, 36 pitchers, six catchers and three others, clip-clopping up the wooden dugout steps, gloves and bats and balls in hand, all of them wearing the team's black, silver and purple uniforms.

"There," he said, beaming with paternal love. "The Colorado Rockies. How about that? I've got chills up and down my spine, you know? This is a little like the way I feel when I stand up and sing the national anthem. Just chills, everywhere."

Of course, it was too much to ask for these players to understand their unique role in Rocky Mountain history. Sure, they knew they were part of the first expansion since 1977, knew they were part of a club bringing baseball to a huge geographical area that had never had a major-league team, an area residents of the region referred to as "The Time Zone Baseball Forgot." But what did they truly know, or even care, about Denver? These were young men looking for employment, a chance to resurrect their careers. For most of them, Denver was a snowy western outpost where the Broncos played football. They did not know, could not know—not the way Howsam, the 74-year-old patriarch of Denver baseball, knew.

"We've been waiting for this day—what?—32, 33 years?" he asked, fully knowing the answer. "We've been so close so many times. We thought we had the A's. We thought we had the Giants. The list goes on. And now, to see this . . . I've been going to spring training now some 25 years in the majors and another dozen in the minors. But watching this spring training, the first day of the Colorado Rockies, this is my biggest thrill."

Down on the field, the team engaged in the most rudimentary

drills—just like every other major-league team, including their expansion mates, the Florida Marlins. They played catch, or, as the modern parlance goes, "long toss." They ran sprints. They played pepper. Little League stuff. For Howsam, the man who built the Big Red Machine, the dominating Cincinnati Reds teams of the 1970s, this was the most beautiful exhibition of baseball yet.

He was there at the beginning of Denver's quest for big-league baseball—or quite close to it—as the owner of the minor-league Denver Bears from 1947 until 1961. And now, he was sitting in the stands, the morning sun beating down on his rosy cheeks, seeing his labors of love coming to fruition.

"I can still remember the day when we lost the Bears," said Howsam, remembering back to the day in 1961 when the expenses became too burdensome and his family sold the club to Gerald and Allan Phipps. "That was one of the most difficult days of my life. I just sat alone in old Bears Stadium and I was devastated. I felt like we had tried so hard to do right by Denver and bring major-league baseball to the area, and now we were out of the whole process. It felt very empty."

Howsam's face brightened. "But as I sit here today, it was all worth it. We helped build the foundation that made this possible."

Indeed, Denver is not an arriviste baseball town. It boasts a long and storied baseball history, going back to 1886, when a team called the Denvers won the first Western League title. For the next 60 years, baseball was an off-and-on phenomenon, with teams called the Denvers, the Skyscrapers, the Grizzlies and the Bears dotting the landscape, boasting players like Joe Tinker—of Tinker-to-Evers-to-Chance fame—and Charles "Babe" Adams during the early years. Denver lost its Western League franchise, though, in 1932 because the Depression was at hand, and the easternmost teams in the league found it too costly to travel to both Denver and Pueblo, Colorado. The teams were dropped, and Denver did not see the Western League again until 1947.

Enter Howsam.

And enter "The Governor." Edwin C. Johnson not only spent

34 years in public office serving the state of Colorado, including a term as the state's chief executive, but also happened to be Howsam's father-in-law. After World War II, Howsam followed The Governor to Washington and dipped his toe into politics. He found himself singularly uninspired. But The Governor had another passion beyond politics: baseball. He was helping to revive the old Western League, and he wanted Howsam to go to Denver for a six-month stint as the league's executive secretary. "I was thrilled when he asked me about the assignment," said Howsam. "Politics just wasn't in my blood."

But baseball was. Soon after joining the league office, Howsam, his brother Earl and his father, Lee, bought the Denver Bears. Their first decision was to move the club out of miserable Merchants Park—"Another few years, the termites would have consumed the whole thing," said longtime Denver baseball reporter Frank Haraway—and into spanking new Bears Stadium, which still stands today as Mile High Stadium. The new edifice was the jewel of the Western League, and the city responded in 1949 by setting a minor-league attendance record.

"The whole time we owned the Bears, even when we were Class A, we were always thinking about the major leagues," said Howsam. "I can still remember talking to the architect, Buckminster Fuller, about building a roof over Bears Stadium so we could be ready for major-league baseball. I've always felt Denver deserved a major-league club. I used to tell people, 'Look at our attendance. Look at our location.' But for whatever reasons, politics, things like that, we didn't get it for the longest time."

It was not for a lack of trying. By the early 1950s, the country was in the midst of great changes, buoyed by postwar euphoria and rising incomes. Baseball, which rarely kept apace of the times, was changing too. After a half-century of the status quo, franchises were shifting. In 1955, the Philadelphia Athletics moved to Kansas City, leaving Kansas City's Triple-A team, a powerful New York Yankees farm club, without a home. Howsam bought the club. Suddenly, Denver was a Triple-A town. And the Bears' roster boasted names like Ryne Duren, Tony Kubek, Bobby Richardson, Ralph Terry and a manager named Ralph Houk. They were great teams, but for Howsam, they were hard times.

The problem, primarly, was television. Why would any baseball fan pay to watch Triple-A ball when he could get the major leagues for free on national television? Finding himself with rising costs and flat attendance, Howsam soon came to the conclusion that if he could not beat major-league baseball, he would try to join it.

"I had read a magazine article by Branch Rickey and he talked about expansion and the possibility of forming a rival league," said Howsam. "I had known him for years when I was in the Western League and he was working for the Pirates. So I talked it over with my father-in-law and we decided to call the man."

The meetings produced results. Howsam, Rickey and others decided to form the Continental League, with teams in Atlanta, Buffalo, Dallas, Denver, Houston, Minneapolis, New York and Toronto. By 1959, Rickey and his group had put together a minor-league feeder system, signed players and scheduled games.

"The idea was we would be Triple A for three years, then become major league," Howsam said. "We weren't doing it to force anybody's hand. We just felt there were so many deserving cities that could support major-league baseball. We were all ready to go. But baseball stepped in."

Baseball, as in Major League Baseball. Ordinarily, the big dogs could have cared less about the Continental League. They had a monopoly. They were exempt from federal antitrust laws. They were golden. Except for one problem: At the time, Congress was questioning why baseball required that cherished antitrust exemption. Suddenly, the major-league powers thought it might look good if they accommodated the Continental League. And so they relented, the American League expanding to Los Angeles and Washington in 1961 (with the original Washington Senators franchise relocating to Minneapolis) and the National League accepting the Continental League's New York and Houston franchises. Ultimately, the major leagues promised, they would expand to all the Continental League towns, including Denver.

"Almost 30 years later, they had added all those cities to the major leagues," Howsam said. "Except Buffalo and Denver. All these years, I kept hoping. I wondered, too, but I kept hoping."

After selling the Bears in 1961, Howsam himself moved into the major leagues. By 1964, he was the St. Louis Cardinals' general manager, overseeing a team that would win three pennants in five years. And in the seventies, he was the architect of the Big Red Machine. Now he is retired, with homes in Arizona and Colorado. On the night Denver received its long-awaited baseball team, Bob and Janet Howsam were in their home in Glenwood Springs, on the western slope of the Rocky Mountains, and celebrated with a bottle of champagne.

"Look at those kids," he said now, pointing to a group running short sprints on the dewy outfield grass. His voice softened. "Wonderful," he said wistfully. "Isn't it?"

EIGHTEEN MONTHS.

Eighteen exhilarating, frustrating, fast-food eating, ass-kicking, mind-bending months. Rockies general manager Bob Gebhard, a fellow who is the human equivalent of an unmade bed, reached for another in an interminable line of cigarettes, pulled deeply and considered what he and his inner circle had been through.

"Hell," he said, laughing.

But as he sat in the Rockies' dugout and looked out onto the field, watching *his* team, *his* handiwork, he knew this to be true, too: He would not have traded the experience of building an expansion franchise from scratch for any job in the universe.

"I can't tell you how many general managers, many of whom are very successful, have said, 'Hey, Geb, what a great opportunity. That's something I've always wanted to do,' " he said. "Andy MacPhail told me the only job he'd leave the Twins for would be expansion. Because you get to set your own standards. You don't inherit somebody else's problems." He paused. "It also keeps you awake at night," he said, smiling.

By the end of Gebhard's 18 months in baseball purgatory, his sleeplessness had become something of a standing joke. A reporter would see Gebhard in the morning and the dialogue would remain the same.

REPORTER: "Morning."

GEBHARD: "Morning."

REPORTER: "How'd you sleep?"

GEBHARD: "Had two 45-minute rests in there. You know, 45 minutes, wake up, have a cigarette, write some notes . . . 45 minutes, wake up, have a cigarette, write more stuff down."

He came to the Rockies in September 1991 with a reputation as a down-and-dirty, hands-on "ball guy." Here was a man with two education degrees and a top front-office pedigree, having worked five years as MacPhail's chief assistant with the Minnesota Twins. But style was not his style. This was a man who grew up playing the game, first as a kid in Minnesota, then as a baseball player at the University of Iowa. He pitched three seasons in the majors, with the Twins and Montreal Expos. He was a player/coach in the Expos' organization in 1974 and 1975 before becoming the Expos' minor-league field director and pitching coach.

"You know when he's happiest?" a friend said of Gebhard. "When he's pitching batting practice."

He was the right fit for the Rockies for a number of reasons. Gebhard had cut his teeth on the Expos and Twins, two organizations short on dollars but long on scouting and developmental acumen. While the Rockies would ultimately prove to be an incredible money-maker, they approached their inaugural season with a small-market mind-set. They figured that, with the small market plus the $95-million expansion fee *plus* a full year without national television money, they would have to play it close to the vest.

The philosophy was simple: Build from within. Spend wisely. Stretch a dollar. Gebhard had had experience in Minnesota, having helped build the 1991 World Series champions with low-level free agents like Chili Davis and Mike Pagliarulo. The Rockies would move in a similar direction.

He had been hired in September, but with the agreement that he could remain with the Twins until the end of their season. This was, after all, a team he had helped build. So when Gene Larkin's sacrifice fly scored Dan Gladden in the 10th inning of the seventh game of the most remarkable World Series in recent memory, Gebhard was torn. He joined the raucous clubhouse celebration for a time, lit up a celebratory cigarette and swilled some champagne. And then he walked outside the Metrodome on a cool, wet night, his son by his side, and cried.

Gebhard arrived in Denver a day later with close to nothing, just some forms he'd taken from the Twins' offices (with their blessings, of course), some stationery with Rockies letterhead and a couple of hundred pages of notes he'd made during those many sleepless nights.

A skeleton crew began to take shape those first few weeks. He imported Chris Rice, his administrative assistant, from Minnesota. He hired Pat Daugherty from the Expos' organization, a rowdy leprechaun of a man, as his director of scouting. His assistant general manager was Randy Smith, whose father, Tal, had been the architect of the 1962 expansion Houston Colt .45's. And he brought in Paul Egins, a young Atlanta Braves employee who had ascended the corporate ladder, as assistant director of scouting and player development.

"I started out keeping a diary of each day," Gebhard said later. "What was said, the great arguments we had, but after a couple of weeks, I just didn't have the time or energy. By the time I got to bed, I was brain-dead. I will tell you this, though. The very first entry into that diary was, 'Are there only 24 hours to a day?' "

Often, the answer was no. The task seemed hopelessly daunting.

"There was incredible excitement in those offices, but we were exhausted, too," said Gebhard. "We'd go back to our apartments eleven o'clock or midnight, we'd be back by 6:30. The thing that was hard was Opening Day seemed like it was 16 years away. We had to find a way to keep everybody geared up. I mean, we were skidding around in the foothills and that peak looked so far away.

"When I would finally get to bed at night and think about the big picture, knowing where we wanted to be five years down the road, where we had to be at the start of spring training and then Opening Day, yeah, it was overwhelming. The only way we could deal with it was to break it down and identify target dates —the June amateur draft, the expansion draft in November and then Opening Day."

Gebhard had spoken with two old friends, John McHale, Sr., and Jim Fanning, who had helped build the Montreal Expos from the ground up, and to Tal Smith. But Gebhard knew, too, that times had changed since the last expansion in 1977. The financial landscape of the game had changed most dramatically, with free agency and arbitration forcing the smaller-market clubs to scramble for scraps.

"There was no how-to guide on how to build an expansion team," said Gebhard. "Even if there was one out there, it would have been outdated. The game has changed so much. We had to write our own how-to guide as we went along."

Gebhard knew that the how-to guide could only be a rough draft, but the Rockies would have to live with their mistakes. No editing, no rewrites.

IT WAS 4:53 A.M. Don Baylor looked outside the window in his Tucson condominium and checked for rain. "Dry," he thought. "Finally." He had been waiting for this day most of his professional life, since the day he stepped onto the field in 1970 as a hot-shot Baltimore Orioles rookie, perhaps even longer. The rain, which had been pelting the desert Southwest for weeks, would not deny him this moment, the day of the Rockies' first-ever spring-training workout.

Don Baylor, manager.

Nothing, he would say, could ever sound so sweet.

"The most exciting thing for me, ever," Baylor said, sitting behind his desk in the renovated Hi Corbett Field clubhouse. "The seventh game of the World Series, you're standing all alone in the batter's box and that's special, but now I need these guys to help me be successful."

Baylor knew the score: He was not, by any stretch of the imagination, a typical manager—and for a lot of reasons.

For one, he is black, and would be joining a rather small fraternity of six minority managers, including his old friend Dusty Baker, the new manager of the San Francisco Giants.

Second, he was joining the expansion Rockies with absolutely no managerial experience. The top veteran managers are, by and large, former fringe players who quit the game early in their careers to hop the slow track to major-league managerial status. Tommy Lasorda. Jim Leyland. Sparky Anderson. Baylor, conversely, was an All-Star player, having toiled 17 full years for the Orioles, A's, Angels, Yankees, Red Sox and Twins. He quit the game after the 1988 season, taking his 1987 Twins World Series ring and his 1979 American League MVP trophy with him before moving on as a batting instructor in Milwaukee and then St. Louis.

Finally, expansion managers tend to be older, more experienced hands who have been on the managerial merry-go-round for years. They are men who are hired to be caretakers and teachers, company men who are willing to sublimate their egos and their desire to win for the chance to remain in the game. The conventional wisdom is you bring in an older manager, let him absorb the losses and regale the media with funny stories about the old days, before firing him four, five years down the line. Then you bring in the guy you really want and let him guide the team toward the playoffs.

The Rockies' unofficial list of candidates included a number of men deemed temperamentally suited to expansion baseball. Tom Trebelhorn, the former Milwaukee manager, had a reputation as a fine teacher of young players. Bill Virdon, who'd been around the game since time immemorial, had impressed the Rockies' brass with his energy and knowledge. Russ Nixon, a veteran coach and a member of baseball's old-boy network, was another who knew the game and understood how to handle losing—he'd had plenty of practice managing bad teams. The list went on.

But there was one name that had stayed with Gebhard from the beginning, one he kept remarkably private despite all the media scrutiny. That was Don Baylor. Gebhard first met Baylor in 1987, when Baylor joined the Twins as a designated hitter and played a pivotal role during the club's World Series drive. What Gebhard saw was the same thing everyone else in baseball saw: a leader. Players came to Baylor. The media came to Baylor. He was disarmingly honest and painstakingly professional. If something had to be said, Baylor said it. If someone needed his butt kicked, Baylor kicked it.

Later, Gebhard would admit, "I told myself, 'If I ever got to this spot, I would pursue Don Baylor.' "

The irony is that Gebhard would be taking a risk with Baylor —he had no managerial experience, after all—and Gebhard is not known as a risk-taker. Conservative? Consider this: "I buy him shirts with a little color or a pattern, and he takes them right back to the store," said his wife, Nancy. "It's straight colors. White shirt. Navy jacket. Very conservative. I found it so out of character when he started talking about Don Baylor."

Gebhard had three requirements: He wanted a teacher (Baylor had been a very effective hitting instructor with the Brewers and Cardinals); he wanted someone who had a burning desire to win, even though this was an expansion team (Baylor had played on seven division winners and in three World Series. In 22 years as a player and coach, he had never been a member of a last-place team); and he wanted someone who could be patient (Uh, well, Baylor was working on it . . .).

When the day dawned and Gebhard and the grounds crew had finally swept some of the mud off the concourse, Baylor and the Rockies were ready. And a little bit nervous.

"We all came here by three different routes," Baylor told his team that first day. "Some by chance, some by choice and some by good fortune. . . . This is a unique opportunity for all of us because the Rocky Mountain region has been waiting more than 30 years for major-league baseball. You have a chance to become new heroes to the people in this region. . . . What I want from this team is to set a new standard for expansion teams. We'll focus on fundamentals and stamina, and we'll keep our expectations high. If you lower your expectations, that's how you'll play. There is nothing out there that says an expansion team has to lose a hundred games."

History, Baylor knew, was not on his side. None of the 10 previous expansion teams had avoided 90 losses, the average being 102. But the Rockies would be different. They would set goals. They would think of themselves as something other than an expansion team. Mind over matter. Privately, Baylor wanted the Rockies to eclipse the expansion record of the 1961 Los Angeles Angels, who went 70-91. The front-office people, folks like Gebhard and Smith, were thinking more realistically about 63 victories: 63 and 99. Avoid 100 losses. That would be a successful maiden season.

Baylor looked around the spanking-new clubhouse, gazed at the newly laundered practice tops and considered his players. Who were these guys? *Some by chance, some by choice, some by good fortune.* But Baylor knew this, too. There was a reason these players were available, whether through the expansion draft or through free agency: Other people didn't want them. These were drifters and castoffs, has-beens and never-weres. Some had confounded coaches and managers with an inability to turn talent into production. Others never had the talent to start with. Winning 70 games would be one hell of a trick.

Who were they?

At first base, Baylor had Andres Galarraga, the "Big Cat," the man he had personally tutored back into form during the latter stages of the previous season when the pair worked in St. Louis. Galarraga, once a Most Valuable Player candidate, had fallen on hard times and lost his swing and his confidence. The Rockies picked him up as a free agent because he was available and he was cheap.

The second baseman was Eric Young, a hard-nosed former

Rutgers football player whose purported defensive deficiences moved the Los Angeles Dodgers, the worst defensive team in modern history, to make him available for the expansion draft. He had unquestioned offensive skills, but could he catch the ball?

Shortstop Freddie Benavides was a fellow the scouts call a good "catch and throw guy," which essentially means he'll make the routine defensive play, but won't hit his weight. Which isn't much to begin with . . .

The steal of the expansion draft, though, was third baseman Charlie Hayes, who had batted .257 with 18 homers and 66 RBIs for the Yankees in 1992. A solid offensive and defensive player, Hayes brought with him another endearing characteristic: a relatively small contract. When the Rockies selected Hayes on draft day, Yankees general manager Gene Michael's face took on a sickly pallor, and he was besieged by outraged New York reporters. Word was The Boss had made the call, George Steinbrenner ordering that Hayes be left unprotected as he pursued free-agent Wade Boggs. "Somebody's head ought to roll for this," said one general manager at the expansion draft. Informed it was probably Steinbrenner's call, the GM smiled. "All the better," he said.

Baylor had left fielder Jerald Clark, a long, lean athlete whose career had been marked by offensive inconsistency. A good first half followed by a torporous second half. An unproductive first half followed by a hot-hitting second half. A guy who had never quite put it together.

In center field was Alex Cole, a mercurial sort who wore gold-rimmed designer glasses. The Cleveland Indians had been so overwhelmed by his hitting and base stealing in the latter part of the 1990 season that they moved the Cleveland Stadium fences back to take advantage of their speedy new star. Problem was, Cole flamed out. He had minimal baseball instincts and showed a strange inability to keep track of the number of outs. Once, Cole had caught a fly ball with a man on second and one out, only to drop his head and jog toward the dugout as the runner sped around third and came home.

Right field was reserved for Dante Bichette, obtained in a draft-day trade with the Milwaukee Brewers. He had strong hands, a rifle arm and a heavy-lidded look that left you wondering whether he was planning to join the rest of the human race on this planet anytime soon. Bichette was an enticing package, a good kid who cared about learning the game—but raw, very raw.

Behind the plate was Joe Girardi, the club's most cerebral player, an academic all-American and owner of an engineering degree from Northwestern. He could catch a nice game and handle a pitching staff and was blessed with a manager's grasp of the game. Hitting, well, that would be a bonus.

And Baylor had pitchers. Lots of them. There were 36 in all, by far the most at any spring-training site. But the numbers were deceptive. There had been a dearth of quality pitching *before* expansion came along, and now the talent base was truly depleted. With the exception of David Nied, the first player chosen in the expansion draft, these were pitchers other teams were content to lose.

The team of strangers sat and listened to the speeches, from principal owner Jerry McMorris, from Gebhard and from Baylor. And then they went around the room, introducing themselves like a bunch of shy schoolboys. Welcome to the quietest clubhouse in major-league history. Of course, it wouldn't stay that way forever.

"I feel like I've just been dropped off at kindergarten," said pitcher Butch Henry. "Except I don't think my mother will be picking me up today."

2

"Hi, My Name Is . . ."

ANDY ASHBY, a Rockies pitcher, and his wife, Tracy, were sitting at the bar at T.G.I. Friday's, the fern-laden bistro just across the parking lot from the team's spring-training hotel. Moments later, a teammate, pitcher Calvin Jones, entered the bar.

"I see you in the clubhouse but we've never met," Ashby said, extending a hand to Jones. "I'm Andy Ashby. This is my wife, Tracy."

"Calvin Jones," came the response. "Nice to meet you. Man, I need a drink bad."

"Bad day?" Tracy Ashby asked.

"I'm here two days, they steal my car right out of the parking lot," Jones said, shaking his head. "That's the second one I've had ripped off. My wife kept telling me, 'Calvin, there are some people driving around and around out there in the parking lot, you ought to check it out,' and I kept saying, 'It's nothing. I'm going to bed.' Get up the next morning, it's not there. I'm thinking, 'Hey, I wasn't drinking the night before, it's not like I forgot where I parked the car.' They just took it. Probably down in Mexico by now.''

Ashby ordered a couple of beers. ''You need these worse than we do,'' he told Jones, placing both bottles in front of him.

Jones had been born under a bad sign. His spring training started badly and only got worse. He not only lost his wheels but his arm was not cooperating either. He was 29 years old, a once-promising pitcher for the Seattle Mariners, and here he was, trying to salvage a career that had gone south rather quickly.

''Nice guy,'' one Rockies coach said. ''You hate to see it happen, but it happens to all of 'em. There's nothing left in that arm.''

The way Jones groused during the spring, you could almost sense he knew it, too. One day, he would say he couldn't find the strike zone because his back was stiff. Another day, he would rationalize failure by saying he was trying a new pitch. Maybe all of that was true. But as the spring wore on, Jones was still getting pounded, in intrasquad games and in Cactus League games. At night, he would get away to the bar next door, leave the wife and kids behind for an hour or so, grab a quick beer and talk about anything but baseball—usually politics or the combustible situation in south-central L.A.

Two weeks before the end of spring training, he was released.

One less name to remember.

''Can you imagine poor Casey in a spring training like this?'' Don Zimmer was asking one day. Zimmer, whom Don Baylor had hired as his bench coach, had been in the game for 45 years, never collecting a paycheck from any business outside of baseball. He had previously managed four different teams, and as Baylor's bench coach he would serve as both confidant and game-day strategist, initiating ideas and critiquing them. Zimmer was a baseball lifer and a wondrous storyteller to boot; Steve Rushin of *Sports Illustrated* once wrote that if baseball had its own currency, Zimmer's face would be on the one-dollar bill.

''Casey would have been totally lost in this camp,'' Zimmer was telling writers one warm Arizona morning, recalling his days with the worst expansion team of them all, Casey Stengel's 1962 Amazin' Mets. ''We've got so many guys here, I can't even tell

you who's who. But Case, even when we got our roster down to
size, he'd be calling Jim Joe and me Bill and Bill Bob. I think,
honestly, he *knew* who we were, he just couldn't get the names
right."

Expansion camps are unlike any other camps in baseball. In
these days of guaranteed and often long-term contracts, most
ballplayers show up to the spring venue knowing who will and
who won't make the club. Athletes like to say, "It's a numbers
game." Often, that number has six zeroes after it. The competition is left open for maybe two or three players—more for a
second-division team, fewer for a top team—to make the squad.

In this sense, the Rockies resembled the Mets in 1962. As
camp opened, the team was a veritable baseball employment
agency, for the Rockies had very few spots guaranteed beyond
free agent Andres Galarraga at first base; Charlie Hayes, a surefire starter at third; Daryl Boston, a free agent pickup in the outfield; David Nied, the staff ace (they hoped); and reliever
Darren Holmes, the closer and the only man given a two-year
contract.

"This clubhouse is totally different from anything I've ever
known," said catcher Joe Girardi, who emerged early in camp as
the club's most vocal leader, forever yapping and cajoling. "Usually, you've got cliques, the established guys in one corner, the
young guys in another, and the young guys are kind of afraid to
approach the guys making the big money. But here, everybody's
in the same boat. There are no stars here. Guys need to rely on
one another. They go out to dinner together, do things together.
There's the saying about the Boston Red Sox, '25 players, 25
cabs.' This team, nobody makes enough money, so they've got to
share a cab."

First, though, they had to learn one another's names. Casey
would have been proud. On the second full day of camp, Bryn
Smith, the wizened 37-year-old pitcher, handed out those hokey
"Hi, my name is . . ." name tags that you find at computer-sales
conventions. Jeff Parrett, the veteran reliever, found room to add
his wife's name, his kid's names and his hobbies. Rookie pitcher
Curtis Leskanic made light of an off-season arrest on a weapons

charge—the whole matter eventually was dropped—by printing a mock prison number on his badge. After two days, players were swapping name tags, just to keep everyone confused.

"Lemme see your roster list," players would ask reporters. "Who's that guy?"

Who knew?

On February 23, though, Baylor issued a "no-beards" edict, further confusing the issue of who's who. Parrett and Smith, the two best-known and most easily recognizable players, were the primary victims. "Great," a clean-shaven Smith said the next day. "Just when everybody knew who I was, I've got to reintroduce myself. I may have to reintroduce myself to my wife and kids. I look so young, I almost look 30." Baylor's proclamation met with no resistance. When reporters quizzed him on the measure, he growled, "It's my team and I make the rules."

For two weeks, the Rockies' clubhouse was a curious place filled with pockets of camaraderie. Smith, the veteran, sat next to Nied, the rookie—a pairing fostered by Baylor and pitching coach Larry Bearnarth to keep the youthful Nied close to the veteran Smith. The catchers, who speak a private language, had their own corner. The black players congregated together while the Latin players tended to stay on their own. Roberto Mejia, a 20-year-old Dominican second baseman who emerged as the spring phenom, did not speak a word of English and found refuge in Gilberto Reyes, a bilingual veteran catcher who was more than happy to translate for reporters.

Early on, Baylor and his coaches noted that the groups were almost completely determined by race—blacks with blacks, whites with whites, Latins with Latins. "You see it in every clubhouse," said third-base coach Jerry Royster, "but more so here, because this is expansion and all these guys are strangers. It's natural, then, when you don't really know people, you tend to stay with people you know the best." When the rosters were cut, Baylor had the clubhouse architecture altered to break up the racial cliques.

The Rockies' locker room also lacked the usual clubhouse give-and-take. Personalities were still being established. Weaknesses were still being discovered. How do you dog someone when you haven't determined his psychic Achilles' heel?

"The first week or two, that was the dullest clubhouse I've ever seen," said Leskanic. "You would think it was instructional ball. But it'll change. It better, because I'm getting bored entertaining myself."

IT WAS NOT LONG before the Hi Corbett clubhouse had a new addition on one of the walls. It was a photo of a Palestinian stone thrower. The penned-in caption read, "Take note, Gents. Excellent release point—LB."

His name is Larry Bearnarth, but everybody calls him "Bear." Not The Bear. Not Larry. Just Bear. For Bear, life is a succession of mornings after. But, then, lording over a group of 36 expansion-quality pitchers is enough to send any man to the closest pub for a taste of the mother's milk of sanity. Bear's official title was pitching coach, but he was much more.

Bear is a walking contradiction. He is, at times, your basic baseball man, talking shit, grousing about release points and waxing rhapsodic on the fine points of throwing a baseball. When his days turn into nights, the drinks flow and the cigarettes grow into an ashen heap atop the mahogany bar. He is a medical marvel. "I'll rest when we get to Yuma," he keeps saying, referring to the Padres' sleepy spring-training site.

But Bear is this, too: a man with a degree in English literature from St. John's University. Author of a story about winter ball for *Sport* magazine. ("Aw, hell, I didn't really write that," he says.) A keen devotee of *New York Times* crosswords. When was the last time you heard anyone, much less a major-league pitching coach, refer to himself as a "Hessian"?

Typical Bear.

When a *Sports Illustrated* reporter came to spring training and asked him about attitude, he responded that he liked Michelangelo's attitude, which was to take a slab of stone and simply chip away at the excess. "I don't know why I remembered that," Bear said later. "I took this art class in college. It's the only thing I remember."

He also noted that Michelangelo sculpted the David from stone rejected by another sculptor. "Not sure if it's true," he said, "but it sounds good."

He is not, however, a fellow who wears his insights on his sleeve. One day, he was asked what he was currently reading. Bear spit on the dugout floor and said, "You know, the usual shit. *Sporting News. Baseball Weekly.* Stuff like that."

Right.

"When we were both in the Montreal organization, I can still remember our intrasquad games during spring training," Gebhard recalled. "Those games are usually pretty dull and nobody gets into them. But Bear went home every night after those games and wrote up a game story that he posted on the clubhouse wall the next morning. And they were incredible. They were better than anything you read in a newspaper."

Bear was brought to Denver for one reason: He had a reputation for saving careers. He had resurrected Dennis Martinez, the Montreal ace, after the right-hander had fallen prey to drugs and other bad pitching habits. He had helped bring Bryn Smith back to life after some flat years. Bear, who had had a short major-league pitching career, almost all of it with the New York Mets, spent 20 years as a pitching coach in the Montreal organization, the last seven at the big-league level, before joining the Rockies in 1992 as Gebhard's special assistant, scouting major-league talent. More incredibly, his entire career had been spent with expansion teams: the Mets (he actually joined them as a player in 1963), the expansion Expos, who were born in 1969, and now the Rockies.

"What we did in the expansion draft was go after some young guys who we thought had good, live arms—the raw material—but guys who, for some reason, the light had never gone off in their heads," said Gebhard. "We thought, with Bear, here's a guy who might give a guy some kind of tip, whether it was physical or mental, and we might have a guy who had a five-something ERA last year down to three-something for us."

Bear's spring-training philosophy was simple: Watch and listen and learn. Find out about mechanics and personalities. Then watch and listen and learn some more. Don't start doing surgery until later in spring training. First, win their trust.

"The biggest thing early on is you hope they tell the other guys you're not a jerk," Bear told Jack Etkin of the *Rocky Mountain News*. "If they do nothing more than that, at least they're telling the other guys I'm here to help. It opens lines of communication. If you come on too strong you lose your credibility real quick."

Bryn Smith, who was signed by the Rockies with the hope that he would provide stability and some veteran leadership, first met Bear in 1979, while still mired in the minor leagues. They met again in Memphis in 1980, and came together once again when Smith, then in Montreal, was at a critical crossroads in his career. The two talked and worked, and Smith went 81-60 over the next seven seasons.

"The thing about Bear is there's nothing phony about him; he's real down to earth," said Smith. "He wants you to do well, and he'll do whatever it takes to get you there. With me, it was a matter of teaching me how to pitch and giving me a pitching philosophy. I've never been a guy who could get away with trying to blow people away, and Bear taught me how to work the plate and be a student of the game. I give him a lot of credit for the success and longevity I've had in baseball."

Parrett, another veteran, could have signed almost anywhere. He came to Colorado. "Because of Bear," he said. "It's that simple."

Bear listens to all this and shakes his head. "It's not fuckin' brain surgery," he says. "They do it. I don't do it. I give them one or two little things and they do the rest."

The conversation ceases. It is happy hour somewhere.

A FUNNY THING happened on the way to last place: The Rockies spent spring training looking like a damned decent baseball team.

Their final record was 18-14, best in the Cactus League. The folks back home in the Rocky Mountain region were even more encouraged: Of the nine televised spring-training games, the Rockies won eight.

But Baylor knew the truth. He knew that in spring training an expansion team's players tend to play with a bit more purpose and gusto than those on an established team. He knew that the 1962 New York Mets had a respectable spring-training mark before going 40-120. He knew that because the Rockies trained in Tucson, some 90 miles south of the spring-training vortex in Phoenix, a lot of teams sent their minor-league players to compete against the Rockies at Hi Corbett Field. On at least one occasion, Gebhard filed a complaint against the Cubs for sending a no-name minor-league contingent to play the Rockies in front of a sellout crowd in Tucson.

"Don't tell me about spring-training records," Zimmer was saying one day between ground balls off his fungo bat. "My Cubs team in '89, we were terrible in spring training. We couldn't beat anybody. Everybody was picking us last, and I couldn't blame them. Then the season started and we won the National League East."

From the first day of spring training, Baylor pounded his players with the incessant drumbeat of optimism. "No reason we should look like an expansion team." "No reason we should play like an expansion team." It became their mantra. They even started believing it. Intelligent souls like Girardi were moved to say, "This team has a real chance of playing .500 baseball."

But who could blame anybody connected with the organization for taking a leave of his senses? Once the rains cleared and players learned one another's names, spring training was a wild ride through virgin territory. The games started, and the crowds came en masse. The Hi Corbett parking lot was teeming with cars bearing license plates from states throughout the Rocky Mountain region, not just Colorado. The Rockies were, in every respect, a regional franchise. That was how they had presented themselves to the National League expansion people, and that was how they marketed themselves to the region. Season-ticket buyers came from 33 states.

The love-in had begun.

"When the Indians was here, you'd meet a couple of people from Cleveland and that was it," said "Tucson Lenny" Rubin, Hi Corbett's resident gofer, bon vivant and jack-of-all-trades. It was said of Tucson Lenny that his unlit cigar always arrived five minutes before he did. He drove around in an old beater that was seemingly held together by cheesy bumper stickers. "Wit' da Rockies, Christ, they come from everywhere. Never seen nuthin' like it. I never met nobody from Wyoming before. I didn't even know they had people in Wyoming."

This wasn't a team; it was a phenomenon. When the Rockies played their first-ever exhibition game against the San Francisco Giants, there was pomp and ceremony to equal a World Series game. Colorado newspapers sent not only sportswriters but newspeople and feature reporters and enough photographers to shoot a war. And TV? There wasn't enough hair spray to go around.

Outside the stadium, scalpers were offering tickets for thirty dollars each. The only person who didn't seem to have a stake in the club's grand opening was the homeless man who spent every morning with his forlorn look and his cardboard sign reading, WHY LIE? I JUST WANT A DRINK.

Of course, the Rockies won, 7–2, before an overflow crowd of 7,726 in a performance that couldn't have been scripted any more beautifully.

Before the game, the players had tried to minimize the importance of the contest. Just another meaningless spring-training exercise, they said. More important to the people of the region than it is to us, they said. And then they were introduced, player after player after coach after player, and the metal stands shook.

Afterward, Girardi was still beaming. "It was the most exciting spring-training game I've ever been involved in," he said. "It was incredible."

Bearnarth had a dreamy look in his eyes. "I thought it was a beautiful scene," he said. "Sixty-five guys running out, maybe about 75 if you count the minor-league people, running out to congratulate a baseball team. When have you seen that?"

The Rockies spent the rest of spring training opening eyes— mostly their own—and serving notice that their style of ball would be somewhat different from the rest. The writers, desperate to endow a formless team with a defining characteristic, quickly took to calling it BaylorBall. Definition: We're gonna run when you expect it, and we're gonna run when you don't expect it. Baylor, who was a surprisingly good base stealer himself despite his reputation as a power hitter, wanted to play National League ball on an adrenaline rush. He wanted baseball at 78 rpm —and more. And he got it.

Everything was looking up: Galarraga awoke from an 0-for-12 start and hit the ball the way he did during his near-MVP years in Montreal. Eric Young, rumored to be a defensive liability, not only made the plays afield but turned into a perfect leadoff hitter with speed and the ability to make contact. Benavides, known for his defense, was pounding the ball. Hayes returned from an early-spring thumb injury and hit the ball hard despite some unwanted girth. And Girardi was solid as he learned his pitchers.

The outfield presented an unusual problem, especially for an expansion team. There were too many players deserving of at-bats, and too few spots. Clark, who was penciled in as the starting left fielder, missed the early part of spring with a hand injury, but he returned to hit the ball solidly—with some prodding from Baylor. Cole, the enigmatic center fielder, woke up and produced. Bichette had injury problems early, and was distracted by his spring-training wedding, but he showed flashes of promise. The best two outfielders, though, were Boston, the longtime fourth outfielder for the White Sox and Mets, and free agent pickup Gerald Young, who was a phenom once upon a time with Houston, but had flamed out to the point of being released the past year during winter ball.

Pitching was supposed to be the problem, but nobody told the Rockies pitchers. Nied, the wunderkind, had emerged as the real deal. Smith, who had had arthroscopic knee surgery early in the spring—"I guess I'm getting old," he said—threw well upon his return. Bruce Ruffin, another free-agent signee, had once been a rookie star in Philadelphia, but had fallen off the face of the earth; he, too, was getting people out. Ashby, another strong-armed Philly reject who was taken in the expansion draft, looked good from day one. Butch Henry, a left-handed change-up artist out of the Astros organization, proved almost unhittable. And the bullpen looked solid top to bottom.

"Everybody keeps telling me we've got a bunch of rejects on this pitching staff," Bearnarth said one day. "Except somebody forgot to tell these guys they were rejects."

But Bearnarth and Baylor and the Rockies' brain trust knew this, too: March is a mean-spirited temptress. March is baseball's cruelest month. They could not have envisioned how cruel.

3

Opening Day

New York, Monday, April 5, 1993.

GEBHARD, the Man Who Never Sleeps, awoke from his usual restless slumber in the City That Never Sleeps and turned to his wife, Nancy. They had finally made it to New York, the two of them. While he had been putting together a team, she had been selling one house in Minnesota, buying another one in Denver and generally maintaining sanity on the home front. The night had been a long and fretful one, but Gebhard was running on adrenaline.

"Bob," Nancy said. "I think I forgot some makeup. I think I left my foundation home."

Bob growled. "Yeah."

"Could you run to Angie's room and get some foundation for me?" she asked sweetly. "It'll only take a second."

"Yeah," Geb said, reaching for the first of the day's 60-something cigarettes.

Ten minutes later, Geb returned from his daughter's room with foundation.

"Honey," Nancy said, "I forgot some other things, too. Could you run down to Julie Glazier's room and bring some makeup back for me?"

Bob stared a hole through her forehead. "Wait a minute," he said. "I've waited my entire adult life for this day, I've waited almost 50 years to get to this point, Opening Day for a team I built, and you want me running around this goddamn hotel early in the morning looking for makeup?"

Later, Gebhard stood in the hotel lobby and smiled. "I'll tell you what," he said, laughing. "She really needed that makeup, too."

Meanwhile, Baylor was receiving a 6:15 A.M. wake-up call: "I used my old fly-to-Japan trick, stay up the night before," he said. "I slept a good four hours. Usually, it's a toss-and-turn." By 7:15, Baylor and his coaches were in a limousine, wending their way to Shea Stadium. When they arrived, they found a stadium tightly secured. "There was nobody around," Baylor said later. "I thought we'd have to break in."

Soon enough, the Shea security people showed up, and Baylor was behind the desk in the visiting manager's office—or, more appropriately, cubicle—by 8:00 A.M. The game was still more than six hours away, but Baylor wanted to attend to every minute detail, including filling out about 50 individual lineup cards to give to his players, coaches and support staff. This was a slice of history, and he wanted them to feel special, to know they were part of something grand and unique.

He also needed time to do something else: to think. Mostly, on this day, about his mother, Lillian, who had since passed away.

"My dad and I have a good relationship, but she was the one I was really close to," Baylor said. His father, George, had some difficult years. He worked as a baggage handler, and went through periods where he gambled and drank too much. At one point, when Don was in junior college in Brenham, Texas, his father spent time in a mental institution. His father's troubles never visited upon the son, though. They remain close, and life has gotten better for George Baylor in the ensuing years. "If she was alive, I'd have had her here. As it is, my dad will be at the home opener in Denver. But if my mom were alive, she would be here, sharing this moment. She was a very special person for me. She was kind of the stabilizing influence on me. She never got too excited. Whatever calm I do have, I got it from her."

All children require parental guidance, but Baylor, a black child growing up in Austin, Texas, during the seismic social changes of the 1960s, required something special. Lillian was his rock and the source of his quiet strength. She was a pillar of good standing in the community and the church, a hard-working woman who began as a pastry cook and moved up to become a cafeteria supervisor at a local high school. When the Austin schools finally desegregated in 1962, Baylor was one of three black children to volunteer to cross racial lines and attend the all-white O. Henry Junior High School. During those early months, he was taunted and degraded, but he fought back. His was a strength that was both physical and moral, and soon Baylor was just another student and athlete, unwittingly shattering a barrier.

"I wish she were here today," Baylor said wistfully. "But I know she is. I know she is."

Baylor couldn't help but consider another memory as he walked through the bowels of Shea Stadium: 1986.

What a year. He was with the Boston Red Sox then, the star-crossed, martyred and much-beloved Red Sox. Boston had ridden to the American League Championship on the strength of Dave Henderson's heroics in Game Five of that series—a two-run homer in the top of the ninth and a game-winning sacrifice fly in the 11th—setting the stage for two easy victories back home in Boston, capping the improbable comeback. The town and the team were on a ridiculous high. The Curse of the Bambino would be exorcised, once and for all.

And then came the World Series, and Game Six, the Red Sox poised *this close* to winning the whole damn thing for the first time since 1918. Baylor was sitting in the dugout, shut out of the game because the designated hitter sat in National League towns. He watched and writhed as the Mets, just one out away from elimination, staged their hysterical last-inning comeback.

"I can still see the ball going through Buck's legs," Baylor said, recalling Mookie Wilson's simple ground ball that had slipped through Bill Buckner's wickets.

As he sat in the tiny manager's room six and a half years later, Baylor felt something different from what he used to feel as a player. Opening Day as a manager was different, strange, maybe better than it was as a player. It was something he couldn't quite figure.

"As a player, it's you against nine other guys, and you can somewhat control that with what you do on the field," he said, still filling out those souvenir lineup cards. Then he recalled his first major-league game in September 1970. "My nerves then came from coming up with the bases loaded against Steve Hargan in Baltimore. I swung at the first pitch. I thought I hit it to left, but it went between first and second and drove in two runs.

"Managing, though, you're going out there, standing on the baseline, now I have nine guys who will follow me. You stand there, and you hope you picked the right nine guys. You do what you can to manage, but they're the ones who have to get good jumps. They're the ones who have to steal bases and execute. I have to rely now on someone else."

By 10:00 A.M., the quiet moments, the times for reflection, were difficult to come by. The Rockies' clubhouse soon became like every other clubhouse. Guys shooting the shit. A Mets clubhouse guy, greeting his old buddy Daryl Boston. "Yo, D-Bo, what's up?" he asked. Boston smiled. "Same shit," he said. "Ain't playing." Boston had come to Denver and the stadium where he had last shown the promise of becoming *a player*. As a member of the Denver Bears in 1984, Boston hit a robust .312, with 21 doubles, 19 triples, 15 homers and 82 runs batted in. All spring, Baylor had tried to push him, make him dissatisfied with being an extra outfielder. Boston responded with a brilliant spring, but his history suggested that he would fall into the same old habits, that he would play only hard enough and only well enough to warrant a position as a fourth, maybe fifth outfielder.

If history was being made, you could never tell by the protagonists. Another day, another ball game.

Yeah, right.

"You can't even find a lousy baseball around here," yelled Darren Holmes, the reliever, as he joined teammates for pregame stretching exercises on the Shea Stadium grass. There were no baseballs. Just reporters. Hundreds of them. More than 300 press credentials had been issued, and most of those newshounds seemed to be on the field. One false move, and a second baseman would require surgery for the removal of a Nikon lens from his ear. Never had a stretching routine been so thoroughly chronicled by so many.

Welcome to New York. "Might as well open in the media mecca," Gebhard said. "Opening Day in the Big Apple. Let's do it in style."

The players were not so sanguine.

"Cameras get off the fucking field," Bryn Smith said angrily.

"Hey, easy, he's a writer," someone said. Just then, a note-pad-carrying man—presumably a writer—was pushed to the ground by a crazed photographer attempting to shoot a picture of Mets manager Jeff Torborg shaking hands with Don Baylor. The two managers eyed the scene and glared at the errant reporters.

"Easy, boys," Torborg said, somewhat bemused.

Meanwhile, Zimmer was doing what he does best: leaning on his fungo bat and telling baseball stories. He had a special place in the hearts of New Yorkers; not only had he been a member of the 1962 Mets but he had begun his career as a reserve infielder for the sainted Brooklyn Dodgers. In fact, the first batter ever to face the Mets hit a grounder to Zimmer, the team's Opening Day third baseman. Zimmer fielded it with grace and élan.

He threw it five feet over the first baseman's head.

Zimmer also brought his problems afield to the plate with him. He began the season in an 0-for-34 slump. When he finally singled, he hugged the base. His was only a momentary respite; he soon found himself slumping once again. He was hitting a lusty .077 when he was dealt at mid-season.

"I'll never forget Case," said Zimmer. "After that 0-for-34, I get a few hits, then I got into another terrible slump. Then, one day, I think we're in Pittsburgh, and I get two hits and we actually win a game.

"So I'm in the shower there and I'm feeling pretty good, the whole team is celebrating, when I see Case motion to me to come out of the shower. So I come out, I've got the towel wrapped around me, and I'm standing in the middle of the clubhouse with Case and his arm around my shoulder. He's saying, 'Son, you're going to like the outfield. The center-field wall is soft, and it's a good town and I really think you're going to like it.' And he's going on and on, for five minutes like this, when I finally say, 'Case, what the hell are you talking about?'

"Well, Casey jumps and says, 'Oh, yeah, we've traded you to the Cincinnati Reds.' "

Zimmer laughed. "Everybody thought Casey wasn't on top of things, but let me tell you, he knew baseball," Zimmer said. "One of his problems, though, is he loved to stay out all night with the writers and tell stories. He'd show up to the park the next day, he'd just nod off for a couple of minutes now and again. It became a little game with us. We'd see him in the dugout, and you could see those eyelids getting heavy. But make no mistake: He was a good baseball man."

While Zimmer was recalling the bad old days, the new Rockies were reveling in the novelty of the experience. Eric Young, a New Jersey native, was scanning the early-arriving crowd to find his family. Kim Girardi, Joe's wife, was leaning over the railing behind home plate, taking pictures of Girardi and Freddie Benavides. "Oooooh," she said. "You guys look sooo good."

Baylor, who seemed to understand better than anybody what the day meant, talked with his good friend, former commissioner Fay Vincent, whose in-house attempts to spur minority hiring had gone largely unnoticed by the outside world. "I haven't been to a baseball game since I left," said Vincent, referring to his self-imposed exile in England after his ouster from the commissioner's chair in 1992. "But for Don Baylor, I'll come back."

And this being New York, there were celebrities. Mustachioed sports artist LeRoy Neiman prowled behind the plate. Glenn Close hobnobbed with star-struck ballplayers.

Just then, a gold cart passed by carrying Dennis Byrd, the former New York Jets defensive lineman, and his wife. Byrd had suffered a devastating injury in a game the previous fall, but he had fought back from what doctors initially believed to be permanent paralysis below the shoulders. Now he was walking and smiling and talking about returning to a daily jogging regimen.

"Opening Day is about renewal," someone said to Girardi.

Girardi was moved as he watched Byrd walk, haltingly and with the aid of a cane, onto the field. "This is what it's all about, isn't it?"

TWENTY-THREE INNINGS.

David Nied pondered that number, twisted it this way and that in his mind and tried to make sense of the whole thing. He had pitched all of 23 innings in the major leagues—all of them in 1992, when he was called up to the mighty Atlanta Braves from Triple-A Richmond—and now here he was, just a few hours away from being the Colorado Rockies' Opening Day pitcher. The first pick in the expansion draft, he had been anointed staff ace. By the end of spring training, he had fully earned the title.

Still, it seemed strange; too much too fast. One day he was just another rising star in the Braves' pitching-rich farm system. Now he was the man expected to carry the load as the Rockies' unofficial poster boy. He was 24 years old, a nice, quiet, baby-faced kid from Duncanville, Texas, who didn't know whether to embrace all the attention or deflect it.

There were 75 players taken in the expansion draft, but there was only one man chosen first. Nied was a pawn of history. He wasn't the best pitcher in baseball, wasn't even in the top 50. But he was the best pitcher an established team could afford to leave unprotected. He was one of the few players coveted by both the Rockies and the Florida Marlins, both of whom had tapped Nied as the surefire top pick in the expansion draft. Had the Marlins won a coin flip, Nied would now be enduring the scrutiny of South Florida's media and fans.

"I know it makes him crazy when he sees a cartoon in the paper where he's pushing John Elway out of the limelight," said Mark Knudson, a veteran pitcher who lives in the Denver area and knows the whys and wherefores of the local media.

But Nied understood. He understood because he is intelligent and affable. He understood because he was there, at the very beginning, when thousands jammed a downtown Denver convention hall on expansion-draft day and greeted Nied as if he were the second coming of Sandy Koufax. He understood because he had been one of the Rockies who had gone on off-season caravans throughout the region and had seen, firsthand, how completely crazy the area had gone. The bus would pull up in a place like Scottsbluff, Nebraska, or Santa Fe, New Mexico, hours and hours from Denver, and the fans would be lined up around the block, asking for autographs.

He was part of a phenomenon. It didn't have to make sense. It just was. Nied had two choices: Make the best of it or spurn it. In the end, there really wasn't any choice.

"I know what this team means to the area," Nied was saying during spring training. "I mean, the day of the draft when I was introduced at the [Denver convention] hall, I have never, ever had my adrenaline flow like that. Not when I was on the World Series roster last year, never. That was the best of all time. I just hope people are realistic."

Nied had not settled into his locker stall at Hi Corbett before embarking on a spring-training ritual. Every morning, there were letters. Loads of them. There was a truckload waiting when he arrived, and just when he thought he was making a dent in the stationery, another 25 or even 30 would come every day. Nied was the Rockies' first hero, their standard bearer, everybody's pen pal. Nobody wanted to know about Armando Reynoso. They wanted Nied.

"This whole thing is amazing," he said, rummaging through the stacks of mail around his feet. "It's like my whole life changed in one day. It's like winning the lottery, you know? One day your life is one way, the next day it's totally different. It's weird. One day. It wasn't a slow process, just such a drastic change. At times, it's been tough to come to grips with it all. In one day, I went from a pretty private person to a person who's having his life dissected publicly."

During his days in the minors, a reporter might happen by and ask a question or two after a start. Now Nied was becoming the team's designated spokesman. The *Rocky Mountain News* ran a daily postcard from Nied in which he gave readers a blow-by-blow account of his day. ("Today, I threw on the side . . .") The Denver newspaper wars between the *News* and *The Denver Post* once had been waged on the football field, with John Elway the unwitting target of stories about everything from the length of his hair to his breakfast choices. Now Nied was getting a taste.

The reporters knew Nied was approachable and a good quote, and asked for his insights on a regular basis. And when the national guys came in—*The New York Times, Sports Illustrated, USA Today*—Nied was an obvious target. He was unfailingly polite and accommodating, but he wondered when the pressure would ease.

"The hardest thing is I don't want to come off like a jerk and tell people I won't talk, but I don't want these guys, my teammates, looking at me and saying, 'Hey, he's only a rookie and look at the attention he's getting,' " Nied said. "I'm already getting a lot of stuff about it. Good-natured, but I understand how they might feel. And the guys in this room are the most important people to me. Sometimes I just want to tell them, 'Go talk to Andy [Ashby] or give some press to another guy.' The bottom line is, I haven't done anything in the major leagues to deserve this kind of attention."

Twenty-three innings.

"All of a sudden, my life is under a microscope," Nied said. "I didn't really understand it until I saw an item in the paper about my engagement. That's when I thought, 'Whoa, this is a whole different deal here.' Don't get me wrong. I'm not complaining. For the most part, it's been fun. It's just I wasn't completely prepared to handle all this.

"Basically, I'm learning as I go along. I'm learning I've got to watch my step and be more responsible than the average 24-year-old. I learned a lot during the caravan. I'm like most people, I like to go out, have a few beers, be with the guys. But now I'm trying to be more responsible, like I won't have beers—even a few—and drive anymore. People are watching me now. They want to see how I act. I have to understand that."

Nied also hoped Denver would understand. There were times, he admitted, when he wanted to take a megaphone and tell the region to kindly back off, to give him room to breathe. "That's the really scary part of this whole thing," he said. "I think I'm going to do real well, but I hope people don't judge me on one game or even one season. I'm still real young. I know there are high expectations, but the way I've been built up, I feel like I have to win every game and pitch a perfect game. It's kind of unfair, in a way."

But it was the way of Nied's brave new world. A few hours before the first day of the rest of his and the Rockies' life, Nied was sitting quietly in front of his Shea Stadium locker stall, signing baseballs, signing cards, signing away. Soon he would begin warming up for the 24th inning of his big-league career.

ERIC YOUNG knew he would be first. He had displaced Alex Cole as the leadoff man late in spring training, so he knew he had a chance to make Rockies history. He would lead off. He had the first shot. He could be the one.

This was special, too, because Young is a Jersey guy and played football at Rutgers. He spent many afternoons watching the Mets at Shea Stadium. By the time he was done trading out complimentary tickets with teammates—each guy gets only six apiece—he had finagled 30 tickets.

"Who knows?" he said before the game. "Maybe I'll cross everybody up and lay down a bunt."

At 2:18 Eastern Time, the Rocky Mountain region's baseball dream was finally realized when Young dug into the batter's box and took a called strike from Dwight "Doc" Gooden, the Mets' once-legendary right-hander. One strike later, he laid down that bunt. Catcher Todd Hundley sprung from his crouch, corralled the ball and threw Young out at first base.

The tone had been set. For most of the afternoon, the Rockies flailed away rather lamely against Gooden, who was trying to come back from the first losing season of his career. The Rockies managed but four hits against Gooden, who retired the final seventeen Colorado batters.

Meanwhile, Nied was struggling. Surviving, but struggling. He threw an incredible 105 pitches in the first five innings. He walked too many people and allowed a home run to Bobby Bonilla, but he kept his team in the game despite five consecutive innings of threats.

"I think he set a record for five innings and number of pitches," said Girardi. "All you can ask for is your pitcher to keep you in a game, and he did that. It was a gutty performance for not having your best stuff."

Nied had guts, but Gooden had stuff. This was not the old Doctor K, not the same young man who once blew away opponents with a rising fastball and a back-breaking curve. He was imperious then, a beautiful athlete to behold, secure and wise beyond his years. But the years and the pressures had slowed him; there was the much-publicized visit to the Smithers Institute for drug abuse, and then there were arm problems.

"It's almost like you should put an asterisk next to Doc's record for 1992," Bonilla said. "All those injuries, it's almost not fair."

For one day, though, the birth of the Rockies was fading into the background, and Gooden's triumphant return was demanding the media attention. Gooden was alternately overpowering and guileful, leaving Baylor to wonder whether the Rockies had left their bats in Tucson. Colorado had threatened just twice. In the third, Gooden struck out Andres Galarraga with the bases loaded to end the inning. Then, in the ninth, with the score 3–0, Galarraga continued a bothersome trend that had begun during spring training: bad baserunning. Down three runs, Galarraga tried to stretch a single into a double and was thrown out.

"I knew the field was really bad from when I went down the line earlier to get a pop-up," said Galarraga. "I knew the grass was so wet and Joe Orsulak [the Mets' right fielder] would have to catch and throw. And I knew we want to be aggressive."

Sure, Baylor had emphasized aggressive baseball all spring, but this was stupid baseball. "Being aggressive is one thing, running out of control is another," Baylor said. "That's not what beat us, but it took us out of a chance. It was a rookie mistake, and he's a veteran out there."

Back in Denver, though, the Rockies could do no wrong. It didn't matter that Nied struggled or that the bats were somnolent or that Galarraga was earning the nickname "Crazy Legs." It was enough that the Rockies existed. The city took a civic holiday.

They filled sports bars, arriving in the morning to earn a good seat. They took the day off—the purple flu—and stayed home in their easy chairs. One company, Vessels Oil and Gas, noted that twenty of eighty employees could not find their way to work that afternoon. At one high school, the principal gathered the students in the cafeteria and dedicated the afternoon to watching Colorado baseball. It was, well, history.

After the game, Baylor could find room in his competitive heart to feel something positive. It felt counterintuitive, but Baylor knew this was just one of 162, that his players were tight, that Doc Gooden on Opening Day at Shea is something special.

"Now we have a little history of our own," he said. Then he broke into a broad smile. "Of course, now I'm known for having the longest losing streak in Rockies history."

Later, he sat in the manager's office and considered what he might do with Galarraga. Yes, he said, Galarraga was a veteran. No sense in embarrassing him or browbeating him. He knew he messed up, didn't he? Or did he? "I'm going to talk to him when we get back tomorrow," Baylor said. "My mom would have been proud of me, the restraint I showed with Galarraga."

Back in the clubhouse, Nied was surrounded by a phalanx of reporters. Dressed in a silk, flowered shirt buttoned up to the top, he was quietly, patiently answering the same questions.

Dante Bichette, the unofficial team goof, sat before his locker stall and admitted his team was tight. How do you play baseball when you're making history? But, then, all the media attention was good, he said, because it would prepare the Rockies for the World Series. Nobody was sure whether he was serious.

On Wednesday, Bichette finally gave the Rockies some offense, hitting the team's first home run into a gale-force wind. A tent-company owner named Bill LoPresti of Flushing, New York, caught the ball, but traded it back for a ball autographed by Butch Henry, who happened to be in the bullpen at the time. "If the ball is worth $100,000 in a couple of years, then I guess I'm the idiot," said LoPresti. But he was not about to deny the Rockies a piece of their history by demanding an exorbitant price. "Aw, hell," he said. "What do I care, right? Give it to the team. I got a ball. I don't know who the hell this guy is who autographed it and it's probably worth nothing, but, like I say, what the hell."

What the hell.

The Rockies lost again that day, dispatched easily by another Mets ace, Bret Saberhagen, by a 6–1 count. They were 0-2 and going home to Denver and a greeting they could never properly comprehend.

"They're throwing us a parade?" Bichette asked when told of Thursday's planned festivities. "That's pretty cool considering we haven't won yet. Imagine if we'd have won a game."

Bill Madden, a longtime baseball writer for the New York *Daily News,* saw both games and came away singularly unimpressed by the mighty Rockies. On the way out of town, the Colorado players saw Madden's screed; the Rockies, he wrote, may very well be worse than the 1962 Mets. John Franco, the Mets' reliever, suggested his team could fatten up its record with early-season games against the Rockies and Marlins.

The Rockies didn't have time to take offense. They had to go home, find their new apartments, figure out where to buy milk and attend a parade, followed by a batting practice open to the public. Bichette couldn't wait. "It's gonna be nuts, isn't it?" he said.

4

Mile High Madness

THEY KEPT HEARING about it during the quiet times in Tucson. Baylor would tell them, Gebhard would tell them, "Wait until you get back to Denver. You can't imagine the atmosphere. You can't begin to fathom the mania." It will be crazy, they were told. It will be unlike anything they've ever known in baseball.

The Rockies shrugged. This was a disparate group of baseball nomads who knew little of Denver. They would ask questions, would shake their heads when Mark Knudson or pitcher John Burke, the two Denver guys, would tell them about the force of nature back home, but they were largely uninterested.

They wanted to know about more mundane issues: where to live, how the real estate market was shaping up, how the weather might be upon their arrival. Most of these men were camping on the fringes of a major-league existence, older players running on the fumes of long-gone talent, or youngsters whose lack of experience would have earned them another couple of years in the minors back in the days before expansion.

Nied, who understood the lunacy back in Colorado better than most, would just shake his head. "Don't take this the wrong way," he would tell Colorado-area reporters. "But all of this is more important to you guys and the fans back there than it is to us."

The Rockies could be excused if the romance somehow eluded them. Athletes are transient animals, especially in baseball, and never more so than in an expansion situation. There were no George Bretts here, no Robin Younts or Kirby Pucketts or Cal Ripkens, great athletes who were synonymous with their cities. Truth was, most of the Rockies would be gone within a year or two. The lesser lights would be dispatched, released, waived or demoted to the minor leagues, replaced by other bodies. The better players would be traded off to contending teams in the heat of a pennant race, moved in return for top minor-league prospects who could help in the future.

"You think about going to Denver and buying a house, settling down," said Eric Young. "But who knows? I've known guys who've played for years, they've always rented furniture. There's no stability in this game. There are no guarantees."

The whole crazy thing was a whirlwind in the hours after the first pair of games. The Rockies flew into Denver Wednesday night and found themselves in the middle of a gathering storm. The city was planning a ridiculous civic celebration of baseball, planning to honor a team that was 0-2 and hitting a collective .102. The players, though, had simpler desires. Like finding a new home. Like finding a bed. They arrived in Denver and were taken to two major apartment/condo complexes. Once one player decided on a place, the rest followed like dutiful lemmings. But it made sense, not only for the athletes but for the girlfriends and wives. Who could they lean on but other baseball wives and girlfriends? While the fans were contemplating the merits of the Rockies' starting rotation, the players and their significant others were wondering where they might buy a loaf of bread.

The noontime parade on Thursday drew more than 20,000 people, many of whom had been waiting hours to pay homage to this ragtag collection of baseball players they yearned to call their own. By 3:00 P.M., the Rockies had assembled at their new baseball home, Mile High Stadium. The itinerary indicated there would be batting practice open to the public. The Rockies figured a few stragglers might happen by. What they found was a crowd more than 5,000 strong, waiting to give them a standing ovation for doing arm circles.

Strange—wasn't this the sport that was supposed to be dying from within? You couldn't pick up a magazine, couldn't spend ten minutes in a bookstore, without reading of the game's imminent demise. Baseball was in moral and fiscal decay, dying on the vine. There was no commissioner, only an acting commissioner whose job it was to keep his co-owners fat and happy. There was no direction. Large markets would not share revenues with small markets. The television contract was running out, and the new one would not pay even half the current rate. The owners were crying their usual "got-the-free-agency-and-arbitration blues." The union wasn't buying. And the prospects remained for a strike or a lockout somewhere down the line.

Once upon a time, Madison Avenue deemed ballplayers to be the most marketable athletes to promote their products. But now, even they were becoming wary. The game no longer held an allure. The kids, especially, looked to Michael Jordan or Shaquille O'Neal or Joe Montana. The Nintendo generation had tuned out, video grazed right past the baseball game of the week —when they could actually find it on CBS—and opted for Shaq versus Mr. Robinson. So desperate had baseball become that they decided by mid-season to go with an expanded playoff format— to make more money by getting more teams involved in the postseason.

All these tales of doom and despair had their place. Baseball was in trouble, intent on killing the golden goose, incapable of finding the basic solutions that had helped both football and basketball reach new and prominent places in the American sports psyche.

In the Rocky Mountain region, though, baseball was fresh and new and utterly without blemishes. Whereas fans in other cities viewed the game through jaundiced eyes, Denver offered its Rockies nothing short of unconditional puppy love. The game's myriad problems were somebody else's problems. This was, in a sense, baseball as it used to be, free of cynicism and recrimination. There was no talk of bloated free-agent salaries or questionable work ethics, no murmuring about trades and clubhouse infidelity—just baseball, through noncritical eyes. For once, there was a sense of symbiosis between city and team, a connection that went past the simple donning of a uniform bearing a region's name.

This was the age of innocence. It was also, as the Don Henley song went, the end of the innocence. From within the joy there came the sense, too, that it would never be quite this way again. Sometime, maybe even very soon, Denver would be like every other baseball city. For now, though, it was as perfect as a crystalline spring day in the high Rockies.

"I tried to warn the players in spring training what they were going to walk into," Baylor said at that first workout. "I think they got a sense of that today."

They had an idea coming in, at least some of them. The Rockies had sold themselves on being a regional franchise, and bused a handful of players around the region—from Wyoming to New Mexico, Utah to Nebraska—on an eight-state, 23-city caravan designed to spur far-flung interest.

"Every player I spoke to before the caravan, I tried to prepare them and tell them, 'You've never seen anything like this,' and they all sort of looked at me and said, 'Yeah, sure,'" said Mike Swanson, the Rockies' public-relations director. "Once we got going, they saw the incredible support, and we would sit there and say, 'Are you believing this shit?' Coming here, there were eight guys who had some idea what it's going to mean to be a Colorado Rockie. The rest of them are now finding out for themselves."

Baylor, who had been the point man in the club's public-relations tour, had it drummed home to him during a Utah Jazz game at the Delta Center in Salt Lake City. He was leaving the basketball game when a man introduced himself and congratulated him on becoming the team's first manager.

"Don't you know who that is?" the man said, turning to his wife. "That's the manager of our new baseball team."

Our team. In Salt Lake City. That's 525 miles from Denver. It was beginning to dawn on Baylor just how regional, just how far-reaching this team's allure would be.

"You know what made the point for me, was when we went to Grand Junction, Colorado," Eric Young said. "What's that— four and a half hours from Denver? And there's all these people there with season tickets. It's unbelievable how many season tickets they've got. To think people will drive that far . . . it's unheard of."

Swanson recalled one trip when the caravan pulled into a Santa Fe, New Mexico, grocery store. The parking lot looked empty.

"I think this is going to be the first zero," Nied told Swanson.

Nied then traded conspiratorial glances with Eric Wedge, a catcher whom the team took from the Boston Red Sox in the expansion draft. "We're in a grocery store in Santa Fe in the middle of nowhere in the middle of the afternoon," Wedge said. "No way."

When they walked inside, they encountered the usual mob scene. "There was a line all the way back to the produce department," Swanson said.

It was like that wherever the wandering Rockies roamed. Dante Bichette and friends were accorded a standing ovation in the Wyoming statehouse. Baylor, Nied and Wedge were blown away by a tumultuous welcome at a Denver Nuggets game. Girardi made a swing of cities he said he didn't know even existed; when he returned, he was stunned to learn there were Rockies fans in Rapid City, South Dakota. *South Dakota.*

Now here they were, back in Denver, getting an early taste of it all, getting a sense, finally, that they were a part of something far bigger than a simple baseball team. "Jerald Clark and I were talking," said Nied after the workout, "and we were so thankful to get to be a part of this team and this event because no matter what happens, no one can take away from being in such a history-making event—the first game in Colorado."

JERRY ROYSTER couldn't make the plane move fast enough. He was stuck there in his seat, anxious, unable to believe he was actually missing this. He had gone to Montreal for a few days to attend his mother-in-law's funeral, only to get stuck for two and a half hours in New York because of fog. Now here he was, 30,000 feet over—what?—Scottsbluff, Nebraska, or something, missing Opening Day.

"I was dying," Royster said. "Then the pilot comes on the PA system and says Eric Young hit a home run in the first at-bat and we're winning. I was going crazy."

The plane finally landed at Stapleton Airport, where Royster was met by security people and given a police escort to Mile High Stadium. As he neared the stadium, he noticed an unusual amount of traffic, especially for a game that had already begun. "I'd been hearing, 'Big crowd, big crowd,'" Royster said. "I figured I'm gonna get there, we'll have maybe 45,000 or something."

Royster ran into the clubhouse, threw on his home Rockies uniform, white with purple pinstripes and the distinctive CR hat, peeked out and began the long trek down the left-field line and toward his regular spot in the third-base coaching box. He was overcome by a wave of sound, by a force. "It's like it just hit me," he said. "I looked up and they had 80,000 people. For a baseball game. Eighty thousand. I couldn't believe it. We'd been hearing the people in Colorado were crazy for baseball, but I was overwhelmed. It was unlike anything I've ever experienced."

The number is etched in Rocky Mountain history: 80,227. It was an Opening Day record, obliterating the previous record set by the Los Angeles Dodgers when they played their first game out West in 1958. It was all made possible by the addition of temporary stands out beyond center field, stands that were still being erected just three hours before game time. Colorado wanted it that way, for the fans, the ones who made this possible, to make a statement.

"ANYBODY HERE get any sleep?" asked Gebhard as he pranced onto the field early in the morning.

Nobody among the clot of reporters raised his hand. Even the cynical, jaded media found room in their collective heart to be excited. What had been bigger in the region's history? The 1978 Super Bowl? There was mania, but the game was played outside Denver. No, this was the biggest. This was the ultimate. This was the greatest sports moment in regional history. The Time Zone That Baseball Forgot was telling the Lords of Baseball that they had made a monumental error by failing to discover the Rocky Mountain fans earlier. They had already bought 28,250 season tickets, all but assuring more than 2 million fans for the season. Now, this . . .

As to be expected, Gebhard had spent the night sweating minor details. At 3:00 A.M., he popped out of bed and thought, "Maybe I should check with the groundskeeper to make sure the sprinklers don't go off during the game." Gebhard had ample reason to worry about stadium operations. For one, the infield had been pronounced hard, chalky and damn near unplayable after the team's first practice on Thursday afternoon. By late in that workout, Charlie Hayes was surrounded by groundskeepers listening to the third baseman's lecture on proper soil composition. Worse, there was a cosmetic disgrace in right field, where patches of unsightly poa grass had left a number of large brown spots. "It looks like a bad haircut," said Bichette. Team owner Jerry McMorris was especially incensed. One week earlier, he had offered to pay $38,000 for resodding. The grounds-crew chief, Tom Lujan, said it was unnecessary. Lujan was wrong.

Around 10:00 A.M., Gebhard looked up at the scoreboard as they ran a test.

LEAGUE: National
DIVISION: West
TEAM: Colorado Rockies
PLAYER: Rudy Seanez

One problem: Seanez was on the 60-day disabled list with a sore shoulder.

None of this mattered a bit, though, to Bryn Smith as he sat in the clubhouse before the game with his headphones pounding to the music of his favorite band, Rush. After 250 starts in the majors, after scuffling and persevering and hanging on through bad times and good, Smith was preparing to pitch in his personal World Series. In an age of long-term, guaranteed contracts, Smith was an anachronism. He had gone 15 straight years on one-year contracts, always on the edge and insecure, until receiving a three-year contract from the Cardinals in 1990.

His was a story of survival. He spent seven years in the minors, taking odd jobs in the off-season—mowing lawns, hauling lumber—to make ends meet for his young family. He did not make his major-league debut until he was 26, but he managed to combine guile and baseball intelligence to forge a better-than-workmanlike career, winning 106 games. He also knew a little something about huge crowds, having once toured with Rush and their lead singer and his friend, Geddy Lee.

"I wish all of the 80,000 could be on the same ride, and they will be, in a sense," Smith said. "If you want to strap it on with me, let's go. I want 80,000 people standing on their feet being at the best concert they've ever been to." Smith had only one fear: "I would try to throw the ball 200 miles per hour. Or I would be in the middle of my windup and fall off the mound."

By 1:15, he performed the impossible: He fell asleep listening to Rush as the music pulsed through his headphones. "Do it all the time," he said later.

Eric Young attempted to relax his own way, by playing catch with his son, Eric Jr., behind home plate some two hours before the game. In Arizona, Young impressed the Rockies on a number of levels. For one, he continued to show he could be an offensive presence—he rarely struck out, and he could run. Second, while he was no Roberto Alomar in the field, he did make the basic plays at second base. Best, though, he had a work ethic. He brought a football player's mentality to the park every day. Two months into the season, the syndicated baseball columnist Peter Gammons would call Young "the best pick of the expansion draft."

The Mile High gates finally opened at noon, and raucous cheers for the most mundane feats came cascading down from the nosebleed seats. A player walking in from the clubhouse would get a round of applause. Two Rockies playing catch would inspire an ovation. The town had waited 33 years; this was a primal scream, more than three decades' worth of frustration and excitement and anxiety rolled into one afternoon of mindless exuberance. It was baseball as baseball had rarely been before, baseball as baseball will likely never be again.

"I've been playing the introductions over and over in my head," said Swanson. "They go through the Expos starters, then the extra players, the trainers, and then the announcer says, 'Ladies and gentlemen, your 1993 Colorado Rockies.' I know I'm going to be in a corner crying like a baby, and I know Geb and Randy and everybody else who's been a part of this . . ." He shook his head. "I'm not sure there's going to be a dry eye in the house."

One by one, the players were introduced, and Swanson was right: These people were present for a birth. Who can stifle a tear when a baby is born? Most of the fans couldn't give you the statistical breakdown on Danny Sheaffer or Charlie Hayes, but they knew the Rockies were *theirs*—their team, their town—and they cheered wildly, almost defiantly, as if to say, "For 30 years, Major League Baseball has jerked us around, and now here we are, 80,000 maniacs, blowing away the all-time attendance record and showing everyone that we should have had a team here a long time ago."

By the time Baylor was introduced, the stadium was rocking.

"It was like Chicago Stadium when they announce Michael Jordan's name," said Girardi. "You could barely hear his name."

For one moment, any leftover squabbling over the business of running the team was washed away by a glorious cacophony. The city had given up a lot for baseball; the taxpayers from a six-county area had voted on a one tenth of one percent sales tax to build a new stadium that would replace Mile High in 1995. The promise of substantial private funding for the new stadium was broken, due, in some measure, to the exorbitant and largely unanticipated $95-million expansion fee that the Rockies had to pay Major League Baseball for the privilege of joining the club. More, the Stadium District, which was responsible for overseeing construction of Coors Field, had to transfer to the ownership group nearly $15 million that Coors had paid for the right to name the new stadium—that's what baseball wanted and that's what baseball got. And the taxpayers ended up holding the bag.

On this day, though, there were no second thoughts.

It had been worth it.

Even the most ardent contrarian was swept up in the frenzy that accompanied the first Rockies batter, Eric Young, who hit an exclamatory home run over the left-center-field fence. First batter. First home run. Perfect. Up in the radio booth, play-by-play announcer Wayne Hagin could hardly restrain himself. "The snow on Pike's Peak is falling off!!" he screamed.

"All these people wanted baseball for so long," Young said later as his team savored its victory, 11–4, over the Montreal Expos. "They fought the war to get the majors to Denver, and then counted down the days to the first game. I wanted to give something back, do something that would say, 'Here you go. This is for you.' "

Said Baylor: "When Eric hit that home run, it felt like I had hit it."

At first blush, Young figured it was going to go to the warning track, maybe land for a double or be a long out. He hit it well, but this was not a Ruthian clout. This, after all, was a man who had hit just one home run in his major-league career. Young sprinted for first base, and when he rounded the bag, he shot a glance at Zimmer, who was replacing Royster in the third-base coach's box. Zimmer was gesturing, making a circle with his index finger pointing into the air—the signal for home run. Young circled the bases quickly—he had not perfected his home-run trot—returned to the dugout, then answered a curtain call.

In the visiting dugout, Expos manager Felipe Alou thought about his days in Denver (he had once managed the Bears) and about all the home runs and the doubles and triples into the gaps of the spacious outfield—and about Young's altitude-aided home run. "I thought, 'Oh, boy, they're going to have some long games here,' " he said. "I can't wait to see what kinds of numbers they put up."

While the Rockies were playing long ball and BaylorBall—they stole two bases in the first inning—Smith was justifying Baylor's oft-criticized decision to start him. After all, Smith had been rocked in his final exhibition start, getting lit up by the Twins at the Metrodome. But Baylor was insistent; he wanted someone who had been there before, someone who could cut through all the pomp and ceremony and keep his wits. In the end, Smith went seven innings, allowing no runs, six hits and no walks.

It was the best concert the fans had ever attended.

"In the fifth inning, I was backing up a play at third base, and I turned to some fans and said, 'Isn't this great?' " Smith said. "They said, 'Yeah!!!' I tried to use those 80,000 people. They wanted to enjoy this from the first pitch to the last, and now we can grow as one."

By that fifth inning, the Rockies were leading, 8–0, and the partying had begun. One of the warmest moments came late in the game, when Baylor sent up Dale Murphy, acquired from the Phillies just one day before the start of the regular season, as a pinch hitter. The crowd stood and cheered as if Murphy had hit all 398 of his lifetime homers as a Colorado Rockie.

"That's when I really got a sense of the city's baseball sophistication," Baylor said. "The way they reacted and the ovation he got, you could tell they knew what Murphy had done through his career. I thought it was one of the classiest moves I've seen in a long time.''

Later, the Rockies' coaches sat in their little anteroom, comparing notes, immersing themselves in a day they wished would never end. "The fans stayed until the very end, didn't they?" said Bearnarth. "I'll tell you what: I've been in the game 32 years. This was an absolute turn-on."

Indeed it was.

5

A Baseball Town

FRANK HARAWAY could have expected it. Why, he wondered, were people so surprised that Denver and the entire Rocky Mountain region would react this way to the arrival of major-league baseball? Of course they were going to embrace the game. They always had, even in the minor-league days, even way back in the forties and fifties and all those decades when he was chronicling baseball for *The Denver Post*.

"I get so tired of people saying professional baseball has finally come to Colorado," he says, pronouncing it "Colarada." "We've had professional baseball here for longer than I've been alive."

Which is saying something. Haraway is a walking museum of baseball. His home, which he shares with his baseball-widowed wife, June, is a shrine to the game's past in these parts. For years and years, he was a dutiful beat man, pounding out his copy, fighting with editors for more space for those minor-league reports. But as major-league baseball became more of a reality, the

76-year-old Haraway had become a required feature story for every out-of-town reporter who passed through Denver.

"Isn't it something," he said on Opening Day. "When I was a young scribe, they said I was an idiot who didn't know anything. But now that I'm old, all of a sudden I'm some sort of baseball sage."

Haraway has followed Denver baseball since he was a sickly child in the 1920s. He suffered from tuberculosis of the hips, and once overheard a doctor tell his mother he would never reach the age of 12. But he was determined to follow baseball, and his father received permission to park the family car down the left-field line at old Merchants Park, where Frank, entombed in a cast from hip to toe, would watch the game, every game, scorecard in hand. It was his passion. It was his escape. "I could see the third baseman's hemorrhoids," he said. So much for romanticism.

During a period when Haraway was bedridden, the great New York Yankees came through Denver on a barnstorming tour. Haraway's father asked Babe Ruth and Lou Gehrig to sign a baseball for his son. When Ruth asked where the son was, the elder Haraway told the Bambino the story of his son's illness.

The next day, Babe Ruth was in Frank Haraway's bedroom.

"Can you imagine," Haraway said, looking down on the field at Mile High, "a player doing something like that today?"

Haraway became a *Denver Post* writer in 1938, and married June in 1961. Four days after the wedding, he ruled an error on the Bears rather than giving a hit to Louisville Redbirds hitter Howie Bedell. Ultimately, Bedell, who is today a Rockies minor-league manager, lost the league batting title to Denver's Don Wert by four tenths of a point. When Haraway arrived in Louisville for the playoffs, a local headline read, HONEYMOONING SCRIBE COSTS BEDELL THE BATTING TITLE.

In 1974, he was back in the soup again when he ruled an error instead of giving a hit to Pete LaCock of the Wichita Aeros. LaCock showed his disappointment by hurling a ball at Haraway in the press box. It missed Haraway, but almost beaned Governor John Vanderhoof, who was sitting nearby.

"I should have ruled the throw an error, too," Haraway said.

He was there at the beginning, when Howsam was building his team and his new stadium and everything was looking up. And he was there in 1961, when Howsam was forced to sell the team. Haraway found Howsam sitting alone in Bears Stadium that night, tears in his eyes, crestfallen in the belief that he had somehow let Denver down.

And, indeed, through the 1960s it appeared that Denver had faded from view in the eyes of Major League Baseball. The city continued to be graced by terrific minor-league clubs, winning the Triple-A crown in 1960 with the Yankees' minor-leaguers and later featuring Minnesota Twins minor-leaguers like Graig Nettles and Bob Oliver. But the big leagues weren't calling.

Everything changed, though, in the oil-boom decade of the 1970s. Denver was riding high, a burgeoning metropolis with millionaires abounding and opportunity lurking around every corner. Denver wouldn't have to wait for baseball to come looking for them; Denver would simply take its huge resources, and a billionaire oilman named Marvin Davis, and offer struggling franchises a chance to move to Denver and join the party. The entire sports landscape of the city was changing. The Broncos were emerging from their days as a laughingstock with vertically striped socks and were marching toward their first Super Bowl. The Nuggets, an ABA power, were moving into the NBA in 1976. Baseball would simply round out the schedule, make Denver the big-league town it believed itself to be.

By 1977, Denver was so convinced the Oakland A's were moving to Denver, they had made up schedules. "It was a done deal," said Haraway. "The wire services reported it and everybody believed it. But there were two problems. One, [A's owner] Charlie Finley was going through a divorce, so his assets were tied up. Two, [Raiders owner] Al Davis was talking about taking the Raiders from Oakland to Los Angeles, which left the stadium in Oakland with just one team. When the people in Oakland heard that, they were ready to do some things to keep the A's there."

Denver kept coming close time and again through the seventies and eighties. More to the point, Denver was used time and again through the seventies and eighties—by the Pittsburgh Pirates, by the San Francisco Giants and by the Chicago White Sox, whose owners threatened to move to Denver as leverage to win better deals from their home cities.

"Marvin Davis finally gave up," said Haraway. "This was a man who could make a billion-dollar business decision in 10 minutes and that was it. But baseball was completely different, and it really frustrated him. They weren't doing business the way he was used to doing business."

Tired of waiting for another team to transfer, frustrated by attempts to lure struggling franchises to Denver, the city and state politicians opted for a new tack: pressure. Big-time pressure.

They would threaten to challenge baseball's cherished antitrust exemption.

Major League Baseball had not expanded since 1977, and that expansion came only when litigation filed by the state of Washington forced baseball to find a replacement for the Seattle Pilots, who had fled the city in 1970 after only one season of operation. To head off a lawsuit, the Seattle Mariners and Toronto Blue Jays were grudgingly added to the American League roster. The National League had been even more conservative, its last expansion having occurred in 1969, when it added the San Diego Padres and Montreal Expos.

It hardly seemed to matter that the population base of the country had, in that time, moved from the Northeast corridor to the South—specifically Florida—and the Southwest. The owners were quite content with their game as it was constituted, a small and marvelously lucrative little club whose members had grown fat and happy on the game's financial success in the mid-1980s.

Clearly, baseball was not going to budge on the expansion issue. They gave it lip service, but little more. In the summer of 1987, National League president A. Bartlett Giamatti created a five-man committee of NL owners to study expansion. But as American League president Dr. Bobby Brown said, "On the scale of importance, on a scale of one to 10, expansion is way down at the bottom of the list."

Of course it was. This was an old political ploy, creating a committee to study the feasibility of creating a task force to study the feasibility of moving ahead with a new study. A politician, of all people, recognized the ruse and took action.

He was Senator Tim Wirth of Colorado, a tall, patrician sort with a passion for sports and good public relations. As an editor at the *Rocky Mountain News* once said, "When Tim walks his dog, we get a fax." But Wirth's latest foray had substance.

Tired of baseball's foot-dragging and intransigence, and mindful of Denver's sad history of frustration in trying to lure existing franchises, Wirth decided it was time to force baseball to expand, to open its borders to cities like Denver, Miami, Tampa–St. Petersburg and Phoenix. In November 1987, Wirth formed his own 14-member task force to promote major-league expansion.

And their primary weapon? The threat of lifting baseball's antitrust immunity. They didn't say it out loud, didn't get in Commissioner Peter Ueberroth's face and say, "Expand or lose your antitrust exemption," but the threat, thinly veiled, was implied.

And Major League Baseball knew it.

"I happen to think that unless they face up to expansion, the pressures could indeed mount and Congress might remove the exemption," said Robert C. Berry, former chairman of the sports-law division of the American Bar Association. "I think Ueberroth would probably do something in terms of expansion if it was left to his office. I'm sure he feels the heat more than anyone else in baseball and would try to accommodate the pressures from Washington."

Finally, on June 15, 1989, the door opened a little further. Major League Baseball announced it would outline a timetable for a two-team National League expansion. Former Denver Mayor Federico Peña called it "the news we've been waiting for."

It was time for Denver, and at least another dozen cities thirsting for baseball, to go to work.

* * *

I<small>F</small> <small>THERE</small> had been a handbook on how to put together a successful expansion package, it would have been a best-seller in cities like Denver, Orlando, Tampa—St. Petersburg, Buffalo and countless others. As with any other major civic or business undertaking, Denver's bid to win baseball's favor was filled with anger, recrimination, subterfuge, intrigue, back-alley maneuvering and chicanery. Too many issues. Too many vested interests. But the job got done, somehow.

"I look back sometimes on the months we spent, and I can think of at least five or six times when I thought, 'We've reached a dead end; this thing just isn't going to fly,' " Colorado Governor Roy Romer would later remark. "We had no money, it seemed public support was flagging. . . . I got to the point where every time I went to a function with local businesspeople, I'd ask, 'So, you think you could spare a couple million?' "

Denver, like most every other city vying for membership in "The Club," did it, in Romer's words, "totally back-asswards." There were so many issues to resolve, and in such a short time:

Would Denver need to build a new baseball-only stadium, as stipulated by Major League Baseball? Or would existing Mile High Stadium, a 75,000-seat multipurpose complex used by the football Broncos and a minor-league baseball team, be suitable?

If baseball insisted on a baseball-only stadium—the better to guarantee a favorable revenue stream and preferred scheduling dates—then how to finance it? Publicly? Privately? Both? How would the citizens of Denver, a city slowly crawling its way out of the economic morass of the oil-bust 1980s, react to public subsidies for a baseball stadium?

And who would comprise the team ownership? Baseball required a broadly based, locally dominated ownership core. But Denver is not a city of billionaires. Most of the major movers and shakers lost their shirts when real estate went the way of oil.

With Davis out of the picture, having moved to California, Denver was left with limited options.

The whole issue, quite naturally, was money. Remember: Baseball expanded only because some powerful politicians held the gun to its head. The owners were facing huge fines for having colluded against free agents in the 1980s; the expansion money would help pay those fines. Expansion was not an act of goodwill or charity. If baseball was going to open its doors to new members, it was damn sure going to bring in members who could pull their financial weight. The new team had to feature an owner with deep pockets, and a stadium whose revenue streams would guarantee that those pockets remained deep.

On every important issue, Denver moved from the gate slowly, unsurely. Rumors swirled that the Mile High City, once a shoo-in for an expansion team, had blown a huge ninth-inning lead. Truth is, most of those rumors were right. At least for a time.

• *The Stadium:*   The critics had a point. Years earlier, tax dollars had been used to refurbish Mile High in order to make the stadium more user-friendly for baseball. Why, they wondered, build a baseball-only stadium to appease baseball's aristocracy? Moreover, multipurpose stadiums were in use throughout professional sports. Even Senator Wirth, the consummate optimist, was crestfallen when he heard of baseball's requirements. "I mean, that really eliminates us," he said in 1988. "With all these things we have to do in Denver, we're not about to assume that the taxpayers are going to pony up 80 million dollars for a baseball-only stadium."

• *The Ownership:*   Other cities had it easy. Buffalo boasted frozen-food giant Robert Rich. Miami offered up Blockbuster Video mogul Wayne Huizenga. But Denver? The leader of its bid was a small, unassuming fellow with bulging eyes and a ramshackle real estate office. John Dikeou, who had owned the minor-league Denver Zephyrs, was not everybody's idea of the perfect man to lead the city's charge. His problem wasn't a lack of money, at least initially, but that Major League Baseball wanted a dynamic personality, a front man who would fit in well with the boys at The Club, and Dikeou did not fit that bill. He gave interviews grudgingly, not out of arrogance but sincere shyness. His idea of a big night on the town was pitching for his softball team, then retiring to his favorite pub, Rodney's, for a couple of cold ones. While Rich and Huizenga were leading the cheers for their cities, Dikeou was keeping his usual low profile.

Even Major League Baseball was dropping quiet hints to Denver baseball organizers about Dikeou's suitability.

And then the bombs started dropping in the summer of 1990. Dikeou was in financial trouble. First, he was sued for defaulting on a bank-loan balance of $7.2 million. Then, in the next two weeks, there were four foreclosure suits and two other actions taken against Dikeou. Always a man who treasured his privacy, he finally decided to step aside, fearing that more negative publicity would hurt his business and his family. His detractors suggested a more sinister agenda: Dikeou, they claimed, had no intention of owning the team, and was simply staying on board with the idea of winning territorial-rights dollars—money the new major-league club would have to pay the owner of the existing minor-league team.

It was time, once again, for Denver to scramble. The taxpayers had held up their end of the deal, approving a stadium tax despite the tumult surrounding the club's potential ownership. Governor Romer and his aides had less than two weeks to find a dozen or so deep pockets who happened to love baseball and didn't get physically sick at the thought of a $95-million initiation fee. The Denver proponents would have to make good right away on a $100,000 fee to Major League Baseball, just for the honor of being included in their sweepstakes. An ownership group was hastily pieced together; it would change a number of times in the next few months and would ultimately be led, at least by the time of the expansion decision, by Boulder attorney Steve Ehrhart and businessmen John Antonucci and Mickey Monus, who hailed from Youngstown, Ohio.

It was the bottom of the ninth. Denver's bid was trailing. Things were getting desperate.

Rumors flew everywhere. One Chicago columnist wrote that Denver's bid was dying because of "a failed stadium referendum." Failed? It had won, 54 to 46 percent, at the polls. Misinformation was everywhere. Orlando's people ripped Miami's people. Newspapers in Denver trashed Buffalo's weather. Talkshow jocks in Buffalo questioned Denver's altitude.

Meanwhile, Denver was busy trying to gets its act together. A stadium site was chosen, an old, abandoned railroad yard in Lower Downtown. A tentative lease was signed with the Stadium District. And finally, after a lot of begging and a lot of posturing, Coors, the beer-brewing conglomerate, stepped to the plate by agreeing to transfer $15 million in naming rights over to the ownership group. Almost overnight, Denver's ownership group went from being shaky and led by out-of-state interests to being rock-solid and local in flavor. A Coors Silver Bullet was raised in pubs all over town.

It all set the table for what promised to be the biggest day in Denver's baseball history. March 26, 1991: the day the expansion committee came to town.

This eight-person contingent—NL president Bill White, Doug Danforth of the Pittsburgh Pirates, Fred Wilpon of the New York Mets, Bill Giles of the Philadelphia Phillies, NL senior vice-president Phyllis Collins, NL public affairs VP Katy Feeney and two league secretaries—had already toured the other five cities on the expansion shortlist. They had heard speeches. They had seen dog-and-pony shows. They had been wined and dined. And after each visit, local writers were left looking for hints in the most innocuous comments. But the expansion committee wasn't showing its hand.

Around 10:15 in the morning they arrived by private jet at Stapleton Airport, where Mayor Peña gave Danforth a baseball bat in the shape of a key. From there, four helicopters took them over East High School, whose band marched in the form of a baseball. A few moments later, the helicopters dipped low toward the stadium site, which had been gussied up for the day's appearances. Ordinarily, the railroad yard was a favorite spot for winos on a week-long binge. But on this day, the winos were gone, and kids were playing baseball on a chalk-outlined field. One helicopter pilot, Peter Peelgrane, noted that his group of baseball executives remained eerily silent throughout the flight.

By 10:35, the contingent had landed on the outfield grass at Mile High, where they were met by about two dozen Denver dignitaries and baseball proponents. The pitch began: about Denver's baseball history; about the efficacy of playing at Mile High while waiting for the completion of the new stadium; about the quality of the clubhouses. Someone said, "And, of course, we should mention that Mr. White here hit .276 for the Denver Bears the year he played here."

"Really?" White said, shaking his head. "I thought I hit at least .300 that year."

Peña, ever the politician, came to his defense. "Sir," he said to White, "if you think you hit .300, then you hit .300."

The whirlwind stadium tour completed, the group moved on to the governor's mansion, where it was surprised to meet not only Colorado's leaders but also the governor of Wyoming and representatives from Nebraska and Utah. "By the time they were done with the number crunching," Danforth recalled, laughing, "they had us convinced there were about five million people in the region this franchise could draw upon. I'm just glad they didn't suggest they would draw from California. That might have strained their credibility just a tad."

After lunch, the group marched over to the atrium of the United Bank Center, where they would engage in serious discussions related to the Denver ownership's financial situation. But first, they were met by a raucous crowd of more than 5,000 fans, loudly applauding them as if they were visiting royalty and singing "Take Me Out to the Ball Game."

"Do you believe this?" Wilpon said to Danforth, the two men engulfed in sound.

"I never get an ovation like this back in Pittsburgh," Danforth said.

Denver was not supposed to do this, actually, what with the committee's prohibition about prestaged rallies and the like. "It was like Schwarzkopf walked in," said Paul Jacobs, the team's legal counsel. "I'll tell you: I got choked up and they got choked up, too. I think it was one of the most important things that happened."

Denver planners had gambled and won. One of the committee members later admitted that the huge crowd had made their day—made their trip, actually. The "impromptu" rally had driven home an essential point: While Denver did not have the single, well-heeled owner or the overwhelming population base, it had the spirit, it had the people—folks who had voted to tax themselves during a time of tax revolts in order to win over baseball.

When the high-level meetings up on the 31st floor went long —way long—the rumblings began in the pressroom, where the reporters waited for the puff of white smoke. "What do you think this means? . . . It's got to mean good things for us. . . . Why else would they stay up there so long? . . . How long did they meet in Buffalo? . . . In Tampa? . . . In Orlando?"

Governor Romer, exhausted, moved off into a corner and fell completely asleep.

Two hours and 40 minutes later, the expansion committee emerged and held a press conference that mimicked their previous press conferences in Orlando, Tampa and the rest. The answers were well rehearsed. Denver was wonderful. Denver was viable. But, then, they'd said all those same things about the other five cities on the shortlist.

Rockies executive John McHale, though, sensed something good happening that day. "I have had or been part of meetings with baseball people and owners on literally hundreds, if not thousands, of occasions and I have some sense of when people are merely being polite or when they're interested," he said. "These people were interested."

Now came the worst part: the waiting. Word was the expansion committee would make its recommendation to the 26 team owners in early June, then hope for a rubber-stamp approval at the June 12 meetings in Santa Monica, California. What to do until then? Not much. Argue about the team name. Argue about the team colors. The time was right for some major-league speculation. The media in all six expansion cities were only too happy to fill that void.

In time, word began to filter out that Orlando, Buffalo and Washington were out of the running, leaving three—Denver, Tampa–St. Pete and Miami—to make two. So, would the owners go with the obvious geographic move, placing one Florida team in the National League East and Denver in the West? Or might the owners look strictly at the Southeast region's growth potential and place both teams in Florida? If, indeed, the National League tried to monopolize Florida, might the American League owners—upset not only about losing the Florida market for themselves but angry about receiving less than half ($75.6 million) of the $190 million in expansion fees—block the Florida land grab?

By early June, word had leaked that Denver and Miami were in. The clamor continued on June 6 when it was announced that the final decision would not be made at the Santa Monica meetings, after all. The delay, it turned out, was little more than an American League power play designed to protest Commissioner Vincent's decision on the division of expansion monies. Still, though, the people of Denver remained dubious. They remembered 1977. They remembered the close calls.

The process dragged on, owners battling other owners on the financial front, but in truth the decision had been made. It was Denver and Miami. When the vote finally came on July 3, it was something of an anticlimax. But Denver was in the mood to party anyway. After 30 years of waiting and praying, Denver was finally major league.

"We said it all along," said Ehrhart after the official coronation. "This was not a race, but a marathon. We fell behind at times, but we never slowed up or lost sight of the finish line. We just kept chugging away."

Back home in Denver, Frank Haraway looked at all those marked-up old scorecards, the ones that bore the names of people like Marvelous Marv Throneberry and Tim Raines, minor-leaguers in a major-league town. "I'm going to have to make more space for the new scorecards," he said, joyously.

6

Rough Drafts

T HE PROCESS of building a ball club began in late October 1991, shortly after Gebhard had settled in behind a desk in the club's half-finished corporate offices in downtown Denver. Rockies scouts were dispatched all over the North American continent and the Caribbean in search of young talent for the June 1992 amateur draft. These would be the kids—the babies, really —who would provide the franchise's foundation, the ones who would go to A ball in Visalia, California, or labor in Mesa, Arizona, playing those 8:00 A.M. games in order to avoid the stifling summer heat, many miles and a good three, four years, or more, from a chance at The Show.

Scouting ballplayers is a not-so-sweet science that just happens to look a little bit like a crapshoot. The numbers are not in a scout's favor. Like the game itself, scouting is grounded in failure. A batter who succeeds three times in 10 ends up in the Hall of Fame. A scout who is right once every 10 tries is hailed as a genius. Anybody with a television and decent vision could tell you Shaquille O'Neal would be an "impact player" in the NBA. But how do you project where Johnny Smith, age 17, all-world high school shortstop from West Hellhole High, will be at age 24? Bodies change. Attitudes change. And pitchers start throwing the curve on 3-1 counts.

Gebhard assembled his area scouts and cross-checkers and inculcated them with the Rockies way of doing things. His philsophy was simple: Look for arms, look for college kids and be right once every great while.

"What I told them, among other things, is this," said Gebhard. "I told them with the thin air in Denver, the way the ball carries, we felt we would be able to sign free-agent hitters who would want to come to Denver. You look at a Galarraga or a Boston—if you can still play, you can ring up big numbers. The area that concerned us most—and everybody else in baseball, obviously—was pitching. We decided we didn't have a system full of prospects, so we had to be on the fast pace and draft college players as opposed to high school players. Everything being equal, we decided to go with college kids, especially pitchers, with the hope they would make it to the majors in three, four years."

One day in early May 1992, the Rockies scouts—the nomads—found themselves back together on the 17th floor of a downtown Denver high-rise, glancing toward the snow-capped mountains and remembering the places—too many to recall, really—they had been. The Pits. Nowhere. West Nowhere. Damned Close to the End of the Earth. One town after another, one rental car and motel room after another, all that time spent scouring the baseball landscape in the hopes of mining a baseball gem.

There was Randy Smith, the assistant general manager, a 30-year-old perpetually tanned wunderkind. He had the bloodlines, and he had the background, having previously served as the Padres' scouting director.

There was Pat Daugherty, the Rockies' scouting director, a fellow who had spent all his life on the field as a coach and scouting supervisor. Now here he was, Gebhard's second choice for the position—after Montreal's Frank Wren, who ended up with the Marlins—attempting to make the move to the administrative side.

There was Herb Hippauf, the team's national cross-checker, an avuncular fellow with an easy manner and a reputation for thoroughness.

And there were stories:

DAUGHERTY: "I'm guessing if we sign 40 players and three make the big leagues, that'll be a helluva draft."

HIPPAUF: "I think the average is two and a half players per draft."

SMITH (laughing): "And that half is a helluva player."

HIPPAUF: "I'd say 10 percent or so get to the big leagues, but only 2 to 3 percent spend a year or more at that level. About one of 18 draftees, basically. It may sound like it's a crapshoot, but there's a definite method to it. It's not a piece of cake, looking at an 18-year-old and projecting what he'll be like when he's 23, 25 years old. Especially projecting what kind of hitter he'll be."

DAUGHERTY: "Oh, yeah, the aluminum bat has made it so difficult to scout a hitter. And a pitcher. It's been a monster for scouting people."

SMITH: "It shows up everywhere. You've got guys swinging light aluminum bats, the pitchers don't throw inside, infielders lay back on balls because balls jump off the bat. So it shows up in pitching, hitting and defense."

DAUGHERTY: "It's a vicious cycle because a kid pitches inside, a guy hits a shot off the handle for a double, so eventually he goes slider away, slider away, all breaking pitches. As a result, he loses arm strength because now, of 100 pitches, 75, 80 are sliders, and that's all brought on by that bat."

SMITH: "There are only two things in scouting that are scientific. That's velocity, which is radar, and running speed, where you use the stopwatch. The rest is instinct and judgment."

DAUGHERTY: "And traveling. I've forgotten what my family looks like. This is all very new for me and it's killing me. You start with that damn 5 A.M. wakeup call, you get in your rental car, you've gotta find the airport, you check in, you check your luggage in, you arrive at the destination, get your baggage, get the rental car, try to find out where the fucking game is, get to the ballpark, hope it's not gonna rain or the kid's not sick or the coach isn't gonna change his mind and use somebody else, go get a motel and try and find someplace open to eat. Then you check in and wait for that 5 A.M. wakeup call again. The only time I relaxed was at the game, but by the seventh inning, I start worrying, 'Where the hell is the hotel?' "

HIPPAUF: "My favorite is you go to see a hitter, he gets up four times, they intentionally walk him twice and you see all of two swings."

SMITH: "I was the rain man this year. I probably hit rain five times. I had one trip where I was rained on, hailed on and snowed on in 24 hours."

DAUGHERTY: "And shit on."

HIPPAUF: "There are so many flights and hotels, I remember calling my wife and leaving a message on voice mail one day. I said, 'Hi, I'm in, uh, um, oh shit . . . I don't know where I am.' She must have thought I was crazy. I had no idea where I was."

SMITH: "It's crazy, but you have more fun at those meetings and then draft day. I mean, by the late rounds, you're just giddy."

Come draft day, the Rockies and the whole city were giddy. Their first pick was a local kid, a big, blond right-handed pitcher named John Burke, who starred at Cherry Creek High School. Elsewhere in baseball, the amateur draft is greeted by a huge civic yawn. After all, college baseball has not achieved the same status as college hoops or football. Who knew these players? And the high schoolers were shrouded in anonymity, known only by the hard-core baseball cognoscenti. But in Denver, it was a party. Who was Garvin Alston, or Jason Hutchins? Nobody knew. But they were Rockies. They were *ours*, the region seemed to say. That was enough.

THE MARRIOTT MARQUIS, right off Times Square in New York City, resonated with the usual early-morning buzz, myopic businessmen and women walking in feverish lockstep. Gebhard, rheumy-eyed and teetering on the brink of exhaustion, watched the miasmic swirl. He was mainlining black coffee and cigarettes, his voice sounding like he'd gargled with whiskey and razor blades.

"Two hours' sleep," he croaked as he gazed at the ersatz potted palms.

It was November 18, 1992, and the expansion draft was over. Finally. More than 100,000 man-hours' worth of work, more than 3,000 players scouted, more than 5,000 bags of airline peanuts, enough frequent-flier miles to earn seven trips to Bali and a few thousand nights at the Motel 6 in West Bumstock, Alabama —and this was it.

The end.

And the beginning, too.

The Rockies and the Florida Marlins had rounded out their roster just one day (and night) earlier, giving shape and form to what had heretofore been a crazy concept. Major League Baseball hadn't expanded since 1977, when it added the Toronto Blue Jays and the Seattle Mariners. And now, 15 years later, they were back at it in a Marriott ballroom bursting with a color scheme of Marlins teal and Rockies purple and a wood filigree trim, the ultimate made-for-ESPN event.

For many baseball observers, the draft was a victory of flash over substance. Peter Bavasi, the man responsible for the Blue Jays' 1976 expansion draft, said, "This is not a pretty sight. At first glance, it seems like a better deal than in the past, but really the opportunity for the newcomers is simply dreadful." Herk Robinson, the Kansas City Royals' general manager, couldn't keep his tongue out of his cheek: "This is the most celebrated, ceremonial, sophisticated, heralded draft in the history of mankind," he said, stifling a laugh. Added Bavasi, "These expansion teams are simply getting shafted."

Gebhard gazed at his expansion list of has-beens, never-weres and might-bes and drew a deep, happy sigh.

"This feels like Christmas Day," he said, taking a long pull on another cigarette. "There's all that anticipation, wrapping the presents, waiting for the big day to come, and then it comes along and that's it . . . you just go flat.''

Do not misunderstand: Gebhard, a stoic Minnesotan (is that redundant, or what?) was not unhappy with his choices. He did not wake up this ''Christmas'' morning to find a lump of coal. Alex Cole, yes. But Gebhard was not displeased. He came away with his 1993 starting lineup, using the first round of the draft to pluck young veterans, such as former Yankees third baseman Charlie Hayes and ex–San Diego Padres outfielder Jerald Clark. He also got prospects, notably David Nied, the number-one pick of the entire draft, and catcher Brad Ausmus.

The Rockies' and Marlins' philosophies were markedly different. The Marlins used the first round to take what they deemed were the best young prospects—kids two, three years away from the majors. They figured this: With a huge financial war chest, they could always fill out the roster later by paying for high-priced free agents or nontendered free agents, the latter being players—usually veterans on the downside of their career—not offered a contract by December 20.

The Rockies took a different approach. Denver was initially viewed as a small market—at least by basic demographic standards—and Coors Field, which would produce sizable revenues once ready for the 1995 season, was still a mere hole in the ground. The result: The Rockies figured they'd better get the best major-leaguers early or take a chance on a disastrous 115-loss season. ''We don't have the luxury of going out later and filling out a roster with free agents,'' Gebhard said at the time. They were ever mindful not only of salary today, but arbitration tomorrow. In the end, the Rockies' Opening Day payroll was $8.7 million, far and away the lowest in all of baseball.

''From day one, we talked about being a young club,'' Gebhard said later. ''But once we saw the protected lists, we felt like we could kill two birds with one stone. We could stay with our basic philosophy of going with young players, but at the same time get guys with major-league experience who could represent us better in the early years.

"We knew we weren't going to go out and get a $3- to $4-million player, but we knew would get some guys who might be coming off bad years and get them at a reduced price. So we didn't really stray from what we said we were going to do. Guys like Joe Girardi, Jerald Clark, Charlie Hayes, they all figure into our future. And we felt a definite responsibility to our fans. We're going to break a lot of attendance records, and I just couldn't throw a bunch of Double-A guys out there and say, 'Hey, be patient.' We owe them something now. And we found a way to do that, with the Clarks and Girardis, without straying from the master plan."

After the draft, the Marlins went after two high-salaried free agents, catcher Benito Santiago and Japanese home-run king Orestes Destrade. They had also drafted Angels reliever Bryan Harvey, who the Angels' doctors insisted was still damaged goods. The Rockies went after none—in fact, Santiago, Destrade and Harvey together made more than the entire Colorado payroll. They also passed on folks like Danny Tartabull and George Bell.

"It's not just us," said Gebhard. "We asked a number of teams, 'If we take Tartabull, if we take Bell, what will you give us in a trade?' Nobody wanted them. That's the state of baseball these days. Everybody is trying to trim payroll."

The consensus was this: Economics dictated the dramatically diverse philosophies.

"The Rockies just drafted a team that will be respectable in 1993, 1994 and maybe 1995," said one general manager at the draft. "The Marlins just drafted a team that will lose 100 or more games the next couple of seasons, but they'll be consistent winners once the kids mature."

Gebhard disagreed with this analysis. He knew the lessons of history. The Toronto Blue Jays drafted young and took their lumps early, and subsequently put together 10 straight winning seasons and a World Series championship in 1992. The Mariners, conversely, went the competitiveness-now route and did not reach the .500 mark until 1991.

"Honestly, even if I had an unlimited budget, I wouldn't have gone any other way," Gebhard said. "First of all, we got a lot of the young kids we really want on the later rounds. Second, if you look at these players we're all calling 'veterans,' hey, they're 27, 28 years old. These aren't washed-up, old players. The other advantage is it gives us the luxury of not having to rush our young kids from the minors. We can let them develop and still put a competitive team on the field. Plus, we felt very good about our amateur draft."

There was nonetheless a growing sentiment, within the Rockies organization and without, that Colorado was behind. And they were behind because they had started later—Gebhard had been allowed to remain with the Twins until the end of the 1991 World Series—and because they hadn't spent nearly the kind of money that the Marlins had. Florida jumped from the gate in every area, flooding the country and the Caribbean with a superior number of scouts at the amateur, the minor-league and the major-league levels. Team owner Wayne Huizenga could boast of deep pockets, and he was willing to spend.

Meanwhile, the Rockies were just emerging from a long and tortuous change in ownership. One of the managing general partners, Mickey Monus, had become the target of an investigation into alleged fraud at the Phar-Mor pharmaceutical chain and was forced to drop out of the picture in August. Soon thereafter, Monus's friend and business associate John Antonucci, another Rockies managing partner, was forced to give up some of his ownership share; a lot of his money was tied up in Phar-Mor stock. Antonucci stayed past the expansion draft as the club's front man and most visible managing partner, but trucking executive Jerry McMorris slowly was emerging as the real power and money behind the operation.

The Marlins came out of the gate with six minor-league teams; the Rockies, four. The Marlins had five major-league scouts; the Rockies scouted the majors with only Gebhard and Bear. The Marlins had 31 scouts and an entire Latin American operation that included 17 people on staff. In nearly every administrative area, the Rockies were outmanned.

Question is, who was responsible?

Gebhard would never say publicly that he was fiscally hamstrung. "I'll let you say that," he said to reporters. But which was the truth? The day after the expansion draft, Gebhard was vehement that he'd been given all the resources he required. When McMorris said in a July 1993 interview that the Antonucci-led ownership group had slowed the club's progress with a tight budget, some Rockies employees still loyal to Antonucci bristled at Gebhard's failure to defend the people who had hired him. "Geb's a small-market guy," said one member of the club's staff. "If he wanted something, John wasn't going to turn him down. But Geb never asked. He's conservative by nature."

Daugherty, the team's director of scouting, said, "I'm hearing all this stuff after the fact that we were hamstrung. But I can tell you, there was never a time when me or Geb went to John to ask for something and didn't get it. Our philosophy was, Why hire all these part-time guys who just want to sit around and make an easy paycheck and aren't willing to work hard? Sure, we had a smaller staff than the Marlins, but I felt good about what we had. We stretched guys out—sure. But we went for a smaller group of guys whose judgment we knew we could trust."

McMorris's view was this: "John [Antonucci] always used to say, 'They [the Marlins] have gone way overboard.' He would say, 'We're doing it just right.' And Geb never complained. He came from Minnesota, which is a small market, so he's used to operating with a streamlined scouting staff. I guess only time will tell."

Gebhard would never bitch and whine for public consumption, but he told friends he was, indeed, shackled by a rather limited budget. The constraints were not a source of discouragement, though; he had worked in small-budget organizations before, and he understood why Antonucci and company were conservative in their estimates of the team's first-year fiscal success. "John had no way of knowing it was going to be like this," Gebhard said later in the season. "Fifty-five thousand a night? Nobody did."

One day after the draft, Gebhard knew the truth: The pickings were slim. Each expansion franchise had paid out $95 million in fees. And for what?

The feeling among some analysts was that the Marlins and Rockies would come away with the best expansion teams in baseball history. The pundits noted that the expansionists would be the first ever to draft nobodies from both leagues, as opposed to previous expansionists, who chose only from within their league. They forgot to note, though, that the Rockies and Marlins were going three-deep into an already-depleted 26-team pool. Baseball's country-clubbers took the expansionists' exorbitant entrance fees and told them they were getting a diamond in return, but the expansionists knew better.

They were getting a cubic zirconium.

"These clubs have a chance to be the most competitive expansion teams ever," said Toronto Blue Jays general manager Pat Gillick. "If they're willing to spend the money."

Right. If they're willing to spend the money.

Sure, the Rockies could have broken the bank to purchase Tartabull and some other established, high-priced stars, even some free agents. But what sense did it make? The Rockies arrived with 28,500 season-ticket holders. They were guaranteed box-office hits, sure to revel in a civic honeymoon for two, three years and maybe longer. These weren't the 1962 New York Mets, who felt compelled to win the town over by bringing in players with local ties. These weren't the 1969 Seattle Pilots, who brought in veterans Don Mincher and Tommy Davis to lure the locals to the ballpark.

"What good would it have done us to bring in a big name at that salary?" Gebhard asked. "We're not that concerned about next year. We want to know where we'll be three, four, five years down the road. You look at recent history, and it shows that free agency is not the cure-all. The Mets and Dodgers had two of the highest payrolls in the game. Where did they finish?"

On the morning after, Gebhard's eyes were at half-mast, puffy slits through which the world seemed an odder place. He was lost in a fog of cigarette smoke and postdraft dementia. One night earlier, manager Don Baylor had stood before a packed house of baseball journalists and unveiled what he viewed as his Opening Day starting lineup.

"Andres Galarraga at first, Eric Young at second, Freddie Benavides at short, Charlie Hayes at third, Jerald Clark in left field, Alex Cole in center field, Dante Bichette in right field, Joe Girardi catching and David Nied pitching . . ."

An expansion team cannot be judged over the short term. Indeed, free agency made it possible to enjoy earlier success; if a team had a bottomless pit of money, it could snap up all the big-name free agents and present a highly competitive team. But history suggested that expansion teams are better off using the early years to stock their farm systems, to live with the losses and wait till next decade. On the average, it took expansion teams eight years to reach .500; only the Angels bucked the trend by hitting that mark their second year.

Gebhard knew, though, that next year's lineup, or record, really wouldn't matter. This was about laying the foundation, about plotting a course for the future. Today's decisions would affect the Rockies for years to come. Gebhard, exhausted and satisfied, didn't seem to mind that burden.

7

Cat Man Do

DON ZIMMER SAT as he always did, like a Buddha with his omnipresent fungo bat, surveying the gray expanse of Montreal's Olympic Stadium. Then his gaze was averted to his first baseman, Andres Galarraga, who had opened the season hitting .406. The Rockies were only 3-5 after that inaugural home stand, but the Big Cat, it seemed, was back.

"There's a proud man right there," Zimmer said affectionately. "Isn't anybody here who wants to do better these next two stops than that man right there."

These next two stops were Montreal and St. Louis, two cities that inspired a crazy quilt of emotions for the affable Venezuelan. The Montreal Expos organization had been his home for so many years—seven years in the minors, six in the majors. He had been a star there, and the fans loved his line-drive hitting style, his catlike defense near the first-base bag and his endearing personality. His best years had come in Montreal; he hit .305 with 13 homers and 90 RBIs in 1987, then .302 with 29 homers and 92 RBIs in 1988. But then he began to trail off, slightly during the

1989 and 1990 seasons, and then more dramatically in 1991 before being dealt to the St. Louis Cardinals.

His bat was getting slower. He couldn't handle the inside pitch. The word throughout baseball, the most damning indictment of all, was this: Galarraga was finished, washed up, a brilliant supernova who had flamed out sooner than anyone could have expected. The Cardinals had offered to renegotiate Galarraga's contract, proposing more security at lower wages, but Galarraga and his agent rejected the offer. Baylor, who had worked tirelessly as Galarraga's hitting coach in St. Louis, disagreed with the conventional wisdom.

"About a week, 10 days before the expansion draft, we started talking informally about some guys who might be out there," said Baylor. "When Cat's name came up in conversation, I thought at the time he might be too expensive. He was making, like, two million dollars plus an option from the Cardinals. But we went in with an offer [$600,000 a year plus incentives] and he accepted right away.

"I didn't need to do much to convince Geb. He had him in Montreal, so it wasn't really a tough sell. The tougher sell would be Jerry McMorris, because he probably didn't know who in hell Andres Galarraga was."

Here is who Galarraga was: He was a once-promising star who had lost it. Or so it seemed. His was not a short-range funk, not a typical mid-season 10-game slump. He was lost. He was Steve Blass, a pitcher who forgot how to find the strike zone. He was Mackey Sasser, a catcher who had a problem throwing the ball back to the pitcher. He was a pro golfer who was shanking eight irons, his lifelong strengths having become a weakness. Ever since his days on the sandlots of Caracas, he had always known how to hit the baseball, and hit it a long way. But now it had become a mystery, an unfathomable Zen koan that eluded rational explanation.

The pain seared his soul. He would pick up the St. Louis newspapers and see a chart comparing himself and the man for whom he was traded, Ken Hill. Bad enough that Hill was becoming one of the most accomplished starting pitchers in all of baseball. But at one point, Hill had hit one home run while Galarraga had none.

The Cat is a thick man, but thin-skinned. The criticism was eating him alive. It got to the point where he didn't want to leave the house, didn't want to chat up the fans or leisurely talk some ball.

"I never told anybody, not the media, not my teammates, nobody, but I thought about going home, giving up," said Galarraga. "I thought about it during the season. I couldn't do anything. I was so down, there was nothing I could do. I kept telling people, 'Yeah, I know I can play this game, and I know I can still hit,' but I didn't know, really. And then I just started letting everything bother me. A fan would say something, instead of ignoring it, I took it to heart. I take everything personally. That's one of my big problems."

Worse, on February 22, 1992, his father, Francisco Galarraga, died from stomach cancer. He had been a house painter who worked hard to support his wife and five children, of whom Andres was the youngest. Francisco had never been a huge baseball fan, but he was hugely supportive. Andres acquired a love of painting from him; Galarraga paints portraits in his spare time, and has sold some of his work in galleries.

"The whole year was terrible," he said. "My father died. And then, two games into the year, I break my hand. Then, when I come back, I try too hard, I think too much. I've never had so much trouble hitting the baseball."

He may as well have lost the faculty of speech or basic motor skills. Galarraga incapable of hitting a baseball? This was what defined him. He was a unique athlete, thick through the shoulders and legs but graceful as a lithe shortstop. He was powerfully built, but best suited to hitting the ball the opposite way, to right center field.

"Just listen to the sound the ball makes off his bat," Rockies hitting instructor Amos Otis was saying one morning during a spring-training batting-practice session. Otis, who hit .277 in seventeen years of major-league ball—three with the Mets and 14 with the Royals—had joined the Rockies' coaching staff from the

San Diego Padres organization. "The great hitters, the ball makes a different sound off the bat. Listen to that—*thwack!* It's a different sound. Andres is a hitter."

This was what he did from the time he was five years old, running around his inner-city Caracas neighborhood, rousting friends from their houses and pleading with them to come out and play ball. Any kind of ball. Whiffle ball. Baseball. Stoopball. Whatever. The only time he wasn't playing, he was watching baseball on television. Galarraga remembered watching two, three games a week on the TV, remembered seeing his heroes, like Roberto Clemente.

"I used to get everybody in trouble," Galarraga said with a laugh. "We would play before school, and sometimes, we would play during school instead of going to class. I would say, 'C'mon, let's keep playing,' and we would miss class. I just loved the game so much. It's all I wanted to do."

Galarraga played sandlot ball for his neighborhood, La Florida Champellin, until he was 16 years old, when he was discovered by fellow Venezuelan and former major-leaguer Chico Carrasquel, who was impressed by Galarraga's single-minded drive, his work habits and his ability to drive the baseball. At 16, Galarraga tried out for the Venezuelan National Team; he didn't make it, went home and cried. A few weeks later, the manager called back and asked Galarraga if he would join the team; he refused, asking, "Why didn't you pay attention to me the first time?"

Soon thereafter, he signed with Carrasquel and the Caracas Leones, a winter-ball team that included major-leaguers like Tony Armas, Bo Diaz and Manny Trillo. He was surrounded by fellow Venezuelans who had been in The Show, and he mimicked their every move. "When they did drills, I did the drill," he said. "When they ran, I ran. I learned how they work and what it takes to be a major-leaguer. Armas was especially good to me because he was very similar, a big man who hit for power."

Two years later, Felipe Alou, then a minor-league manager and now the Montreal Expos' manager, scouted Galarraga and talked his organization into signing him. The ink had not dried on his contract when Galarraga, an 18-year-old Venezuelan who had never been outside Latin America, found himself in three countries within a month—Venezuela, the United States and Canada.

"I can still vividly remember Cat at his first spring training," said Gebhard, who was working in the Expos system back in 1979. "He was a skinny kid, but he had a lot of pop in his bat. And he always had that smile on his face. You would talk to him, and I'm not sure he always understood, but he was always smiling and nodding like he knew what you were saying. I remember we had a complex there with three adjoining fields, and Cat had about three home runs the first week there, so when Cat was up, the guys on the other fields, the ones who weren't playing, would come over when Cat was batting."

Galarraga was assigned to West Palm Beach, Florida, where Larry Bearnath was the manager. A few weeks later, he was demoted to Calgary, about 10 light-years away from his beloved Venezuela.

"I didn't speak one word of English," said Galarraga. "Not one. I was completely lost and very scared. I wanted to call home to my parents every day, but there wasn't enough money for that. So I ended up calling once a week. It was terrible, really. I mostly stayed with other Latin players, but we were all very lost. We would go to a restaurant and just point at the menu. We didn't know what we were getting; we'd just point. It was frustrating; very frustrating. I couldn't communicate. And it was so different. When I got to Calgary, it was cold and I didn't have a coat or sweaters. I had to buy some when I got there."

It is a problem many Hispanic ballplayers had, and some still have, being transported at a very young age to a new country, forced to acculturate, to learn a new language without any real help. Kids like Galarraga were sent to West Palm or Calgary or wherever, and asked to produce on the field while they were still trying to figure out how to order a cheeseburger from a menu. That situation has improved over the years, though, with the increasing influx of Latin players. More and more organizations have taken steps to ease the transition; the Expos and Dodgers, for example, hold English-language classes for Latin players after spring-training sessions. Galarraga had none of those advantages.

"When I called home, I tried not to tell my mother how bad it was," Galarraga said. "I would say, 'I'm getting used to it. I'm not doing good now, but I'll be okay.' If I told her how I really felt, if I told her how frustrated and lonely I was, she would have said, 'That's it, then you come back home.' Believe me, I thought about going home every day. Every day. I thought about it all the time. . . . But something inside me kept saying, 'Stay with it. Do something good for your family. Make them proud.' The only time I feel comfortable there is when I go to the ballpark because all I have to do is play baseball. That's where I take all my frustrations. I don't have to speak English, I don't have to talk or worry about anything, just baseball."

In 1981, Galarraga was sent to the Expos' affiliate in Jamestown, New York. "The best thing for me was going to Jamestown," he recalled. "I was the only Latin player on the team, so it forced me to speak English. I was very lonely there, but I learned the language much quicker. I would read my dictionary and watch a lot of TV, read the newspapers. And [pitcher] Randy St. Claire helped me a lot. He would tell me, 'Andres, you don't say it that way, you say it *that* way.' I appreciated that.

"For a long time, probably four years, I always did an interview with somebody translating. Even when I went out, I didn't want to say something in English and say it wrong. I don't want anybody laughing at me and saying, 'He's stupid,' because it comes out the wrong way. After four years, I did my first interview in English. But even now, I still get so nervous, especially on TV. That's why sometimes I ask the TV guys what questions they will ask so I can think of how I want to say it in English."

During the Rockies' spring training, Galarraga could be found offering counsel to Roberto Mejia, the Dominican sensation who was being besieged by interview requests after a fast start. "When I look at Mejia, I see myself," said Galarraga. "That was me 10 years ago. It's very confusing. That's why I try to help our Latin players now, like Armando Reynoso and Vinny Castilla."

As Galarraga's language skills improved, so did his game. He also found security, and serenity, when he was married in 1984. "I used to study at her brother's house," he said of his wife, Eneyda. "I remember seeing her when she was a little girl."

He joined the Expos in 1985, getting only 75 at-bats. But in 1986, he burst onto the scene as one of the finest first basemen in baseball, hitting .271 with 10 homers and 42 RBIs in just 321 at-bats. One year later, he bloomed as a full-fledged star, putting up MVP-caliber numbers.

"I was very happy then," Galarraga said. "Hitting was very simple. Nothing mental. Just go up to the plate and hit the ball."

But something happened, something nearly imperceptible. Before the 1989 season, Expos batting instructor Joe Sparks and manager Buck Rodgers suggested that Galarraga would hit even more home runs and drive in more runs if he lowered his hands in his stance and pulled the ball more often. "I had a decent season (.257, 85 RBIs), but I felt confused at the plate," he said. "I felt like I was losing my natural swing. People started throwing me fastballs inside, and I couldn't get my hands through.

By 1991, Galarraga was completely confused, struggling at the plate and dealing with the knowledge that his father had contracted stomach cancer. He would try something new at the plate every day, look for a new swing key, try a new stance, anything. He listened to everybody and learned nothing. That year he hit .219 with just 9 homers and 33 RBIs. The Expos were all too happy to deal their fading giant for Hill, a promising young pitcher who carried a smaller contract.

Meanwhile, Galarraga's descent continued. His father died shortly before spring training. Minor injuries were bothering him. He had a new hitting coach, Baylor, who had his own ideas about things. And he bore the burden of high expectations; the Cardinals had traded for him believing he could return to his old form.

Baylor looked at Galarraga and asked himself this question: "Why in the hell was he trying to jerk everything to left field?" No wonder he couldn't turn on the inside fastball. No wonder he was striking out at such an alarming rate. Baylor approached Galarraga during spring training and said, "First thing, we're not gonna worry about strikeouts. You're gonna strike out. That's understood. Now, let's get you back to hitting to all fields, starting with hitting the ball back up the middle.''

Baylor learned something else about Galarraga. ''You know what the guy's problem is, is he's too nice,'' said Baylor. ''I don't know how or when it happened, but sometime when he was in Montreal, someone told him he had to be a pull hitter. It wasn't enough he hit 22 home runs, drove in 90 runs. I mean, he's not a pull hitter. He's such a nice guy, though, he never went to the goddamned hitting instructor and said, 'Hey, kiss my ass, I've been successful this way and this is the way I'm gonna do it.' But of course, Mr. Nice Guy listens and all of a sudden, they're jamming the shit out of him and he can't lay off that ball.''

They went back to Baseball 101: hitting off a tee; hitting balls tossed softly on an underhanded lob. They deconstructed and reconstructed and looked for answers. And finally, it became evident to Baylor that the problem could be corrected by opening Galarraga's stance—that is, moving his left, or front, foot, away from home plate, thus turning his entire body toward the pitcher. He saw results immediately, and then the season started.

His hand was broken by a pitch the second game of the year.

''By the time I got back on May 22nd, I was trying too hard, I was thinking all the time, I wanted to do well so badly,'' said Galarraga. ''All these people were saying I couldn't play anymore. 'That Galarraga, he's finished, he can't play.' And really, I was so frustrated, I thought about just going home, quitting. But I thought, 'Okay, let's try it this way with the new stance. Let's shut everybody up and prove everybody wrong.' ''

A year later, the Big Cat started hitting that opening weekend in Denver, kept hitting in Montreal and St. Louis and never quit. By the end of April, he was hitting .412 with 4 home runs and 25 RBIs. Gebhard, who saw the best of Cat while with the Expos, could only smile. ''The man is on a mission,'' he said. ''He's on a mission to show everybody, and himself, that there's a lot of good baseball left in that body.''

''I want to be an All-Star again,'' said Galarraga, remembering his only appearance at an All-Star Game in 1988. ''I want to be able to go in that clubhouse and look those guys in the eye again and think, 'I'm back at this level.' " Galarraga smiled like a Cheshire cat. He tried to find the right words in English. "I am so happy for myself," he said contentedly.

DARREN HOLMES STUNK, and he knew it.

"I would have booed me, too," he said. Holmes, the Rockies' closer and the third choice in the expansion grab bag, had become the answer to a Rockies trivia question: Name the first Rockies player to be booed at Mile High Stadium. In a town in which the Rockies could do no wrong, Holmes had become the first goat.

On April 13, Holmes walked off the Mile High mound to one chorus of boos after another in a series of late-inning disasters. The Rockies were leading the Mets, 4–2, and there were men on first and second with two outs in the eighth. Enter Holmes. Exit the victory. Holmes promptly walked three batters, driving in two runs, before getting the hook. Two days earlier, against the Expos, he had been shelled for seven runs while mopping up in a 19–9 loss.

"I can't believe this is happening to me," Holmes said after a Rockies loss. "I can't believe it." His head was buried deep in his locker stall. "I never walked people like this. Not even in Little League . . ."

Later, Holmes was back by his locker stall, dressing slowly, most of the reporters having left the clubhouse to file their stories. He was composed, solemn.

"When somebody next year asks me for the most memorable moment of my career, I'll say it was tonight, when I walked off the mound and heard all those boos," he said, buttoning up his shirt. "That will always stay with me. I don't blame them. I really don't.

"It was the most helpless I've ever felt on the mound. . . . I couldn't throw the ball underhand and get it over the plate. It was a terrible feeling. I've never pitched like this. Never. And to do it now, in front of all these people. They're just dying to have someone do well so they can go crazy. It's disappointing, but I know I can pitch. *I know it.* I don't know, maybe being told I'm the closer, the two-year contract, everything added up. Who knows? I'm looking for answers like everybody else.

"But I've always been someone who's had to fight for everything in baseball. This was the first time anyone had ever said, 'The job is yours to lose.' I'd never dealt with that before. Maybe I was immature. But I'll tell you this: I want to be this team's closer. I want it as bad as anything I've ever wanted my whole life."

But his mechanics were lousy. His confidence was waning. "You could see it in his body language," said Baylor. "The way he walked, the way he stood on the mound. When you get to the point where you're afraid to throw strikes, you've got a problem."

Whether Holmes couldn't throw strikes or wouldn't throw them was a matter of opinion. All the Rockies knew was that their closer was flaming out. Holmes was one of only two players, Nied being the other, whom both the Marlins and Rockies had coveted. Holmes, a stocky man with a buzz cut and a goatee, had performed well as a middle reliever for the Milwaukee Brewers in 1992. The expansion teams saw a guy with a 93 mph fastball, a nasty slider and curveball that seemed to fall off a table.

The Marlins, meanwhile, felt compelled to take a major financial risk, drafting California's ace closer, Bryan Harvey, who was not only making huge dollars but was coming off arm problems. Most of the baseball world snickered when the Marlins tabbed Harvey. "What's an expansion team need a closer for when they're only going to win 60 games anyway?" Indians general manager John Hart wondered. Another GM shook his head while attending the expansion draft. "Damaged goods," he said. Even Gebhard quietly expressed surprise. "Our doctors tell me he's not right physically," he said.

As the season unfolded, the Marlins were having the first, and last, laugh. Holmes was a disaster waiting to happen, his bullpen compatriots were not much better and Harvey was his old, dominating self. Holmes couldn't find the plate with a 3-and-0 fastball; Harvey was tearing people up with his legendary forkball. By early June, Harvey would record his 17th save, breaking the expansion-team record held by Enrique Romo of the 1977 Seattle Mariners.

The Rockies never wavered in their convictions about Holmes's physical ability. Bad mechanics could be fixed. But they worried about his bruised psyche. They worried that he didn't have that closer's bravado, the necessary arrogance that marks great ones like Dennis Eckersley or Rob Dibble.

Already, Baylor was losing confidence. "I'll try to get him some work on the road," he said of Holmes. "I can't have him going out there with the game on the line and walking the ballpark."

After the Rockies lost the first game in Montreal, moving their record to 3-6, Holmes was called upon to mop up in the ninth inning of a game the Rockies led 9–1. This would be child's play, an innocent game of pitch-and-catch. So, why did Holmes's stomach feel like a Guns 'n' Roses concert was playing inside? Why did the walk from the bullpen to the mound seem so interminable? He had done this a thousand times, and yet he felt like a writer who had forgotten basic sentence construction, a musician who had gone tone-deaf. Three lousy outs seemed like the most daunting job in the world.

"That was the toughest thing I've ever done, going out there like that," he said after giving up two singles, but no runs, while preserving the victory. "Until you throw against someone standing in the batter's box, you don't know how you're going to react."

Afterward, Gebhard walked over to Holmes's locker and patted him on the back. "Atta boy," he said. "Get ahead. Throw strikes. It's coming back." Holmes smiled. His sense of relief was palpable.

"I feel like I got over the hill today," he said. "Don talked to me and said, 'Don't worry about it,' but of course, in the back of your mind, you're worrying. This was a good situation for me to come in. I really wanted to get myself together before we got home. It's important that I get the respect of my teammates."

Baylor, however, was not quite so optimistic. He had been burned by blown saves before, even though the season was just nine games old. "I've got to see him do this a couple more times," he said.

The Rockies would end up losing two of three in Montreal, followed by an identical result in St. Louis. They were playing the way they were expected to play: like an expansion team. There were flashes, most of them supplied by the rejuvenated Galarraga, but there were also those blips of ineptitude, when the Rockies looked every bit like a team of strangers. Already, Baylor was beginning to put together his own book of notes, jotting down areas that needed improvement.

The early notations included—featured, really—one particularly pressing need: the bullpen. Holmes may have felt like he had gotten over the hump. But Baylor quietly sensed that there were a few mountain ranges yet to scale.

8

Fifty-Two Eighty

BACK IN 1991, when baseball was beginning to think about Denver as a possible site for expansion or even relocation, Douglas Danforth, the head of baseball's expansion committee, called his old friend Daniel Ritchie, who was chancellor of the University of Denver. There were some concerns as to whether Denver's light air might make a mockery of the traditional game, cheapening the home run and diminishing the statistical sanctity of baseball.

"Have any studies ever been done on baseball at altitude?" Danforth asked.

Ritchie wasn't sure. So he called Dr. Thomas Stephen, a young assistant professor in the physics department. Stephen, a lean, bespectacled fellow with a taste for the game, had heard about some work done by a Robert Adair, a Yale professor who had been a friend of the late commissioner, Bart Giamatti. But there had been nothing specific, nothing that quantitatively showed how the baseball, whether hit or thrown, would react in Denver's mile-high altitude.

There had always been suspicions about Denver through its many years as a minor-league town. The ball definitely carried farther; any golfer could tell you that after hitting a solid nine-iron 150 yards. But there also seemed to be some other curiosities, like the fact that the pitchers' curveballs didn't seem to curve as much, and the way routine flyballs seemed to take off disproportionately farther than the crack of the bat might suggest.

So Stephen, who spends most of his time as an atomic molecular physicist, designed a computer model that takes into account the variables of ball velocity, the angle at which a ball is hit and air density, and made hundreds of different calculations.

Stephen's study, released in August 1991 and titled "Baseball in Denver: Some Ramifications of the Altitude," soon became required reading, not only by the expansion people but by the folks at the Metropolitan Stadium District, a special district and subdivision of the state of Colorado charged with building the Rockies' future home. It suggested a brand of baseball markedly different from a game played at any other altitude, including Atlanta, which, at 1,050 feet, was the highest major-league site. Here was a game being played where the air was 17 percent thinner than at sea level.

"A ball batted in Denver," Stephen concluded, "will always travel farther than an identically batted ball at sea level. . . . The ball in Denver will travel approximately 9 percent farther."

Some simple math: a 330-foot fly ball, a routine out in most parks, would travel a bit more than 360 feet in Denver—a home run in most parks and a sure four-bagger with Mile High Stadium's short left-field porch. The Rockies would play their first two years at Mile High, where the left-field and left-center-field dimensions were not adjusted to accommodate altitude. By season's end, statistics would show Mile High to be a right-handed power hitter's heaven. The Rockies would go on to hit 77 homers at home as opposed to 65 on the road. Opponents, who rather enjoyed Colorado pitching, had 107 homers at Mile High and 74 elsewhere. By season's end, Mile High would prove to be the National League's easiest park in which to hit a home run, with 184 total homers. The next easiest was San Diego (176) and

Chicago's Wrigley Field (170), which was as much a commentary on the pitching staffs as it was on the ballparks.

Philadelphia Phillies catcher Darren Daulton was among the legions who feasted on Rockies pitching and the Mile High dimensions. Daulton remarked that Mark McGwire, Oakland's right-handed hitting slugger, "would hit 75 home runs in this place—easy."

"There's no question there are going to be some cheap home runs the first two seasons," said Stephen as he sat at Mile High one evening. "The left-field dimensions are similar to stadiums at sea level. Any home run that barely clears the left-field fence at Mile High is not much of a shot. Maybe they should have a new stat for pitchers, call it DERA—ERA in Denver.

"But when they move to Coors Field in 1995, the dimensions will be altitude-adjusted and that'll create an entirely new kind of game. [Plans call for Coors Field to be 347 feet down the left-field line, 390 in the power alley, 415 to dead center, 375 to right-center-field power alley and 350 down the right-field line]. When they move, the home run won't be paramount, but you'll have an outfield so large, you're going to have an inordinate number of singles dropping in front of the outfielders, or balls in the gaps for doubles and triples. If anybody is going to hit .400, it's going to be in Denver. If the Rockies are smart, they'll put a lot of emphasis on speed."

Stephen, an avid baseball fan, sits in seats behind the Rockies' dugout, not to watch the tape-measure home runs but to take fiendish delight in the altitude-inspired foibles of visiting outfielders. While the thin air affects the distance of a batted ball most dramatically, the altitude also plays more subtle havoc on pitching and defense.

"I love watching a visiting outfielder camp under a fly ball for the first time in Denver," said Stephen. "He'll stand there, think he has it, think he has it, and . . . it's gone, over his head. And he can't understand why."

But Stephen knows why: At altitude and at sea level, a fly ball remains on the same trajectory for the first third of its flight. That's when an accomplished outfielder judges the ball's distance, often basing the judgment on the sound of the crack of the bat.

"This is accomplished by a feedback process from the inner ear as the player watches the ball on its way up," wrote Stephen. "The player's response is then learned in response to the visual and inner-ear reactions." It is not until the ball is halfway through its flight that altitude comes into play, the ball seemingly taking off. "The learned response would then place the player too far in and force him to back up quickly in the later portion of the ball's flight," wrote Stephen.

The Rockies and their competitors learned the lessons early and often. During the very first home stand, Dante Bichette and Montreal right fielder Moises Alou, both decent defensive players, misjudged routine fly balls, only to see them fly over their heads and beyond their reach.

"This is going to be murder on opposing teams," Bichette said after his first excursion into the unknown. "We'll learn how to adjust for altitude because we'll play here all the time. But visiting teams are in for a surprise. What I've figured out already is, when in doubt, break back on the ball. It's always going to go farther than you think. I mean, I might as well just play on the warning track, you know?"

The thin air also affects long throws and pitches. "Notice how many times we've seen overthrows of cutoff men?" Stephen asked. "It's not that they're missing cutoff men, but they don't take into account the 9 percent additional distance the ball is going to travel."

The few pitchers who have had success in Denver have claimed that the whispers about altitude and its effect on the game are overstated. It's all in the mind, they say. Stephen quantitatively proves it's not.

"The pitching game will be enhanced slightly by an increase in the average speed of fastballs," Stephen wrote. "This will cause a 100 mph fastball in Denver to cross the plate 0.003 seconds sooner than its 0.432 second travel time at sea level.

"The slight edge a pitcher gains with his fastball should be more than compensated for by the decreased effectiveness of his curveball. A pitch that will curve 14 inches at sea level should only curve about 11 inches in Denver."

And knuckleballs? Stephen could have predicted that Pittsburgh knuckleballer Tim Wakefield would have been pummeled during an early-season visit to Mile High. "No drag, no resistance," he said. "The ball doesn't dance."

After only one month of baseball, Rockies pitchers weren't in the mood to do a jig either. It didn't take long before they were spooked by Mile High's oddities. The short left-field porch was one matter; routine fly balls were leaving the park, bloating earned-run averages and wreaking havoc on the pitchers' already-diminished self-images. These were not accomplished pitchers; otherwise they wouldn't have been available to an expansion team. But coming to Denver, standing helplessly on the mound and craning their necks to watch ball after ball go into orbit over their right shoulders, was only making matters worse.

The field dimensions offered another quirk that proved unfriendly to pitchers. Center field and right field were pushed way back, and while few home runs cleared those fences, outfielders were forced to play quite deep. This meant Rockies pitchers were being dinked, pinged and pecked to death by seeing-eye base hits. And when a ball was hit well into the cavernous gaps between center and right field, a batter could run forever.

"I have never, ever seen so much room in an outfield," said Cole, a speedster who played in Cleveland Stadium, a field so huge that Babe Ruth once complained, "You need a horse in the outfield." "Right center field here is trouble. I'm going to be cheating that way as much as possible. That's the biggest right-center-field gap I've ever seen. You're going to have lots of doubles and triples in this park, and some inside-the-park home runs, too."

In fact, for all the talk of Mile High as a home-run hitters' paradise, statistics over a three-year span showed that the minor-league Denver Zephyrs, who were the Milwaukee Brewers' Triple-A affiliate, and their American Association competitors hit about the same number of homers in Denver as they did at sea level. The real difference came in the area of singles, doubles and triples—batters hit .297 in Denver compared to .249 throughout the rest of the league.

The Rockies, though, were being brutalized by every sort of offensive thrust. Averages were high, home runs were soaring . . . and all of it was preying on their minds. Soon, the pitchers began to become too cautious, afraid to challenge batters, pitch them inside. There were walks. Pitchers fell behind in the count. Nied was the first to complain about Mile High, drawing a stern rebuke from Baylor. The other pitchers agreed, but expressed their sentiments privately.

"Tell them I know what they're going through," said Pirates reliever Bill Landrum, who pitched in Denver during his minor-league days. "The problem is, you get lit up there, and you take that mentality on the road with you, too. That's where you really get messed up." Atlanta lefty Tom Glavine agreed: "I really feel sorry for the guys who have to pitch there all year. There are going to be some bloated statistics."

Bob Tewksbury, the St. Louis Cardinals starter, called a friend in Denver. "My next start is at Mile High," he said. His friend laughed. "Isn't it cold-and-flu season?" his buddy wondered. "Maybe you should miss that start."

There is no question; altitude plays games real and imagined, working on an athlete physically and mentally. The Denver Broncos own the most lopsided home-field advantage in all of football—almost unbeatable at Mile High and merely pedestrian on the road. There has always been talk of the ghosts of Mile High, the apparitions who weave their magic and lead the home team to victory in the desperate, waning seconds. More likely, the ghosts are sucking what oxygen is left in the atmosphere. The Broncos have won a number of games late in the contest not only because of John Elway but because the opponent is literally out of gas.

The Denver Nuggets, the local NBA team, also have maintained a sizable home-court advantage, and, at one time, put an oxygen tank at the end of the opponent's bench—lest they forget they're supposed to be sucking wind in the rarefied air.

By the second week of the season, Baylor already was using

altitude to his advantage, ordering the grounds crew to paint "Elevation 5,280 feet" on the right-center-field wall—just as a friendly reminder.

"Maybe we should put 7,000 feet," he said, smiling.

What's 1,720 feet between friends?

"I'm already going out of my way to mess with [opponent's] heads," said Amos Otis. "Absolutely. Anything to get an edge, get them out of sync. I'll be standing around the batting cage and I'll tell someone, 'You should have seen the shot Galarraga hit the other day—26 rows up in the second deck. Even our pitchers hit 'em out during BP. Ball really flies out of here.' "

The physiological ramifications of altitude are not quite so pronounced in baseball as they are in football and basketball. "Baseball is essentially anaerobic," said Stephen. "When you're running to first or chasing down a fly ball, you're essentially using the oxygen that's already in your system."

But that didn't stop the Philadelphia Phillies' team physician, Dr. Phillip Marone, from suggesting that his team send its starting pitchers to Denver 24 to 48 hours before a scheduled start to help their bodies become used to the altitude.

Los Angeles Dodgers manager Tommy Lasorda, a former pitcher for the minor-league Denver Bears, learned the hard way that baseball in Denver is somehow different. "I pitched the day I got there, and I was out of breath and completely disoriented after I threw my first pitch," he told the *Rocky Mountain News*. "I thought the plate was 90 feet away and I was in a big barn. Strangest feeling I ever had. I broke off one of my best curveballs, it spun two or three times, straightened out and the guy hit it a mile."

And then there is the story of the Phillies' John Kruk, an ungainly man who has been described as a ballplayer in a plumber's body. In a game at Mile High on May 28, Kruk was standing on first when he was given the hit-and-run sign. He sprinted. The ball was fouled off. This happened again. And again. Kruk, who usually saves his athleticism for sprints to the postgame buffet, was gasping.

The batter, Dave Hollins, then ripped the next pitch into the outfield gap for a double. Kruk rounded second, legs churning . . . rounded third, lactic acid building up in every fiber of his being . . . down the third-base line, his chest burning, his legs like dual anvils, before sliding into home plate.

There, he lay on his back, his prodigious midsection heaving, craving even a hint of oxygen. After a few seconds, he struggled to his feet, stumbled to the dugout and put smelling salts under his nose.

"Shit, I must have asthma or something," he said later. "Great town, Denver, I just wish you could breathe in it. I'm so fucking tired right now, I may not be able to go out and drink beer later."

Pittsburgh manager Jim Leyland bet his coaches he could use a fungo bat, usually reserved for hitting groundballs to infielders, and clear the Mile High fence. "Watch this," he said. One at a time Leyland tossed the baseballs in the air, stepped into the swing and watched the balls fly. A dozen balls, two dozen balls, "I'll get one out," he said. Finally, after about 25 tries—folks started losing count—Leyland hit a fungo that barely cleared the fence. He launched into his home-run trot and was met at home plate by a score of high fives.

"Where else can you do that?" he said, his voice cutting through the thin air.

THE LOS ANGELES DODGERS and the San Francisco Giants.

The New York Yankees and the Boston Red Sox.

The Chicago Cubs and the St. Louis Cardinals.

The Colorado Rockies and the Florida Marlins?

By the time the club returned from the road trip to Montreal and St. Louis, they found themselves embroiled in a media-generated, fan-inspired, wholly artificial rivalry with their next opponents, their expansion sisters from Miami, who entered the three-game set on April 23 with a 6-10 record, a half-game worse than the Rockies.

But, then, how could the Rockies get mad at a team whose

manager was named Rene and who wore teal uniforms? Neither club seemed particularly inspired by this contrived rivalry. After all, who speaks of the blood feud between the Expos and the Padres, or, within the class of 1977, the Toronto Blue Jays and the Seattle Mariners?

"It takes time to build," said Baylor, who knew all about rivalries from his years in Boston and New York. "What you need is a bench-clearing brawl or something like that."

Another huge crowd—the first game drew 57,784—saw the Rockies' beleaguered bullpen earn its first victory (by Steve Reed) and its first save (by Holmes). Those efforts significantly lowered both men's ERAs; Reed came into the game with a 17.18 mark, Holmes with a 34.71 number.

The town was abuzz once again. The weather forecast called for clear Colorado skies and warm temperatures, and folks were talking about a sweep of the team they pejoratively called "the Fish." Better yet, CBS-TV was in town to televise the Rockies-Marlins game and to show the country what this Rocky Mountain phenomenon was all about.

And then Saturday morning dawned, and there was snow. Wet, cold, blowing snow. The fog completely obscured the Denver skyline. It wasn't enough that Denver was known for the Super Bowl blowouts featuring the Broncos as sacrificial victims. Now the country—especially the people in the rejected expansion cities like Buffalo and Tampa–St. Petersburg—would take a look at snow falling on the field in late April and declare, "See, we told you Denver didn't deserve a team."

Of course, the minor-league Denver Zephyrs, who occupied the stadium one year earlier, had not been snowed out or rained out all season long. Still, the Marlins couldn't resist a few jabs at the local weather while sitting in their clubhouse, waiting out the storm.

"All I know is, in Tampa, it's 75 and sunny," said Marlins third baseman Dave Magadan. "If you're going to choose an expansion site based on the best conditions for the players, this would not have been at the top of the list."

Catcher Benito Santiago, who had fled San Diego to sign with the Marlins, said, "The people might love it, but they've got to think about making a dome here."

Marlins first-base coach Vada Pinson, the former Cincinnati Reds star, pretended to ice-skate through the Marlins' clubhouse. "It's beginning to look a lot like Christmas," he sang. Throughout the room, Marlins were donning black-knit ski caps. All they needed was a wood-burning stove.

One hour and 11 minutes later, the game began under gray skies, and the mercury stood at 38 degrees. This was a game the Rockies, and Gebhard, were going to play come hell, high water or a plague of locusts. Some three hours later, however, they regretted the change in barometric fortunes.

Of all the bad games they had played through this early mixed bag of a season, this one was the worst—and a grim preview of things to come. Good thing the CBS cameras switched to a Cubs-Reds game, leaving the Rockies and Marlins for the local audience. Worse, the embarrassing 2–1 loss opened a few wounds within a clubhouse that had been, for the most part, an expansion Disneyland. Expansion was supposed to be a lighthearted frolic. But when it ended, there were fingers pointing and heads shaking, and the clubhouse had become a tense place filled with anger and recriminations.

A tone had been set for the rest of the season.

How could the Rockies mess up? Let us count the ways:

THIRD INNING—With the Marlins leading 1–0, Rockies starting pitcher Andy Ashby singled, a rare feat by a pitcher. Then Baylor, forever attempting the unexpected, called for the hit-and-run. Ashby saw the sign, but he did not go. Next pitch, the sign came again. Ashby saw the sign, but did not go. "I don't know what I was waiting for," he said later. Third pitch, Ashby saw the sign. He still didn't go. Eric Young grounded into a double play, one that might have been avoided had Ashby run on the pitch. The next hitter, Alex Cole, singled, which would have scored the run. "I cost us a run," Ashby said. "I might have cost us the game."

Actually, he had plenty of company.

That same inning, Cole showed again why his talent makes scouts salivate and why his lack of baseball smarts drives managers to drink. He opened the season as one of two Rockies (Eric Young was the other) who had the green light to steal whenever they thought it prudent. With two outs, Cole thought it prudent to get into scoring position, so he stole second base. Good baseball.

Meanwhile, on that pitch, Charlie Hayes had worked the count to 3-and-1, the ultimate hitter's count, a count that virtually guarantees a fastball. This is a count where a baserunner stays put. He does not take the bat out of the hitter's hands. Plus, the fastball is the worst pitch on which to steal.

Cole failed to make this basic calculation. He broke for third and was gunned down by the rifle-armed Santiago. End of threat. End of inning.

"That was aggressive baseball," said Cole in his defense. "That wasn't stupid, it was aggressive. He [Santiago] put the ball right on the bag. If that ball is a little higher or wider, I'm safe. Plus, if he throws a breaking ball, I've got it easy."

A breaking ball? On a 3-1 count? The pitcher was Luis Aquino, the fifth man on an expansion team's staff, not Roger Clemens.

When Cole was asked if Baylor said anything to him afterward, he said, "No, because it was aggressive baseball and that's the way we play."

Third-base coach Jerry Royster passionately defended Cole's derring-do. "He's going to be safe more often than not," said Royster. "If you don't put pressure on the opposition, you're going to lose the game."

Problem was, BaylorBall's architect did not quite see it that way. When asked if there was any advantage to stealing third in that situation, Baylor said, "Dumb question. And a dumb play."

He was informed that there were some who saw merit in the move. Baylor shook his head. "Who said that?" he asked. Cole and Royster, he was told. "If they think that was a smart play, I'm going to have to talk to them," he said.

While Cole had the green light, Baylor said he could also slap the red light on his wayward speedster. "We didn't in that situation," Baylor said, assuming Cole would make the correct read. "But I'm going to have to because those plays keep catching me by surprise."

The seeds of discontent had been sown.

SIXTH INNING—Hayes singled to lead off the inning, with the score still 1–0, Marlins. Baylor decided to go hit-and-run. Except for another problem: Galarraga missed the sign and took the pitch. Hayes was thrown out easily at second base. This was not an aberration; while Galarraga was making news with his resurrection at the plate, he consistently made Baylor crazy with his baserunning blunders (as on Opening Day in New York) and his repeated failure to pick up signs. At first, Baylor was patient, figuring a veteran like Galarraga would see the errors of his ways. By the second week of the season, Baylor made this determination: Galarraga just didn't get it.

"What happened there?" a reporter asked the first baseman, who remained silent. "Did you miss the sign? Did you get it and realize you couldn't hit the pitch?"

Galarraga uncharacteristically walked away, muttering, "Write whatever you want."

By now, Baylor had seen quite enough. His coaching staff had literally walked the club through the baserunning basics during spring training, going so far as to take the team, en masse, from home to first, from first to second, and so on, explaining fundamentals at each stop. Now here they were, still a respectable 6-10 after a 2–1 loss to the Marlins, having run themselves out of another victory.

"I don't know what it is, but I've seen more and more of this stuff over the years," said Baylor, referring to players failing to execute the fundamentals. "Maybe it's all the money now. Guys give themselves up, going to the right side, they figure they can't take that to arbitration. The little things like smart baserunning don't show up in the box scores. Everybody wants numbers. 'If I put up good numbers, I can take it to arbitration. . . .' I don't know when or how things changed, but I've seen this trend the past decade or more; guys just don't know the game the way they used to.

"If they're sitting on the bench, believe me, they'll start to figure out how the game is supposed to be played. I guarantee they'll sit there and say, 'Why's he trying to steal third in that situation?' "

Royster, who had come to the Rockies after four years of managing in the Dodgers organization, was asked if the problem might be that players spend less time in the minor leagues these days. With expansion on the one hand and the growing popularity of basketball and football on the other, the game's talent base had been depleting for years. Now young players were moving through the minor leagues far more quickly.

"No, no, no," he said. "Let me set you straight on that. This is what I've seen, at least during my time there. When they're in the minors, they're willing to do whatever it takes to get to the major leagues. They'll do the little things. They become students of the game. Whatever they had to do, they'll do.

"But once they get here, it's like they forget the things they've been taught. It's really hard to understand. For example, the other day I was getting grief for sending Eric [Young, who had been thrown out at home plate in St. Louis on April 22], and I'm willing to accept the blame for that. But when he played for me [at the Dodgers' Triple-A affiliate in Albuquerque], he would have hit third base at full speed. That's why, when the relay was slow, I sent him home. What I didn't know was he slowed down as he came into third. Now, why would he do that? He never did that in the minors.

"Guys just don't prepare themselves to play the game as well as they used to. I notice it when I'm watching other teams, too. It's not like we've got a bunch of guys with multimillion-dollar contracts. We don't have anybody making great money. Maybe if they would prepare themselves better, mentally, become students of the game, they would make the big money. Baserunning is the worst of all. We've got the same signs we had in spring training, and yet we're still here—what?—16 games into the season, and we're still talking about missing signs."

As reporters were leaving the clubhouse, Cole, sensing the coming storm of criticism, sidled over to a writer. "You're not gonna dog me in the papers, are ya?"

The Rockies eventually would rebound from their wretched game with the Marlins, finishing their first month at a very respectable 8-14. Baylor and his players felt they could be even better if they could get Holmes and his bullpen mates out of their current morass.

But they were beginning to learn a basic baseball law of nature: If you're not any good, it doesn't matter whether you're playing at sea level or a mile high.

9

Road Trip to Hell

FOR MOST TEAMS, most players, the road is a necessary
evil, an accepted part of a major-leaguer's life. Some guys
revel in it—the 24-hour room service, the maid service, the
chance to get away and sample the nightlife in such exotic locales
as Houston or El Lay. Other players just survive it; they miss their
families, home cooking and the warmth of the home fires.

"Tell you what I do on the road," said outfielder Jerald Clark.
"I get up, listen to some music, talk to my wife and iron my
clothes. Have lunch, come back to the room, listen to more
music, iron some more, and then it's time to go to the ballpark.
Pretty boring, huh?"

The Rockies, though, entered the league as the ultimate road
warriors. Not only did Denver's location require longer-than-
normal trips—the closest National League city is St. Louis, 857
miles from Denver—but the NL schedule was drawn up with the
idea that the San Francisco Giants were moving to Tampa–St.
Petersburg. Schedule makers thought it would be efficient to pair

the Giants and Braves—Tampa and Atlanta—when teams traveled into the region.

Except for one problem: The Giants stayed in San Francisco.

This meant the already-overtraveled Rockies would have some trips where they went from Denver to Atlanta and back to San Francisco before returning to Denver. The Rockies would have to make that trek twice.

Worse, though, was the fact that the Rockies were beginning to show signs that the home-field advantage was wearing thin; in early May they went 1-7 in four games against the Braves and four more against the Giants during a Mile High home stand, giving up 76 runs. With a record of 11-23, the bloom was certainly off the rose by the time the Rockies embarked on the first of two monster road trips the schedule makers had prepared for them—a 13-games-in-14-days Western Division swing through Cincinnati, San Diego, Los Angeles and Houston.

Were they ready?

Well, their best player, Galarraga, had gone on the disabled list on May 10 with an injured knee. He was hitting a mere .395 at the time. Their bullpen was a complete shambles, in such desperate straits that they had to demote Holmes to the minor leagues to straighten out his head and his mechanics. And the starting staff, which had been something more than mediocre the first month, was starting to wear down and give up really big numbers—the result, in part, of Baylor's understandable reluctance to use his bullpen. The running game continued to hurt the team as much as help it. And the defense, which had been professional if not sterling, was becoming eerily reminiscent of the 1962 Mets, far and away the worst in the league.

On the road again . . .

Cincinnati, Friday, May 14—Reds 13, Rockies 5.

Royster stood on the top step of the dugout and leaned against the railing before the game, casually surveying his team and watching them stretch.

"You can learn a lot about guys' work habits when they do

this," he said. "Look at Galarraga. Great work ethic. Does all the stretches, prepares himself for every game, even if he's not playing. Same with David Nied. He's not even pitching, but he goes through the whole program, does everything correctly.

"Then you look at some other guys. Dante Bichette: We're happy if we can even get him out here on time. Charlie Hayes? Look at the guy. He has a chance, if he puts up good numbers, to make two to three million a year. But he's out of shape, he doesn't take stretching seriously. Some guys, they just screw around. I don't know what happens to these guys because I've managed in the minors, and they do things correctly. But they get here, it's like, 'I don't have to do this anymore.'

"Can you believe this? Vinny Castilla [a backup shortstop] came to me one day and said, 'Can you remind me to stretch every day?' This is a major-league baseball player. This isn't some star player; this is a guy who's with an expansion team. He's on the fringe."

Just then, Royster looked toward a clot of players, all of whom were doing some shoulder stretches. Castilla stood in the middle, completely oblivious to his surroundings, tossing a ball into the air.

"Hey, Vinny," Royster said. "C'mon."

Castilla nodded like he'd just learned the secret to life.

Royster laughed. "Can you believe that?"

Thus did the Rockies begin their Road Trip to Hell. When the whole thing started, Baylor was consumed with wins and losses. Halfway through the trek, he altered his perspective. No longer was Baylor so worried about losing, but rather, about *how* they lost.

They lost this first one bad.

The Reds' Kevin Mitchell, a man with more chins than extra-base hits, attacked the Rockies pitchers like cheeseburger-and-fries combo meals. First, starter Andy Ashby was consumed. Then, Mark Knudson, the local Denver guy, got taken past the drive-through. It was over early—the Reds led, 9–2, after four innings—and it was over ugly. Late in the game, defensive replacement Gerald Young camped under a routine fly ball in right field, only to have it kick off the heel of his glove and roll away on the artificial turf.

"I don't know what happened to Gerald, but it's like he's turned it down a notch after a great spring training," said Gebhard. "It doesn't make sense. His career was going down the tubes, he comes to spring training and shows up out of nowhere to make our club, and then it's like he's not as interested anymore —or something."

Another teammate said, "It's like, 'I'm in the big leagues now. I've made it.' He couldn't be bothered. It was like he was too cool for the game."

Young wouldn't have to worry about the big leagues much longer.

Cincinnati, Saturday, May 15—Reds 5, Rockies 3.

At least it was a game.

In fact, the Rockies led, 3–0, after four innings. And they had their new starter, Armando Reynoso, on the mound. Reynoso, who had been taken in the expansion draft from the pitching-rich Atlanta Braves, had impressed the coaches during spring training, but he had an option left—which meant he could be sent to the minor leagues and recalled without having to pass through waivers. And so the team decided to start Reynoso in the minors and save other pitchers who didn't have options. By this time, though, three of the Rockies' five opening-week starters had been moved to the bullpen—Ashby, who had been demoted after getting shelled one day earlier, along with Bryn Smith and Bruce Ruffin, two veterans who couldn't get anybody out. Now Baylor would go with Nied, Butch Henry, Willie Blair, promoted from the bullpen, and two minor-league call-ups—Reynoso and Lance Painter, a left-hander taken from the Padres in the expansion draft.

Reynoso was struggling, throwing lots of pitches as was his habit, but he was surviving. It was 3–3 going into the seventh when Baylor's queasiness about his bullpen, and his general strategy, backfired. The Reds had men on second and third with two outs when Mitchell, who had gone 0-for-3 that day, lumbered to the plate. The Rockies had first base open; they did not have to pitch to Mitchell, who was one of the hottest hitters in baseball and a man who had enjoyed feasting on Colorado pitching in previous encounters.

Why let this guy beat you?

The book said, "Walk Mitchell, take your chances with Chris Sabo." But Baylor, whose managerial style meandered between playing by the book and playing it on instinct, had a hunch Reynoso could get Mitchell out for a fourth straight time, despite the overwhelming odds.

He was wrong.

Mitchell lined a two-run single and the Reds won, 5–3. "I had a feeling Reynoso could get him one more time," Baylor said afterward.

The Rockies were now 11-25, a brutish 50-112 pace for the season, and the frustration was showing. Even the mellow Dale Murphy was losing his cool. After a strikeout in the eighth inning, Murphy, a fellow widely considered the nicest man in baseball, slammed his bat on the plate in anger. He had struggled all season as a part-time player and pinch hitter, had been plagued by doubts about his efficacy after nearly 20 years in baseball. He was still stuck at 398 lifetime home runs, two short of the magical 400, and was beginning to wonder whether he should really be playing out the string with the Rockies. He felt a vague sense of guilt, knowing he should be thinking about returning home to his seven sons and his wife, Nancy, who was expecting another child—yes, a girl—in October. His zeal for the game was still in evidence, but in private moments he admitted it was beginning to wane. It is the most difficult admission a once-great athlete has to make: He was nearing the end.

Cincinnati, Sunday, May 16—Reds 14, Rockies 2.

The defining moment of the road trip came in the fifth inning.

The Rockies were trailing, 14–0, down by two touchdowns, after a nine-run third inning for the Reds. Ruffin was mopping up when Ashby ascended the bullpen mound in foul territory down the left-field line. Ashby's first warm-up toss was a wild pitch, and the ball rolled onto the field. Play was halted. Play was resumed. Ashby threw again—wild pitch—and the ball rolled onto the field. It was comic and it was tragic. The whole thing was coming apart.

The carnage did not end until Rockies pitchers had thrown 203 pitches—in just 8 innings—including 51 pitches by Smith in one third of an inning's work. And let's not forget the 10 bases on balls.

"How many strikes did we throw?" Baylor asked later.

Somebody jokingly said, "Six."

"You mean that they didn't hit?" he said.

Baylor was steaming. "What I hear is, 'Now we can go on the road, we'll relax and play a lot better,' " he said. "That's not what I'm seeing."

What he was hearing was even more disconcerting. The Rockies were beaten in that game by a fellow named John Roper, a promising right-handed pitcher the Reds had brought up from Triple-A ball. Roper had the easiest job in the park—pitch with a 14–0 lead. Still, he felt emboldened when asked his impressions of the Rockies.

"I've seen better lineups in Triple A," he said. "Nashville and Buffalo come to mind."

One Cincinnati columnist was so impressed by the Rockies, he suggested that all victories over the expansionists should be accompanied by an asterisk.

At this point, who could argue?

San Diego, Monday, May 17—Padres 4, Rockies 0.

By now, the word was the Rockies would win when it snowed in Southern California. And when the Rockies took the field for pregame stretching, they noticed that the right-center-field bleachers were filled with snow.

"A radio promotion," somebody said. "Brilliant, isn't it?"

Mike Swanson, the Rockies' PR director who had come to

know the Padres' fiscal policies all too well after seven years of employment there, rolled his eyes. "The team paid half the expenses [for the snow], about $12,000 dollars," he said. "How do you think that stands with employees who didn't get a raise this year?"

The fire sale in San Diego was not foremost on the Rockies' minds, however: They were still seething over Roper's comments —"Dumbest fucking thing I've ever heard in baseball," said Zimmer—and still seething over being blown out twice in three games in Cincinnati. So they did what all teams do when they have no answers: They held a team meeting. They decided they were sick and tired and wouldn't take it anymore.

And then they went out and got shut out by right-handed pitcher Andy Benes, who, ironically, had been scouted and signed by Randy Smith. "Guy's a stud," said Smith. No kidding.

The only positive sign: The Rockies pitchers did not give up double-figure runs.

San Diego, Tuesday, May 18—Rockies 2, Padres 1.

Willie Blair to the rescue. At a time when the Rockies were searching the far corners of their clubhouse for a starter who could get them into the seventh inning, along came Blair, the wiry, rubber-armed right-hander who had worked as a reliever in 20 of the team's first 35 games. Until this night, he had not thrown more than 43 pitches in a Rockies game, but as he worked into the seventh inning, and the eighth and the ninth, Baylor could not muster the will to remove him. Blair would break the Rockies' seven-game losing streak by throwing 127 pitches and completing nine innings.

Unfortunately, he did not get credit for the victory, but he was more than happy to sit in the clubhouse watching as the Rockies scored the game-winning run in the 11th inning. Vinny Castilla led off with a double, Dante Bichette moved him to third on a single, and Charlie Hayes brought Castilla home with a sacrifice fly.

"I've never managed that hard," Baylor said later, after using four pitchers. "There was no way we were letting that game get away."

Of course, the vultures around the league were not viewing the Rockies' rare victory as the prelude to a turnaround. When teams are going poorly, the more successful teams will not hesitate to take advantage by attempting to swing a one-sided deal. Gebhard got a pretty good indication of that the day *USA Today* ran a note mentioning that Ashby had been moved to the bullpen.

"I won't give you any names, but I got back to my hotel room and I had three messages from GMs wanting to trade to get Ashby," said Gebhard. "One deal, they wanted to give me a 35-year-old pitcher who was coming off arm surgery, was making far too much money and had his best season three, four years ago. I could have 40 cocktails and I wouldn't even consider these deals."

Gebhard's opposite number, San Diego GM Joe McIlvaine, was having problems of his own. The Padres' new ownership group, led by Hollywood mogul Tom Werner, was on the cost-cutting warpath. McIlvaine, who had come to San Diego from the cash-rich New York Mets in 1990, was pulling his hair out, making financially motivated deals that he knew, in his heart, were bad for his team. Here was a Padres team that was on the cusp of becoming a contender, led by steady Tony Gwynn, classy Fred McGriff and a revitalized Gary Sheffield. But money mattered, and McIlvaine had been forced to deal outfielder Darrin Jackson, shortstop Tony Fernandez and others to cut payroll.

"This ought to send off alarms all over baseball," said Gebhard. "There's got to be some kind of revenue sharing. We took a look at our 1987 championship team [the Minnesota Twins] and we figured out that by 1990, if we'd have kept all those guys, our payroll would be 65 million dollars. It's impossible to keep a team together anymore."

San Diego, Wednesday, May 19—Padres 7, Rockies 3.

Zimmer was back in his usual spot, sitting on the bench, surveying the scenery some three hours before the game. The stadium brought back memories of Zimmer's first managerial job, of a time when he was still quite green and in charge of the woebegone 1972–73 San Diego Padres. It was this way in most every park in the National League for Zimmer. Every stadium held a memory, some bad, most of them good.

"It's funny, but I was telling Baylor the other day, I had an acquaintance who managed a team like ours," Zimmer was saying. "No pressure. They were expected to lose. And he told me he loved managing a team that lost 100 games or more because there was no pressure. And I thought, 'Even if I felt that way, which I don't, I would never admit that.' "

The pressure in the Rockies' clubhouse was purely self-inflicted, and it came from the top down. Baylor had preached all year about setting new standards for expansion teams; problem was, the Rockies were setting new standards for ineptitude. For a time, the problem could be pinpointed: It was the bullpen's fault. But then the starting pitching began to crumble. And now, here on the Road Trip to Hell, the bats were falling silent. Galarraga remained on the disabled list—he would not return to action until May 28, the first home game back after the long road trip—and was reduced to spending mornings running in the hotel pool, while Hayes and Bichette struggled mightily.

"Mile High swing," said Baylor, referring to Hayes, whose average had dropped 21 points since the beginning of the trip, from .310 to .289. "It's like playing at home at Fenway. Guys gear their swings to play there. Then they get on the road, start pulling off the ball trying to pull everything to left, next thing you know, you're in a slump."

The only guy hitting, finally, was Boston, who hit three homers in two games in San Diego. Boston, scouts said, was a guy who would break your heart. Great tools, great baseball body, but he didn't have designs on greatness. He was, they said, too happy to be a fourth or fifth outfielder. Of course, he never had the at-bats necessary to prove otherwise; in nine seasons, he had never amassed 400 for a year. "I'll tell you how you get Boston to reach his potential," said one member of the Rockies' staff. "Lock him in his room every night. He's a classic underachiever."

On this night, the Rockies didn't pitch or hit—except for Boston, who hit two home runs—and lost, 7–3. Painter didn't pitch badly in his first major-league start, but got dinked to death as the Rockies lost their 12th game in 14 tries. The statistics didn't lie: Colorado was last among the 14 NL teams in ERA, 12th in shutouts, 13th in saves and last in hits allowed, batters faced, runs allowed, walks and wild pitches. Bearnarth was taking it all quite personally; intellectually, he knew these were mostly cast-offs, but emotionally, he believed he could get them to overachieve.

"Right now," he said, nursing a cold one, "I stink."

He was not alone.

San Diego, Thursday, May 20—Padres 5, Rockies 4.

In the effort to find silver linings amid the gathering gloom, the media had dutifully reported that the Rockies' bullpen, the same one whose ERA approximated the year of Andrew Jackson's election, was getting its act together.

But this was a special day, the day of the last *Cheers* episode, a show that featured a former relief pitcher named Sam "Mayday" Malone, who was known for surrendering home runs during the game and hitting them afterward. The Rockies, ever vigilant about keeping in the spirit of things, took a 4–3 lead into the ninth inning. And then they called on their own personal Mayday, the fallen Mr. Holmes, who seemed to have gotten his act together after a brief sojourn in minor-league Colorado Springs.

Wrong again.

He gave up a single to Sheffield. Then he gave up a two-run home run to McGriff. That was that.

"I don't know why I'm being put through this," said Holmes,

his voice quavering. "Maybe it's all a test. I don't know. But this isn't any fun right now. I know I'm a better pitcher than this."

Los Angeles, Friday, May 21—Dodgers 8, Rockies 0.

The Rockies are the tonic for the troops. So, you say Orel Hershiser hasn't been quite the same since arm surgery? So, you say the Dodgers are falling off the edge of the earth and out of contention? Here come the Rockies with the medicine for what ails you.

Hershiser threw a shutout.

Worse, Nied got shelled, again, and the Rockies were getting desperately worried about the once-and-maybe-future ace. He had handled everything so beautifully during spring training and even early in the season. But now he was struggling, having lost six straight games, and his personal history suggested he didn't handle adversity with that much grace. Baylor knew the story; back in 1989, Nied had quit the game and gone home to Duncanville, Texas, after being demoted in the low minors.

"I worry about David more than any of our other pitchers," Baylor said. "He's never really gone through a slump like this, and I'm not sure how equipped he is to handle it."

Said Bear: "The kid is really hurting, emotionally anyway."

After his quick exit in Cincinnati, Nied had greeted reporters by saying, "I have nothing to say," then walked off into the training room.

After his exit in L.A., Nied showered, dressed and left as soon as the writers arrived. He would not face the music—again—and his teammates were grumbling.

"David took off?" a player asked. "Beautiful. Very mature. We have to answer the questions, but he doesn't. That kind of shit don't fly."

Baylor was as stunned as anybody to learn that Nied had done a Houdini. "We're gonna talk tomorrow," he said, sternly. "Actually, I'm gonna talk and he's gonna listen. That won't happen again, I promise you."

The Rockies were worried about more than Nied, though. They were worried about their offense. Life without Galarraga was worse than they had ever imagined. Hayes was in a deep slump. Boston was Boston—brilliant one day, three K's the next. Clark was his usual streaky self. Eric Young had cooled off considerably. Cole was Cole, still only half-conscious, which drove Baylor crazy. And Bichette was struggling, especially in the field and on the bases. One of the problems was his weight. He was not classically fat in the Kevin Mitchell sense, but he had used the winter to bulk up with the weights, and it had hurt his speed.

"I'm gonna send him anyway," Baylor said after Bichette was thrown out stealing. "Maybe that will get him in shape."

Things were not going well.

"If I've got to turn over a buffet table or do something out of character, I'll do it," said Baylor, beside himself with frustration. "We need a shake-up. We can't keep going like this."

Los Angeles, Saturday, May 22— Dodgers 4, Rockies 3.

Baylor and Nied stood behind a screen in front of second base during batting practice. It was father-son, manager-player, and no bullshit. Nied was hurting himself, Baylor was saying, not only with his on-field performance but with his off-field demeanor. Running out on the press twice wasn't going to work. Showing up to the ballpark wearing a scowl on nonpitching days, sulking—that wasn't going to fly, either. And complaining about pitching at Mile High Stadium wasn't a masterstroke.

It was time to grow up.

All of this meant nothing, though, as the Rockies continued to stumble. There was Young, failing to move a runner on a bunt. There was Parrett, coming in as a reliever, balking on his first pitch, then going to a full count, allowing the runners to move on the pitch, both of them scoring on a single. Same old, same old.

After the game, club owner Jerry McMorris, who flew in for the game, asked Baylor what he thought he needed to make the

Jerry McMorris, the trucking executive who became chairman, president and CEO of the Colorado Rockies on January 26, 1993. (Photo courtesy of the Colorado Rockies Baseball Club.)

The original ownership team, Mickey Monus and John Antonucci, posing with the Rockies' team logo in July 1991, shortly after receiving word that Denver would be awarded one of the two new National League franchises. (Photo by Glenn Akasawa/*Rocky Mountain News*.)

General manager Bob Gebhard, who sweated the details through sleepless nights to assemble the staff and players of the Rocky Mountain region's first major-league team. (Photo courtesy of the Colorado Rockies Baseball Club.)

Draft day, November 17, 1992: Number one pick David Nied appears before a throng of eager Rockies fans at Denver's Currigan Hall. (Photo by Ken Papaleo/*Rocky Mountain News.*)

Manager Don Baylor among a sea of pitchers and catchers at the Rockies' first spring-training workout at Hi Corbett Field in Tucson, Arizona. (Photo by Thomas Kelsey/*Rocky Mountain News*.)

Pitching coach Larry "Bear" Bearnarth in a preseason photo, before the Rockies' Venus de Milo pitching staff began dimming the gleam in his eyes. (Photo courtesy of the Colorado Rockies Baseball Club.)

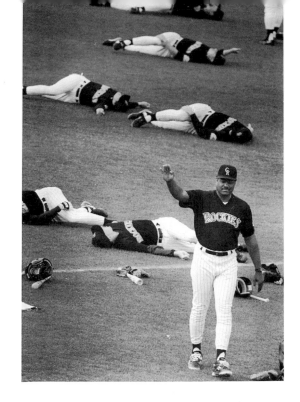

Coach Don Zimmer, scowling for effect. In his forty-five years in baseball, he has seen and done it all and has never collected a paycheck from any other job. One sportswriter has said that if baseball had its own currency, Zimmer's face would be on the one-dollar bill. (Photo by Thomas Kelsey/*Rocky Mountain News*)

David Nied delivering the first pitch in Colorado Rockies history, against the New York Mets at Shea Stadium, April 5, 1993. (Photo by Thomas Kelsey/*Rocky Mountain News*.)

Catcher Joe Girardi tagging out the Mets' Joe Orsulak on Opening Day. (Photo by Thomas Kelsey/*Rocky Mountain News*.)

The 1993 Colorado Rockies, lined up for the National Anthem before a crowd of 80,227 at their home opener, Mile High Stadium, April 9, 1993. (Photo by Thomas Kelsey/*Rocky Mountain News*.)

Eric Young rounding third base after hitting a home run to lead off the Rockies' first game in Colorado. Don Zimmer is the third-base coach. (Photo by Thomas Kelsey/*Rocky Mountain News*.)

Don Baylor and the Rockies celebrate their first victory, in their home opener, beating the Montreal Expos, 11–4. (Photo by Thomas Kelsey/*Rocky Mountain News*.)

The meat of the order: The Rockies' heavy hitters pose for the cameras in a meat locker. From left to right are first baseman Andres Galarraga (.370, 22 HR, 98 RBI), third baseman Charlie Hayes (.305, 25 HR, 98 RBI), left fielder Jerald Clark (.282, 13 HR, 67 RBI) and right fielder Dante Bichette (.310, 21 HR, 89 RBI). (Photo by Thomas Kelsey/*Rocky Mountain News*.)

Second baseman Roberto Mejia, a midseason addition who helped anchor the Rockies' infield. (Photo by Thomas Kelsey/*Rocky Mountain News*.)

The Firemen: Another publicity shot, this one featuring relief pitchers. From left to right are Jeff Parrett, Darren Holmes and Steve Reed. (Photo by Thomas Kelsey/*Rocky Mountain News*.)

Armando Reynoso, who led the pitching staff with 12 wins, running off the mound during a rain delay against the Los Angeles Dodgers. (Photo by Ken Papaleo/*Rocky Mountain News*.)

Curtis Leskanic pitching against the Florida Marlins at Mile High Stadium. Nicknamed "Psycho," he periodically shaved his arm during the season in the interest of "aerodynamics." (Photo © Eric Larrs Bakke/Rich Clarkson & Associates.)

Shortstop Vinny Castilla getting high fives after hitting a home run at Mile High. (Photo by Thomas Kelsey/*Rocky Mountain News.*)

First baseman Andres Galarraga, the first expansion-team player (and the first Venezuelan) to win a batting title, still stroking the ball on the last day of the season, against the Atlanta Braves. (Photo © Eric Larrs Bakke/Rich Clarkson & Associates.)

team competitive. Everything, Baylor told him, but he emphasized pitching. They also conferred on another issue: the composition of the team. Privately, Baylor had been grumbling about
the number of aging players on the roster. Murphy, clearly, was
finished. Smith was running on fumes. Ruffin was always falling
behind in the count. Baylor felt that youth was not being served.

Baylor and McMorris agreed. The problem now was Gebhard,
who seemed painfully loyal to the old horses. And Gebhard questioned whether the club might not hurt the developmental process by bringing up minor-leaguers like Chris Jones, Pedro
Castellano, Brad Ausmus and Roberto Mejia too soon.

McMorris was also losing his patience with the scope of the
debacle. The club expected to lose a lot, and expected occasional
blowouts. But the team was rapidly becoming a laughingstock,
and McMorris was gradually realizing that he would have to
spend more money to set things right. Already, he had given
Gebhard the freedom to add a bullpen coach and another minor-
league club, and had given approval for additional scouts.

"We will have a much larger payroll next season," he promised. "It will be dramatically larger. And we will be active in the
free-agent market."

But that was next year. The 1993 season was already getting
out of hand.

Los Angeles, Sunday, May 23—Dodgers 4, Rockies 0.

It seemed like it lasted only 10 minutes.

After the game, after Dodgers pitcher Ramon Martinez had
blown the Rockies away on a three-hitter, Baylor looked at a
piece of notebook paper. "Oh-for-eight on hit-and-runs this
week," he said. "I've tried it with Hayes, Young, Jim Tatum . . .
oh-for-eight. We're not even making contact."

The Rockies were on a streak that saw them have just one
scoring inning in the last 27. "It feels like we've been on the road
since spring training," said Girardi.

The Rockies were 1-9 on the road trip. They weren't pitching,
weren't hitting, weren't running, weren't fielding. But they were

eating well from the postgame buffet. They were done with the poor sisters, San Diego and L.A. Now came Houston, a winning team, a good team.

Houston, Monday, May 24—No score.

This was an off day, which meant a good day for the Rockies.

It was not, however, a good day for baseball. The Reds had just fired first-year manager Tony Perez after just 44 games. Baylor and all of baseball were outraged at the premature dismissal of one of the few minority managers in the game. How could they do this after 44 games? How could they do this to a local legend? How could they do it over the phone?

The Reds' rookie general manager, Jim Bowden, claimed it was his call, but Baylor saw owner Marge Schott's paw prints all over it. "Would a 32-year-old GM make that kind of call on his own?" he asked rhetorically. Schott, who was serving out a suspension for using racially insensitive remarks, publicly distanced herself from the move. Naturally. "Sure, because if she says she had any say in it, they slap another year or two onto her suspension," said Baylor.

He would soon send Perez a note. "As soon as I can figure out the appropriate thing to say," he said grimly.

Houston, Tuesday, May 25—Rockies 7, Astros 5.

Begin the parade.

Where's Harry Caray when you need him: "Rockies win!!! Rockies win!!!"

Here's how you knew the Rockies would win this game. Along about the seventh inning, a Houston reporter uttered the magic words, "Who's the expansion team here?" This had become something of a running press-box joke. Back in April, when the Rockies were still playing decent baseball, it was inevitable that some out-of-town reporter would say, "Who's the expansion team here?"

It was a question that had not been uttered for weeks. Every night, the Rockies proved who the expansionists were. Proved it in myriad ways. But on this magical night, everything would go right. Nelson Liriano, a former Toronto infielder whom the Rockies had picked up as a free agent during the spring, hit a home run off Pete Harnisch in a ballpark noted for being unfriendly to long-ball hitters. Jim Tatum, who had played for the Denver Zephyrs the previous season, botched a hit-and-run, only to see it turn into a double steal. During that same at-bat, Tatum doubled in both runs. And the bullpen came in, one reliever after another, and shut the door on Houston.

"Look at you guys," Girardi told the media as they entered the clubhouse. "You guys can't wait to get in here now."

He wasn't lying; the losing might have been a source of jocularity outside the organization, but nobody, not even the most jaded writers, enjoyed walking up to the Goat du Jour and asking, "So, what happened on that dropped fly ball in the ninth?"

Murphy sat at a table and picked at some food. "Hey, guys," he said, gesturing toward a stereo that was blaring heavy metal. "Think you could turn that up?"

A happy group. For a change.

Houston, Wednesday, May 26—Rockies 3, Astros 2.

How many *g*'s in *juggernaut*?

There had been a two-game harmonic convergence of BaylorBall and the bullpen. Bichette drove in three runs. Parrett got his first save since man crawled from the primordial slime. The Rockies got another good relief performance from the pen, allowing just one run in three and a third innings.

They were winners of two straight for the first time in a month.

And tomorrow they would have a chance for a sweep, a chance to go home on an upbeat note. They had Nied going, fresh from a good talking-to and self-examination. He knew this was a key outing, what with Baylor saying he was contemplating demoting Nied to the minors if he struggled once again. Nied understood he had been acting badly, understood he needed to find his off-speed pitch if he was going to be successful.

They had crawled out of the abyss. For a few minutes, anyway.

Houston, Thursday, May 27—Astros 8, Rockies 0.

It was late in the morning when Dale Murphy was summoned to Gebhard's room at the Westin Galleria. He found both Gebhard and Baylor waiting for him, and the former great power hitter knew something was wrong. He was not suffering from delusion; he knew he was on the bubble, knew he wasn't contributing as a pinch hitter, his only remaining physical attribute. His wobbly knees now made him a liability in the field and on the base paths; if he didn't hit, he didn't fit.

For Gebhard, the meeting was especially difficult. He had hoped the Rockies might milk whatever was left from Murphy, especially if the former star could hit two more home runs and reach the magical 400 mark as a Colorado Rockie. So far, though Murphy had infused the clubhouse with some professionalism, he had done little on the field. And so it was with a heavy heart that Gebhard and, to a lesser degree, Baylor apprised Murphy of his options.

They were bringing up young outfielder Chris Jones and Murphy would be released—or he could go out with a bit more dignity and retire on his own. Murphy chose the latter, and a quickie press conference was held in an inappropriate setting— in a hotel conference room just down the hall from the Galleria mall. But Murphy wanted it done quickly so that he could return to his family in Paintsville, Georgia. The Rockies and Murphy would do it right a couple of days later, honoring him in a touching pregame ceremony at Mile High.

"I'm leaving this family for my number-one family," Murphy said tearfully. "But it's tough, leaving something you've been so close to for all these years. This has been a fantasy life, and now I'm going back to reality."

Gebhard was moved. "When I think about Dale Murphy, I think about him as a fan would," he said, choking back emotion. "I don't look at him as a general manager. That's why this is so difficult."

Third-base coach Royster had first become close to Murphy when they were teammates in Atlanta, and agreed to give up his number 3 jersey when Murphy was signed by the Rockies. "He's one of those guys who has a way of making everyone feel special," said Royster. "He didn't play here long, but I know there are a lot of guys in that clubhouse who can consider themselves very lucky for having been Dale Murphy's teammate."

Sentimentality gave way to ugly reality within four innings of the trip's final game. Nied used the double-play ball to wriggle out of jams in the early innings, but he still lacked the off-speed pitch. Hitters were sitting on the hard stuff, the fastball and the slider. Nothing had changed. Except this time Nied stuck around and faced the music after the loss.

At that moment, Baylor decided Nied would make his next start when the Rockies played their top farm club, Colorado Springs, on June 3.

The final tally: a 3-10 road trip. Good signs: winning two of three against Houston; the bullpen was no longer making Baylor physically ill; and Galarraga was set to come off the disabled list. Bad signs: Nobody was hitting; the starting pitchers were fortunate to last until the fifth inning; and the Philadelphia Phillies, the best team in baseball, were waiting to greet the Rockies back in Denver.

"I think we'll be all right," said Holmes. "I'm seeing some good things. We just need to get back home."

Yeah . . . right.

10

Simply Amazin'

RICH ASHBURN peered down from his broadcast perch at Mile High Stadium, adjusted the lid of his omnipresent cap, and shook his head. "Jeez," he said as he watched the Phillies dismember the Rockies, 18–1, on a typical Bloody Sunday. "We were never *this* bad."

This was not some idle boast.

The "we" to which Ashburn referred were the amazing, incredible, remarkably inept 1962 New York Mets, the worst team of the twentieth century, an expansion club that managed an almost unfathomable 40-120 record. Most of Ashburn's luminous career had been spent as a member of the Philadelphia Phillies, who have honored Ashburn by retiring his number 1 jersey. But Ashburn is remembered almost as much as the best player on a truly wretched and uniformly beloved Mets team, remembered, too, as a proud veteran who couldn't take the losing anymore and quit at season's end.

And now he sat at Mile High, having watched three Rockies-

Phillies games, the best versus the worst, the Phillies winning 15–9, 6–0 and this laughable 18–1 game, during which Phillies batters were literally sprinting to home plate for a chance at the bat, and he wondered whether the Rockies might not be even worse than those 1962 Mets—as Bill Madden, the New York writer, had predicted back in April.

"What I mean is fundamentally—fundamentally worse," said Ashburn. "Our Mets team wasn't any good, but we were mostly a veteran team and we knew how to play the game. When I look at this team, you have a lot of fundamental violations—people throwing to the wrong base, bad baserunning, things like that. And that's gotta make Baylor crazy, as competitive as he is, as fundamentally sound as he was.

"Who was worse? I don't know because it's tough to compare generations. They're such different teams. The Mets had a bunch of gallant, old warriors, mostly guys at or near the end of their careers. The Rockies are a lot younger, and you just don't know what you're going to get. Some of them will become good players and some of them will fall by the wayside. You would think the Rockies would be better because the expansion process favored them this time. They were able to draft from both leagues, plus they had free agency, which we didn't have back then."

Ashburn turned to the field and watched as the Phillies congratulated themselves after a convincing series sweep, watched as the Rockies, devastated and embarrassed, walked with their heads low toward the sanctity of the clubhouse. He had been there in 1962. He had been part of something that was both special and painful, part of a team that was both loved and laughed at. The '62 Mets would ultimately forge a unique spot in baseball lore, would ultimately become known as the Amazin' Mets and inspire a library's worth of books. But when it was happening, while the losses were piling up on one another, it was oppressive.

"You know who it affects most is the veteran guys," said Ashburn. "I've always said there should be some rule that anybody over 30 can't play on an expansion team. Because it eats you up. If you've ever known success in the major leagues, it's just dismal being a part of all that losing.

"Expansion," he said, shaking his head. "Expansion is something. It's totally different. A ballplayer can't know what expansion is about until he goes through it. But you know what? Even though I retired at the end of the season, it was something I was glad to be part of. I wouldn't have traded that experience for anything. The people I met, the associations, and the fans . . . Lord, the fans were great. It's like the people in Colorado. This was 18-to-1 and it was like nobody left the ballpark. Expansion is great, but I wouldn't want to do it twice."

The Rockies didn't want to hear about the '62 Mets, but the comparisons were difficult to avoid. After a 1-5 home stand—a sweep by the Phillies followed by a 1-2 series against the Pirates —the Rockies stood at 15-38, precisely the same record as those '62 Mets. It was pointed out that the Mets fell off rather dramatically the rest of the season, but the Rockies were showing early signs of collapse, too. After a 10-15 start, quite respectable by expansion standards, the Rockies had gone an atrocious 5-23 as they arrived in Philadelphia on June 4 to play the best team in the National League East.

Comparisons to the '62 Mets:

Galarraga versus Marv Throneberry at first base: an easy edge to Galarraga, who was having a remarkable renaissance season.

Young versus Rod Kanehl/Charlie Neal at second base: a wash. Neal had a fine year, batting .260 with 58 RBIs.

Vinny Castilla/Freddie Benavides versus Elio Chacon/Felix Mantilla at shortstop: a wash. Castilla replaced Benavides early and hit the ball well. Mantilla hit .275.

Hayes versus Zimmer, Cliff Cook and a cast of thousands at third base: edge to Hayes.

Clark versus Frank Thomas in left field: clear edge to Thomas, who had 34 home runs.

Cole/Boston/Chris Jones versus Ashburn in center field: edge to Ashburn. He was at the end of a great career, but he was still better than the Rockies in their prime.

Bichette versus a cast of thousands in right field: Bichette—easy.

Girardi versus Choo Choo Coleman and others at catcher: edge to Girardi.

Starting pitching: Neither team had any—a wash.

Bullpen: Neither team had one—a wash.

Baylor versus Stengel: a wash. This was Baylor's first go-round as a manager, and he was dedicated to making the most of the opportunity. He made some rookie mistakes, but mostly they were errors of commission rather than omission; if anything, his teams messed up trying to make something happen rather than sitting back and playing passively. Still, there were questions as to whether Baylor was temperamentally best suited to managing an expansion team. Stengel, conversely, was the ultimate retread, a friendly old caretaker who kept the writers happy. Only the Old Perfessor could make 40-120 palatable.

Overall: edge to the Rockies. But not by a lot.

"You know, we had a pretty good hitting team," Ashburn remembered. "It wasn't until the 1986 World Championship Mets came along that a Mets team broke our home-run record. But God, we had a 24-game loser [Roger Craig], we had Al Jackson lose 20 games, Jay Hook 19, Craig Anderson 17 and Bob Miller 12. And they were the best we had. There was nothing we could do but just keep running those guys out there over and over again. And our defense wasn't very good, either. I mean, I was at the end of my career, I'd lost a step or two, and I was one of our better defensive players.

"What kept us going, though, was, first, the fans. It was incredible. And I have to credit Casey Stengel because he never let us feel like we were going to lose. You can get to a point where you get totally beat down to the point where you didn't think you can win, and we had some unbelievable losses. But we never got beat down, and that's because of Casey.

"I can remember we had a doubleheader rained out against Milwaukee, and Casey said, 'Fellers, this is a great day for the New York Mets,' and he took us all out to dinner. That's the way he was. And that's probably the main difference between our clubhouse in '62 and yours now. Casey deflected all the criticism. All the focus was on Casey. We would score nine, 10 runs and still lose by seven runs, and the writers wouldn't talk to us— they'd talk to Casey. I think Casey knew, early on, that it was going to be a very long season. Plus, he'd managed some bad teams before, so he knew what a bad team looked like. I think he took it all in stride. The difference with the Rockies is you have a first-year manager who is very competitive—and that's great. But it's probably hard for him to accept the fact there's going to be a lot more losing than winning.

"I think because of Casey, that team became a cult. We had a reunion a couple of years ago, we figured we'll show up at this Manhattan hotel and sign for three hours and that's it. Well, I'll tell you, so many people showed up, they were waiting for blocks in line. We ended up staying Friday, Saturday and Sunday to accommodate them all. Still, to this day, I probably get more mail on my season with that team than any other. It's amazing, really."

They captured the heart of a city that doesn't suffer fools or losers gladly. There was nobility in their losing, in their trying, and, with each telling, the tall tales of the '62 Mets grew in stature. They were a team for the ages in their own ridiculous way.

"Tell him your Piggy story," a friend said.

Ashburn adjusted his cap and laughed. "Piggy," he said. "Joe Pignatano. You want to talk about symbolic. This is the last game of the season, we're in Chicago. We're behind the Cubs by one run, top of the ninth, Sammy Drake leads off with a base hit, then I follow with a hit, so it's first and second with no outs. So Piggy is up, he tries to bunt and fails. So he's swinging away, and hits one of those dying quails to right center field. I take off, Drake takes off, and Kenny Hubbs catches it on the dead run, dives and rolls over a half dozen times. Then he throws it to second, on to first . . . a triple play. That ended our season. A TRIPLE PLAY!"

Afterward, the '62 Mets gathered in their visitors clubhouse, deep in contemplation of the season just passed. Stengel searched for the right words to say.

"Fellers," he said, "now, I don't want you to feel too bad about all this. I just want you to know that no one or two guys could have done all this by themselves. This was a total team effort."

The Rockies felt the same way: This was, indeed, a team effort.

How BAD WAS it getting? Here's how bad it was getting.

"Gimme a Coke," Bear said as he bellied up to the hotel bar in downtown Pittsburgh. "With a slice of lemon."

What? No beer? No sea breeze?

"Why drink?" he wondered. "It just gets me more fucking depressed."

Things were getting worse, especially with the beleaguered Venus de Milo pitching staff. Smith had been released. Nied, who had been hit hard in his Colorado Springs outing on June 3, had been placed on the 15-day disabled list with an elbow problem. Henry had been demoted to the bullpen, incapable of getting anybody out after a decent start. Painter was back in Colorado Springs as fast as he left the place.

"Taking this job was not an act of cowardice," Bear said.

Here's what was left:

Ruffin, the ultimate journeyman, who began the season as a starter, got stuck in the bullpen, only to return—out of desperation—to the starting rotation.

Ashby, another former-starter-demoted-to-the-bullpen-and-brought-back-to-start, who continued to frustrate Bear and Baylor with his lapses in concentration. "Someday," Ashby said after a gruesome effort against his old mates, the Philadelphia Phillies, "the light's gonna go on in my head."

And then there were the two saviors: Blair, a right-hander who began the season in the bullpen, and Reynoso, who threw so many different pitches, catchers ran out of fingers.

The best answer to an innocent question came after the Rockies had fled Mile High for the relative serenity of Philadelphia's Veterans Stadium on June 4.

"What's up?" a reporter asked innocently.

Ashby and Holmes looked at one another and said, "Our ERAs."

Incredibly, the Rockies won the first game in Philly on Friday night, 2–1, as Blair pitched eight shutout innings and the Rockies scored a pair of runs in the ninth. But one day later, Phillies right-hander Tommy Greene was overwhelming, shutting down the Rockies, 6–2, with a complete-game effort. The final game of the set told the same story as Ashby was lit for five runs in the first and nine in three and two-thirds, the Phillies winning, 11–7. So much for the revenge he so desperately desired against his former teammates. "I wanted to stick it up their ass," he said.

Two days later, in Pittsburgh, it was Ruffin's turn to stand at the career crossroads. In fact, Gebhard had flown out to the game to see, firsthand, whether Ruffin was worth keeping or shipping out. The result: Ruffin was spectacular and the Rockies won one of their best-played games, 4–1. On Wednesday, June 9, Blair got typically shoddy run support and the Rockies, led by the overzealous Baylor, ran themselves out of innings and handed Pittsburgh a 4–1 victory.

They were now 17–41. But there was some good news. First, Galarraga, who had returned to play on May 28, was hitting better than ever. By the time Colorado left Pittsburgh, he was hitting a robust .409. And the other piece of good news:

They were only three games behind the New York Mets.

ONE MORNING, Danny Sheaffer, the real-life Crash Davis, and reliever Gary Wayne were sharing breakfast. Wayne was perusing the *USA Today* sports pages when he said, "Man, the basketball and hockey seasons just go on forever."

Sheaffer, a 31-year-old catcher/utility player who had just 82 major-league at-bats after more than 12 years of professional baseball, looked up from his plate and smiled.

"As long as I'm up here in the big leagues," he said, "the season can't be long enough."

If expansion baseball could have a poster boy, it would have been Sheaffer, a squat, earnest and thoroughly professional fringe player who had beaten the bushes forever in the hope that he might one day find semiregular employment in the bigs.

He came to spring training as a long shot—as usual—a non-roster invitee who figured to have difficulty finding a spot with Girardi penciled in as the starter, Wedge as the backup and Tatum as the emergency catcher and backup infielder. Beyond that, there was the emergence of Gilberto Reyes, the rifle-armed former Expos catcher who had come back from alcohol and drug rehabilitation to make a run at a job, and two youngsters with strong pedigrees, Brad Ausmus and J. Owens.

Sheaffer came to Tucson with the same fleeting hope he had brought to every major-league camp. Some guys get a cup of coffee in the bigs; Sheaffer had two, three sips. He made the Boston Red Sox out of spring training in 1987, and hit .121 in 25 games; then, in 1989, he had one hit in 16 at-bats, an .063 average, in seven games, for the Cleveland Indians.

And so every day in The Show was special, a day to be treasured like a dusty old keepsake. It hardly mattered that he rarely played in the early weeks, what with Girardi playing so well. And it hardly mattered that he was getting his most extended playing time ever in the big leagues during this stretch as Girardi nursed an injured hand. He was Here, not There—getting the $62.50 per diem, making the big-league salary, riding charter flights instead of buses, feeling like he'd finally arrived.

"I feel right now like a kid who goes on Christmas vacation and finds out it's three or four weeks instead of one or two," Sheaffer said one morning. "There are some guys in this league who take for granted they're in the big leagues. They complain that they're away from their families a lot, and I understand that part of it. But I played so many years in the minors, in so many different towns—I've nearly lost track of them all—the way I feel, this experience can't last long enough."

Every day *up here* negates a month *down there*. It almost seems like another life, another person, disembodied, toiling for all those years in so many small cities. There was Elmira, New York, and Bristol, Connecticut; Winter Haven, Florida, and Winston-Salem, North Carolina. There was New Britain, Connecticut, and Pawtucket, Rhode Island; Colorado Springs and Buffalo and Portland—12 years of baseball, of believing the call would finally come.

Crash Davis.

Sheaffer laughs. "You know, I've never seen *Bull Durham*, but so many people have told me so much about the movie and about Crash Davis, I don't need to see the movie; I've lived it," he says. "Except for the part with Susan Sarandon. I think his love for the game and mine are identical, though the lifestyles are totally different.

"See, I know what it's like to taste the big leagues, but not taste it for a long time. It's a feeling you can't get anywhere else. You can have a stellar season in Triple A and be an All-Star in the minors, but it doesn't match just one day in the major leagues. It's just a different feeling. You know you're among the elite. You can do what you want with that: You can cherish it and feel very, very lucky . . . or you can boast about it and have it all fall down on you.

"Fact is, there's no other place to be in sports. Major-league baseball is it as far as I'm concerned. It'll wear on you. Yeah, it'll wear on you. But, you know, right now, Triple A seems so far away. Sooo far away. It's funny, when you're in Triple A, you pick up the paper every morning to see how the major-leaguers are doing, who's going where, who's struggling and might be sent down to the minors. You feel a little bit like a vulture, circling over the carcass, because you want so badly to move up a level. Later in my career, I found it more difficult to read the sports pages and watch players who were friends and hope they would fail. It's not the way to be. It's not positive.

"But once you're here, you don't care who's doing what in

Triple A, even when you have good friends down there. It's like you don't even want to admit that Triple A exists or ever existed."

He looks dreamily into midair, considering a thousand memories of floodlit nights on bad fields in decaying cities. "If there's anybody in this game who appreciates being a major-leaguer more than me, I haven't met him yet," he says. "I know how hard I've worked the last twelve years. I had one thing in mind when the Rockies signed me, and that was to not give them any excuse for farming me out. This is like being in Disney World. This is a fun time.

"I've seen a bunch of guys in the majors who take this life and opportunity for granted, and it just rubs me the wrong way, because I know guys in the minors who deserve to be in the majors, who wouldn't take this all for granted. It does bother me to watch people with all the talent in the world and then they don't use it. I feel fortunate because I've used what God's given me, and I think, now, I've been rewarded."

The way Sheaffer figured, if he couldn't make the Rockies, he might consider finally quitting and attending to his wife and young son. He had two successful businesses up and running—a chimney-sweep business and a network marketing firm—and he could live perfectly well off that income. But Sheaffer couldn't truly say this was his last gasp. When the game is in your blood, it is difficult to say, "Enough." Maybe he wouldn't have called it quits; maybe he would have gone to Colorado Springs, given it one more shot.

The choice was a difficult one; Royster later said the decision on the final catcher/utility-man spot produced the most heated debate. But Baylor was unimpressed by Reyes's work habits and distressed by his failure to come to the mound and offer guidance to a struggling pitcher, and he chose the hard-nosed veteran. That night, Sheaffer and his wife, LaDonna, went out for a nice dinner. It was the best moment in his baseball life.

By a long shot.

"I've stayed with it because of love of the game," Sheaffer said. "I've got responsibilities, bills to pay, and a family to take care of. But the main reason is I just love baseball. I've been doing this since I was too young to do anything else. I truly *love* this game. There are times when I've hated it. But, you know, I look at people in some other professions and I wonder, 'What do they have to look forward to? Are they going to be happy in their jobs 10 years from now?' I look at myself and ask, 'Am I gonna be happy in 10 years?' and the answer is, 'Yeah, I will be.'

"Hopefully, I'm going to stay in the game as a coach and then a manager. I mean, I've been playing forever, I've played every position. I've learned a lot about the game. One thing that's helped me, too, is I've been a student of some of the better teachers in the game, like Mike Hargrove, John McNamara, Russ Nixon, Ted Williams. My ears and eyes have always been open, and that's benefitted me.

"Honestly, I knew from day one I'd never be a Hall of Famer. I think I had it embedded in my mind from the very beginning, people telling me I was too small or too fat or too whatever. The only people pushing me to prove somebody wrong were my dad and my high school coach. But even in college, my coach was telling me I wouldn't play ball. Then, every time I jumped a level, they'd say, 'Well, you're not gonna get any higher.' I never really thought I'd be a superstar, but I knew I could play at any level. Still, the whole time, I thought, 'Pick their brains.' When I'm not playing, I'm listening to the coaches and watching what they do."

Sheaffer's is a baseball life lived on the fringes, fraught with insecurity and false hopes. On days like these, he is a major-leaguer, *feels* like a major-leaguer, like someone who has made it and can go eye-to-eye with Barry Bonds and Gary Sheffield. But he knows the truth: He is here because expansion means jobs, and a dilution of the talent base. He is playing because Girardi is hurt, because Wedge seems to be on a permanent rehabilitation assignment. And it's just a matter of time before the young kids develop.

But that doesn't seem to matter now. This is Sheaffer's 15 minutes of fame. This is his just reward for 12 years of fighting and scuffling. The money is one thing; he is making just a tad more than the major-league minimum of $109,000 after five or six years of making between $30,000 and $40,000. More, though, there is a sense of closure, of accomplishment and fulfillment.

"I have some good friends in Double-A and Triple-A ball who didn't make it any higher, and there's always this bitter feeling of 'I could have . . . I would have . . . I never got a chance' and maybe that's true," Sheaffer said. "I've found that guys who've been to the majors, even for a cup of coffee, and then they don't make it back, they're more at peace with themselves. You hear them say things like, 'Well, I can always tell my grandkids about this,' or, 'Well, I got someplace not too many guys reach.' I know, for me, if baseball ended tomorrow, I would leave the game feeling very contented."

Once upon a time, Sheaffer would treat every rare playing opportunity like a personal Armageddon. Either he produced, or he was on the plane back to Elmira. He pressed, trying to hit six-run homers every at bat. "I used to go up there thinking, 'I've got to get a few hits and play flawless defense or I'm in trouble,' " he said. "But I find now, I'm not pressing anymore. Maybe for the first time in my career. The way I look at this, this is extended spring training. This is a blast. Hey, I'm 31. I've been in the game 12 years—I'm gonna press? I mean, yeah, there's pressure when you don't play much, but I know my role and I'm just relishing every minute of it."

The greatest joy comes from playing, but Sheaffer likes to watch, too, to see and to feel the game, to soak up the sensory bouillabaisse of baseball. Life on the fringes means spending lots of time peering in at the vortex of the game's activity. He becomes an exposed nerve ending, his senses heightened.

"I see baseball for what it really is, especially when I'm not playing," he said. "I see the strategy from the bench. I see how many sunflower seeds guys can eat. I can tell you who spits tobacco the best. I can tell you who pays attention and who doesn't, who takes batting practice seriously and who doesn't, who's happy to be here and who isn't. That's the key, you know? There are guys in the majors who aren't really happy. I don't know if it's something at home or if they just don't like baseball, but they're not happy. I can't understand that. I cannot, for the life of me, figure out how this can become a labor. I don't see it. It's a game. And if that's not enough, if you can't get excited after going to the bank the first and 15th of the month, well . . . Money isn't everything, but man, those alarm clocks in the morning, they can get ignorant on you. I know I don't want to answer one of those things.

"When I see guys like that, if I really care for the guy, I'll say something. It's happened before. But some guys, they've got talent but they're just not happy and you can't wait for them to get out of the clubhouse because they can only bring you down. You see a lot of this, too: guys who have the work ethic, put the nose to the grindstone while they're in Triple A, then they get to the majors and it's like, 'Okay, I'm done, I've made it,' and the work ethic is out the window. See it every day. And those guys are back in the minors quicker than they can unpack a suitcase. In the minors, they take extra ground balls, come out for early BP, they have a good lifestyle and get their sleep, then they get to the majors and everything changes. The work habits diminish. The nightlife increases. And then you're back in the minors and the cycle begins all over again."

Sheaffer wants off the treadmill, wants to break the cycle. If he plays, he plays. If he sits, he'll be a sponge, watching and learning and biding his time. The game is too precious. These days, as a major-leaguer, as a Colorado Rockie, are to be cherished. The season can't last long enough.

11

Home Cooking

JERRY McMORRIS was howling.

"Awright, Nate!" he said, high-fiving the hospitality man sitting near his seat behind the Rockies' dugout. "We are rolling."

Then McMorris turned to an acquaintance, his voice barely audible above the Mile High din. The Rockies were putting together another big inning en route to a 15–5 victory over the Cincinnati Reds, the perfect denouement to a splendid 8-4 home stand that brought the club back into the fold of respectability.

"Can you imagine how it will be when we win?" the owner said loudly. "Can you imagine how it will be when we're contending year in and year out, when we really give people something to scream about? I'll tell you what. When this team came back after that long road trip, I wouldn't have given a dime for anybody except Big Cat. Maybe Reynoso, maybe Charlie Hayes and Dante Bichette. But the rest of them?" McMorris shook his head, then broke into a wide grin. "But you know what? We've got something to build on. We really do."

Two weeks had made so much difference. On June 9, the Rockies limped back from the road with a 17-41 record. Now, on June 23, they were 25-45 and on a pace for 58 victories, a far more respectable number.

For one brief moment, a blip on the long continuum of a baseball season, the Colorado Rockies were Baylor's Dream Team, a club that scored lots of runs, wreaked lots of havoc on the base paths and generally set those new standards for an expansion team. Better yet, they were finally giving the multitudes at Mile High something to savor. The crowds kept coming—one million by Mother's Day, two million by Father's Day, crowds unlike any in the long history of baseball, unfazed by the Rockies' quality of play. But now the games were becoming competitive, entertaining, Rockies hitters feasting at Mile High, the pitchers finally getting beyond their phobia about pitching at home.

They were also developing a personality not unlike their manager's. They were becoming angry, feisty, developing an ornery reputation around the league as a team that wouldn't back down. It was as if they had heeded the words of old hockey coach Conn Smythe, who once said, "If you can't beat them on the ice, beat them in the alley."

For 12 games, they were as good a baseball team as the Philadelphia Phillies or the San Francisco Giants.

This team could have come home and gone one of two ways: They could have fallen completely to pieces, especially with Nied out for what was expected to be most of the season, or they could have become a first-rate laughingstock. But instead they returned home and made a statement: "We are not this bad," they said. "We can win at home."

And they did.

JUNE 11—The Rockies beat the Houston Astros, 5–4, as Reynoso, the team's co-MVP with Galarraga, continued to establish himself as the unquestioned staff ace. "He goes deep into the count, but he battles," said Bear. "He's got a lot of guts." And a lot of pitches. Reynoso's games were rarely austere, often lasting 150 pitches or more, but he was emerging as the one Rockies pitcher who was undaunted by Mile High.

JUNE 12—They were down, 7–0, to Cy Young candidate Doug Drabek in the third inning. Game over? Hardly. Forget that Drabek had shut the Rockies out just two weeks earlier in Houston. In one of Baylor's brightest managerial moments, he orchestrated the fourth inning as if it were the ninth, sending a procession of pinch hitters to the plate in a desperate attempt to get the game back under control. For one night, he had the Midas touch. Houston manager Art Howe could only scratch his bald pate as Colorado surged to a 14–11 victory. "It's a strange ballpark," he said. "I guess no lead is safe."

While the music blared and the chatter filled the postgame clubhouse, Charlie Hayes sat in his corner locker stall and considered a reporter's question about reclaiming the home-field advantage. It was a softball question, the kind you take deep out of the park, something that demanded one of those clichéd responses, like, "We feel more comfortable at home now." But no; Hayes wanted to talk about the official scoring at home, about how the Rockies weren't getting home town calls from Haraway. "Dude must be blind, man," Hayes said. "What game is he watching? He's given me at least two, three errors I didn't deserve. You're supposed to get those calls at home. That's what I mean about home-field advantage."

Tough guy to figure . . .

JUNE 13—Black Sunday no more. The Rockies, who had been so miserable on Sundays, rolled over Houston, 9–1, and completed the first sweep in franchise history. They had come into this game 1–8 on Sunday, outscored 94–31, including 60–19 at Mile High. On Sundays, their pitching staff rested and the rest of the league feasted. Not so on this bright and shining afternoon.

The Big Cat wasn't the only one swinging a hot bat now; the entire middle of the order was producing. Hayes was hitting again to the opposite field. Bichette was finding every gap in the outfield. Clark, who always ran hot and cold, was in the zone. And, of course, another attendance record fell. The Rockies drew 60,349, breaking Toronto's 1977 expansion attendance mark of 1,719,566, doing it in just 30 home dates. "We owe these people," McMorris said. "There's no question; we owe them."

JUNE 14—While the Dodgers were continuing their mastery over the Rockies, beating them 9–4, a young man named Mark Zessin was scurrying around the bowels of Mile High, a walkie-talkie pasted to his ear.

"No ballots?" he asked.

"None," the voice said. "None left."

"God," he said. "Now everyone will say, 'Why can't those guys get the All-Star ballots out?'"

The Rockies were not embarking on a ballot-stuffing campaign for Galarraga; it was more like a "ballot maximization program." Yeah, that sounded good. Like a Chicago mayoral election: Vote early and vote often. Incredibly, the major talk on the radio gab shows regarded the lack of All-Star ballots and Galarraga's inexplicable failure to move up in the All-Star standings. He was still in fourth place, far behind the leader, Philadelphia's John Kruk. The fans had to blame somebody.

So they blamed the fresh-faced kids in the goofy Andy Frain usher's uniforms, the people charged with showing fans to their seats and distributing All-Star ballots. They charged the ushers with not giving out all the ballots and failing to collect all the ballots.

Zessin, a Brillo-haired young man who was in charge of the Andy Frains, shook his head. "I wish the Rockies would put in a press release that it's not our fault," he said. "The reason there are no ballots is because they ran out. They ran out early in this home stand. They got about a million from Major League Baseball to start with, but now they're down to calling other teams and having 60,000 or so brought in for every game. I mean, it's 10, 15 minutes before the game, and we're out already. So, now people will call the radio shows and say, 'What's wrong with these people?' It's not like we hoard them and redeem them later. They're worth nothing to us."

JUNE 15—McMorris couldn't wait to show the owners. The 28 major-league team representatives had gathered in Denver for their regular meetings, and McMorris couldn't wait to get them out to Mile High to watch baseball among 55,000 of his closest friends.

They showed up in the seventh inning.

"No sooner had we gotten into our seats than the fights broke out," said commissioner pro tem Bud Selig. "Great timing, huh?"

For the better part of the day, the owners had been talking not only about realigning baseball and adding a layer of playoffs but also about the recent outbreak of bench-clearing brawls. The Mariners and Orioles, in particular, had been embroiled in a fight that was quite violent by baseball's often genteel standards. And now, here they were, settling down behind the Rockies' dugout, prepared for a late beer and a dog and a lazy summer night under the stars, when the punches started to fly.

The fireworks began innocently enough when Dodgers pitcher Ramon Martinez brushed back Galarraga with a pitch under his chin. Moments later, Galarraga, standing on first after a single, broke for second with his spikes high, clipping L.A. second baseman Jody Reed, who later left the game. This constituted an act of war.

One batter later, Martinez retaliated by hitting Charlie Hayes in the ribs with a pitch. Hayes went ballistic, his eyes bulging out of their sockets as he charged the mound. The brawl was on, bodies flying everywhere, Hayes flailing away madly. "For Martinez to do that was gutless," Hayes said later.

The field was finally cleared and a semblance of order restored, but the emotions were bubbling near the surface. In the top of the eighth, the Rockies called on Keith Shepherd, a right-handed relief pitcher who just happened to be a former boxer (who went by the name of "Apache Kid"). He was being hit pretty hard, absorbing blows left and right, when he decided to take the law into his own hands. He promptly threw at Cory Snyder, barely concealing his intentions. Snyder glared at Shepherd but did not rush the mound. Shepherd, in an act of youthful bravado, gestured with his hands to say, "C'mon out and fight like a man." The benches cleared again.

A rivalry had been born.

Two fights, four ejections, big fun.

Dodgers manager Tommy Lasorda was not amused. "Did you see the exhibition that guy [Hayes] put on out there?" he asked. Baylor responded with his quote of the year: "If I'm a hitter and somebody nailed me, I'm going to get me a second baseman or a shortstop. If guys don't like that, get a skirt on." Baylor spoke from experience. As a player he had been hit by pitched balls 267 times, far and away the major-league record.

By the way, the Dodgers won, 12–4.

The owners went back the next day and agreed unanimously: Fighting was bad. Very bad. What they might do about it, well, they had no earthly idea.

JUNE 16—Somebody forgot to issue a verbal ceasefire.

Before the game, Lasorda launched into one of his patented obscenity-filled tirades. For all the talk of Lasorda as a salesman and sweetheart and first-rate schmoozer, he is also one of the few men on earth who can use *fuck* as a verb, adverb, noun and preposition.

"My guy [Reed] can't fucking play tonight," he said. "What did he do to deserve that? That was a dirty fucking shot by Galarraga. He started it by what he did to our second baseman. That's bullshit, and you can tell him I said that. That guy and that team don't give a shit about anybody but themselves."

Lasorda's mood couldn't have been improved by the machinations of his moody superstar, Darryl Strawberry. A few nights earlier, Strawberry had been yanked from the lineup by Lasorda and general manager Fred Claire for failing to show up on time for his pregame workouts to rehabilitate his aching back. Now Strawberry was whining about the unfairness of it all and insisting that he should be restored to his right-field position, with Snyder, the right fielder in his absence, moving back to left.

He wasn't feeling all that hot after the game, either. The Rockies won, 7–6.

JUNE 18—A homecoming and a farewell for Randy Smith. Just days earlier, the Rockies' assistant general manager had achieved a lifelong dream when he was named the second youngest general manager in baseball history, taking over the San Diego Padres after the firing of Joe McIlvaine, who had been openly critical of the ownership's penurious ways. Smith had grown up around baseball, in the Padres' farm system. He had high hopes, but he knew the purse strings were not about to loosen. Even so, Smith's return to Denver was triumphant: The Padres won, 11–1.

JUNE 19—The game was over after three innings. Even Blair, who could have sued for nonsupport in previous starts, joined the hit parade. Rockies, 17–3. John Elway did not play.

JUNE 20—Two million fans. *Two million.* In just 37 home dates. And a 3–1 victory over the punchless Pads. It was the calm before the storm.

JUNE 21—The matchup wasn't Rockies versus Reds. It was Baylor versus Davey Johnson, the newly installed Reds manager who had replaced favorite son Tony Perez. Baylor had been one of many baseball people who were angry about Perez's untimely demise, but he was especially upset at comments attributed to Johnson in the wake of the controversy.

Johnson, it seems, had told ESPN he was puzzled that he had been overlooked for jobs—he had been, after all, a successful manager with the New York Mets—while Perez, Dusty Baker and Baylor all had gotten jobs without any previous managerial experience. Baylor and Baker were not angry that Johnson questioned the wisdom of hiring inexperienced managers; that was his opinion and he was entitled to it. What angered them was that Johnson had singled out three minority hires, all of whom had no managerial experience. Why didn't he mention Phil Garner, the Milwaukee manager who got his job with no experience?

The Reds manager tried to backpedal, saying that he was misquoted, that it was taken out of context, but he repeated the comment three weeks later during a CNN interview.

Baylor told *Rocky Mountain News* reporter Tracy Ringolsby that racial implications were "the only thing I can read into what he said. He can't tell me anything different. He said it more than

once, 'Why not me? Why do these guys have jobs and I don't?'
It was a delicate situation he [Johnson] was in, taking over for a
popular guy and a minority. He takes the guy's job and slams the
other two first-year minority managers, also."

Baker, who is quite close to Baylor, told Cincinnati writers he
had a meeting with Johnson, but it failed to clear the air. "He
failed to mention the names of Phil Garner and the job he did
and he didn't mention Lou Piniella," Baker said, noting that
Piniella had had no managerial experience when he was hired by
the Yankees in 1986. "I wonder why Davey only mentioned
black inexperienced guys."

Baylor had no intention of speaking with Johnson before the
game except for the meeting at home plate and a perfunctory
"Here's the lineup card," but the pair did meet and the conversation was spirited. Baylor did not appear to be appeased. But
the smile could not be erased from his face after a come-from-
behind, extra-inning 5–4 victory. Bichette was the hero, driving
in the game winner with a single in the 10th. The Rockies were
now 7-3 on this home stand, equaling their home-victory total
for the entire year.

JUNE 22—One story was the Reds' 16–13 victory over the
Rockies, a typically wild Mile High game and the sixth in which
the teams combined for 20 runs or more. But the bigger story
really was McMorris's decision to extend Gebhard's contract
from three to five years. Gebhard, that wild man, wore a white
shirt and a blue coat to celebrate the occasion.

"I wore a shirt with some color yesterday," he groused.

It was an important move for the franchise because it not
only signaled the team's long-term commitment to Gebhard but
solidified the relationship between McMorris and Geb. The contract extension closed the book on Gebhard's differences with
McMorris and Baylor over Gebhard's acquisitions of grizzled veterans like Dale Murphy. Also, the move demonstrated the owner's resolve not to make a clean sweep of the people like Gebhard
who had been brought in by John Antonucci, the leader of the
previous ownership group. Anyway, he liked and respected Gebhard. Three years, McMorris decided, placed too much pressure

on the general manager to produce immediately. "I don't know what's right for an expansion team," he said. "Five years? Seven years? It just seemed like Geb needed to get the kind of security where he could make long-term decisions instead of short-term, and feel comfortable about them."

Geb celebrated by smoking a cigarette. Big party guy.

JUNE 23—Print the playoff tickets.

"Give me five, Nate," McMorris said.

Rockies 15, Reds 5. The Rockies had finished this raucous, sun-splashed home stand with a host of new attendance records and an 8-4 mark. They were no longer the worst team in baseball —Let's go, Mets!—and were slowly creeping out of the National League West cellar and gaining on the Padres. They had won more games on this home stand than they did in all of May, and tied April's victory total. The pitching was still shaky, except for Reynoso and some moments of competence from Blair, but the team hit a robust .355 at Mile High.

"This is beautiful," McMorris said as he scanned the cheering multitudes, "isn't it?"

If only it could have lasted forever. Or at least another week.

THEY SIT THERE at every home game, in section 112, rows 32 and 33, right behind home plate. To outsiders, they have no identity beyond "Rockies wives" or "Rockies significant others." They are seen as so many vacuous Barbie dolls, all dressed up in nice, new clothes; nothing more, really, than extensions of their husbands, appendages with bright, toothy smiles. Along for the ride, folks figure. Reveling in the attention and the perks and the big bucks, smiling sweetly, finding an identity in a ballplayer.

Yeah, right.

The women sit in their seats, trying to catch glimpses of the game, trying to keep an eye on hyperkinetic kids, trying to keep order in a business that thrives on ambiguity. What will tomorrow bring? LaDonna Sheaffer doesn't know. Debbie Parrett doesn't know. None of them know—Trinelle Cole, Crystal Jones,

Trina Blair. Security is something enjoyed by other ballplayers, other families. Where are all these riches the people talk about? Where is the glamorous lifestyle they're supposed to be leading? Perks? What perks?

Maybe for Mrs. Ripken. Or Mrs. Puckett. That's somebody else's life. Our life, this life, is far more mundane. Here, fame is ephemeral, success a fleeting temptress.

"These guys, they all make millions and they sit and complain," a leather-lunged fan said during a spring-training game in Tucson.

Trina Blair heard the man, turned to a friend and frowned. "Oh, yes, millions of dollars; very glamorous life," she said cynically. "Let's see, in the past five years we've lived in Knoxville, Toronto, Cleveland, Colorado Springs, Tucson, Houston . . ."

Sure, some of them lead the good life, the ones who got lucky and just happened to fall in love with the players making the serious dough. No question, the money is marvelous, even for those making the $109,000 minimum. Only in baseball can you hear the phrase "Andres Galarraga is grossly underpaid at $400,000 per year." But all conventional measures must be discarded. This is an entertainment business. The numbers are not supposed to make sense.

Still, expansion baseball is different, not only for the players but for their wives and significant others. These are, for the most part, athletes on the fringe of a major-league existence. Their fortunes shift with the wind. One day, you're making a nice buck, at least $109,000, plus that $62.50 per day meal money. Tomorrow, you're back in the minors, making a small percentage of that total. It isn't bad money either way, but how long does it last? How do you commit to a place to raise your kids? Do you base your lifestyle on today's paycheck or tomorrow's?

And then there is the moving. Always, the moving . . .

"Fifteen times," said LaDonna Sheaffer. "Fifteen."

The conversation makes its way down the row.

"Eight," says Debbie Parrett, counting the towns out loud, ultimately laughing at the absurdity of their existence. Trinelle Cole says, "Just six times in the last three years." *Just.* Crystal

Jones checks in with 13 moves. Trina Blair is the leader with 20. Willie has been with four organizations in four years, and has shuffled between the majors and minors while toiling for each team.

"It's a big deal, especially because I have to take care of most of the moving myself," Trina said. "On the spot, he gets called up to the big leagues or he's sent down and has to be on a plane tomorrow morning at 5 A.M., and I'm left with an apartment full of stuff." She packs, returns the rented furniture—Rule One: Always rent furniture—and moves on. "It never gets any easier," she said with a sigh.

Most of them meet when the players are young and still scuffling around in the minor leagues. That means hanging on through more lean years, of living in cities like Peoria and Bakersfield, of making lousy money, of having their husbands on the road for extended periods of time. *Be supportive.* It is like a mantra for so many of them. But how do you make it right for your husband when he knows he's good enough to play in The Show, and the goddamn numbers keep conspiring against him, and the whole world is sticking it to him because that's the way the world is, and there's not a thing you can do about it except to say the things he wants, needs, to hear?

"Look at Danny," said LaDonna Sheaffer. "I mean, when he was in the minors, if he wasn't playing, he'd be in the worst mood. But up here, in the majors, it doesn't matter whether he's playing or not. He's just so happy to even be here and getting this opportunity. It makes life a lot easier for everybody."

The Sheaffers spent their first season together in 1987, the first year Sheaffer made a major-league team out of spring training. "We had just gotten married and went to spring training, and then we went to Boston," she said. "The first road trip, when he left, I thought, 'What have I done? What have I gotten myself into?' I was devastated. Just devastated."

This was her glamorous new life?

Thing is, the wives are the ones who do the grunge work. They're the ones who have to pack and unpack and pack again. They're the ones who have to run around with the real estate people to find yet another new apartment in which to live. They're the ones who have to tell the kids, "Okay, your daddy has a new job now, so we're going to have to move—again—so let's all be good soldiers about it." They're the ones who have to tell the kids not to cry, that it's not the end of the world, that they'll make new friends in Waukesha or Midland. They're the ones who have to convince the kids that their new school will be just as good, if not better, than their old school.

And what do you do when the kids are old enough to attend school? Trina Blair, for one, has a teaching degree and is considering teaching her child. Galarraga's wife remained behind in Caracas so that their child could finish school. Everybody makes arrangements, works around the hellish baseball schedule. Nothing about it is convenient.

That's the thing about baseball: If you're lucky, the payoff can be huge. But it's a lottery. There are so many other people determining how you're going to live and where you're going to live. There are scouts and general managers and managers. Maybe it's based on performance. Maybe it's based on personalities. Sometimes it comes down to something like procedural considerations; for example, a player has an option left, meaning he can still be moved to the minors one more time without being lost on waivers, and so the decision is made on that basis. Another decision, another move, another upheaval. Go tell the kids we're moving back to the Springs.

But their eyes are open. Maybe they didn't know, way back when they met. Maybe they didn't know much about baseball or the life that comes with it. Blair, for one, said she didn't know a thing about the game when she met her husband. "I was so pitiful," she said. But their eyes are open now. There is an air of resignation about them. This is the life they chose when they said, "I do." Nobody is complaining.

"That's the biggest thing about establishing yourself," Willie Blair was saying one day after a third consecutive strong start. "It's great for me, but it's more important for my wife and daughter because they're the ones who've had to put up with all the moves. For me, it's not that much of a hardship. But if I could get established somewhere, make Colorado our home, that would be a way of paying back Trina for all the years when she was moving around with me. She deserves that."

For now, the expansion wives and significant others can only stand together and find refuge in one another, lean on one another to help make sense of a nonsensical existence. The players were strangers when spring training began, but the daily contact bred an easy strain of familiarity. It took just a few weeks before the normal clubhouse give-and-take commenced. The wives, though, stayed behind, complete strangers, wholly unfamiliar with the members of their newly adopted extended family.

"It took a while for everybody to get together," said Terry Reed, wife of relief pitcher Steve Reed. "It was like everybody was afraid to make the first move. Plus, we were all so busy trying to figure out where we were, where the department stores were, where the grocery store was, the basic things you need to live. This is a new city for all of us. It was like, 'Okay, the season's here, you ladies are on your own.' It took some time before we all got to know one another and have each other over when the games were on TV."

It's different with an established team. There is an established group of women, a support group. There is an established pecking order; in some cases, the wives of superstars exist in a different sphere from the wives of average players. Not so in Colorado, where there was only one player, Charlie Hayes, making more than a million dollars.

"We're all part of a new adventure," said Terry Reed. "It's something that brings us all closer together. It's different than what we had back in San Francisco with an established team. This is more of a family atmosphere."

LaDonna Sheaffer eyed her three-year-old, a dynamo in perpetual motion, and smiled. She was asked about Danny's home run, a rare and wondrous occurrence. She smiled. "I missed it," she said with a sigh. "I was still trying to get everything together, we left late and I heard it on the radio."

Very glamorous.

12

The Submerged Whale

THE OWNER STOOD amid a sea of klieg lights, running his hand through his salt-and-pepper hair and smiling for the cameras. The owners' June meetings had just broken up, right down the street from the Rockies' corporate headquarters, at the downtown Hyatt in Denver.

Reporters peppered Jerry McMorris with questions:

What about revenue sharing? How do you feel about the new expanded playoff format? How is the search for a new commissioner coming along?

McMorris stood in the vortex and answered questions with 30-second sound-bite efficiency. He seemed natural, like a man who had done all this before, a man in the limelight, acting as gracious host to a group of baseball owners. This was his party— a coming-out party—for a newly crowned owner, for a fellow who came into baseball as nothing more than a limited and generally silent partner, only to emerge as the Rockies' primary money man and most vocal representative.

It wasn't supposed to happen this way. McMorris was supposed to remain part of a group of low-key Colorado investors who had put up 75 percent of the money for the Rockies. He was supposed to remain firmly entrenched as the CEO of Northwest Transport, the largest private trucking company in the West, a company McMorris grew to epic proportions over the course of three decades.

His philosophy on public life was simple: Keep out of the limelight. "You can't harpoon a submerged whale," he would tell friends.

And he seemed perfectly suited for the role. McMorris is an unassuming presence, a man with an even disposition and a middle-aged paunch. He is the epitome of the stolid midwesterner, given to listening before speaking, his eyes darting about the room, looking for an angle, making a calculation. He speaks with the hard, nasal patois of central Illinois, where he was born.

Not that McMorris was not interested in sports. He had been a pretty good ice-hockey player during his youth, and once had a tryout with the powerhouse University of Denver hockey team before settling north at the University of Colorado in Boulder. But McMorris was more comfortable maintaining a low profile as a trucking magnate and gentleman rancher, retiring to his home in Timnath Falls, near Fort Collins, or his ranch in Red Feather Lakes, an out-of-the-way utopia with horses and nature and everything he loved.

There was another reason, too, for his reluctance to step directly into the fray as a managing partner. McMorris and his partners—especially Oren Benton, chairman of the Denver-based mineral-trading company Nuexco and owner of a Coldwell Banker real estate franchise; Charles Monfort, president of Greeley-based Monfort International Sales Corp., a meat-packing company; and Coors, the Golden-based brewery—had grown to trust the group that had emerged as the managing general partners. They were willing to sit back and watch as Steve Ehrhart, a Boulder attorney; John Antonucci, the CEO of Superior Beverage, based in Youngstown, Ohio; and Mickey Monus, kingpin of the wildly successful Phar-Mor drugstore chain, ran the operation.

"None of us [in Denver] felt we had the expertise or the time to be managing general partners," McMorris recalled. "At that time, they [Antonucci, Monus and Ehrhart] looked awfully good to us."

But trouble was afoot, which was generally the state of affairs for the Rockies' ownership. When Denver was first attempting to lure an expansion franchise, the community's standard-bearer was John Dikeou, a painfully private fellow who did not fit the mold of the Major League Baseball country-clubber. "Dikeou is a good guy to go out and have a beer with after his softball game," said one member of the old Denver Baseball Commission, a grassroots group that helped push the baseball effort. "But can you imagine him at a meeting with these guys, trying to sell the region? He'd been looking down at the floor and shuffling his feet. What we need is someone dynamic."

The Dikeou problem then took care of itself. Just weeks before the August 1990 referendum in which the region would vote to tax themselves for a new baseball-only stadium, Dikeou was felled by an avalanche of stories about loan defaults and other fiscal difficulties. He then dropped out of the ownership picture, citing excessive public scrutiny of his private affairs.

But with Dikeou out of the picture, the Colorado investors were back to square one in the expansion derby. Denver had the go-ahead to fund a stadium, a city filled with fans who had committed to season tickets—and no owner. Yet there were deadlines looming, papers to be filed, checks to be written. Denver had once been considered a front-runner to get an expansion team, but now Denver's bid was seriously flagging. There were no saviors out there, no Marvin Davises to bail them out.

"You know, as I look back and think about that—here's John just two weeks before the stadium vote saying he can't go ahead —but maybe that's what made this franchise what it is," Mc-Morris said. "The public said, 'Okay, we want major-league baseball. We'll help build you a stadium. Now we want the private sector to put the money together to own the team. Will someone from the private sector please stand up?' That was literally the cry."

So, with two weeks left before the expansion application and the $100,000 fee were due, some of the region's best and richest gathered around a long rectangular table in Governor Roy Romer's office in downtown Denver. McMorris sat directly next to Romer. As usual, he kicked back and scanned the room, looked for hints, tried to separate the players from the pretenders.

"It was clear to me there wasn't enough money in the room to get over the hump," McMorris recalled. "But at the time, I was only looking at it for civic reasons. I can remember telling the senior executives at Northwest, my board and my family, 'This is money we're investing in an area that has been awfully good for us.' We looked at it like building a wing on a library or a hospital. And I told my kids"—he has three grown children—" 'Have fun with it. Someday, you might get your money back, but don't count on it. Just enjoy it.' And that was the basis on which I made the initial commitment."

The managing general partnership was put together rather hastily, and the sloppiness showed. The primary managing general partner was a fellow named Mike Nicklous, a man who had initially made his money with a company that builds elevators, later moving on to other successful enterprises, including ownership of the minor-league Memphis Chicks. No sooner had Nicklous been introduced as the Man Who Would Run the Rockies than he disappeared off the face of the baseball earth amid questions about his fiscal health and concerns unearthed by baseball's preliminary background checks.

McMorris had been among those eyeing Nicklous suspiciously from the beginning. "That second meeting we had, when he started backtracking and saying, 'The money is coming, don't worry about it,' that's when I leaned over to Monte [Hutchinson, Northwest's senior vice-president of operations] and said, 'Jeez, if we want to take control of this deal, we ought to just take control of it.' He just found himself in a position and he realized he couldn't handle it, financially anyway."

From the smoldering pile of Nicklous's ashes arose yet another group of ownership wanna-bes, the Ehrhart-Antonucci-Monus group. (In 1992, Nicklous would tell Norm Clarke of the

Rocky Mountain News that allegations about his purported gambling activities had been concocted by Antonucci and Monus to kick him out of the general partnership.) Other Rockies executives insisted, though, that the concerns had been voiced by Major League Baseball. Ehrhart didn't have much of a financial stake, but he was a local tie, an organizer who knew people— people of wealth. Ehrhart and Antonucci knew each other from Ehrhart's days as commissioner of the World Basketball League, a circuit for players six feet five and under, when Antonucci was the owner of the Youngstown Pride. And Antonucci had known Monus and his family for years. At one time, they had been like brothers, running in the same rarefied social circles, enjoying the good life together. Their relationship, however, had changed in the previous five years—Antonucci was married and had two daughters; Monus was leading the swinging single life after a divorce—but they remained partners in a number of business ventures. And there was Paul Jacobs, the razor-sharp Denver lawyer who would become the team's legal counsel, quietly shepherding the monied interests through the murky waters of the expansion process.

It seemed like a strong group at the time. Ehrhart was the local guy who knew the Denver market, a former athlete who had a seemingly endless supply of manic energy. Antonucci was a driven businessman, a competitor in the game of life who would blow his top over a missed putt. Monus was the silent partner, a quiet man who wore loud ties, his long gray mane framing hangdog eyes. He was a counterpoint to Ehrhart and Antonucci, willing to stand quietly in the background. And Jacobs was the brains behind the fiscal brawn, inconspicuously pulling all the strings.

And for a while, it worked. The Youngstown group entertained the National League Expansion Committee when they looked over the city's bid in March 1991. They filed all the proper correspondence with the league. They shook the right hands. And when it came time to announce Denver's admission to the National League, there was Antonucci, standing with his family, a broad smile creasing his face; there was Monus with his father,

Nathan, who was patting his son on the back; and there was Ehrhart, talking a mile a minute, a stream-of-semiconsciousness staccato, going on about the limitless possibilities of this concept they called the Colorado Rockies.

"We did it," Antonucci said, arms raised above his head.

And they had. There was criticism, to be sure, complaints about the Rockies being run by what was perceived as a bunch of eastern carpetbaggers. But baseball was convinced that this group had the right stuff. And so were McMorris and his Colorado investors.

Until early August 1992.

That's when McMorris was sitting in his office, reading a story in *The Wall Street Journal* that mentioned that Monus would be moving to a new position within Phar-Mor. "Something isn't right about this," he thought. "This is one of those kicked-upstairs moves."

He called the Rockies' offices and reached Antonucci.

"What's this about?" he asked.

"Mickey's got problems, big problems," Antonucci said. "I need to talk to you."

McMorris didn't hear from Antonucci for two days, so he called the team's legal counsel, Paul Jacobs.

"Jerry," Jacobs said glumly. "Mickey's not gonna be acceptable to Major League Baseball."

Monus, it turned out, was in deep, being investigated for allegedly defrauding Phar-Mor of more than $400 million. Monus denied the accusations, but questions were being raised —yet again—about the composition of Colorado's ownership group. The franchise already had been awarded, team names and colors and uniforms selected—but could baseball change its mind and take the team away? Would this be yet another near miss in the region's maddeningly frustrating baseball history? Another week, another owner, another fine mess. Jacobs called McMorris a day later from New York, where he was meeting with Major League Baseball to ensure them that everything was still solid with Colorado's ownership. He had called to say, "Jerry, we're going to need some help."

"I can clearly remember sitting there, very quietly, shortly after talking to Paul Jacobs," McMorris said. "And I was thinking, 'Do we start this process all over again, find new investors and new partners?' And then I thought, 'Wait a minute. I know I have the ability to fix this thing. It's obviously going to work. Why not go in and take care of the problem, just me and the other primary Colorado investors?' I could have taken care of the whole thing myself, but I didn't want to make an end run on Benton, Monfort and Coors."

The first thing McMorris did was to put out the fires, telling the media—and, by extension, Major League Baseball—that the limited partners were prepared to take care of the problem, to pick up what would become a $20-million shortfall and take the reins of the managing general partnership. He figured this: If Benton, Coors and Monfort didn't want to increase their stake, he would pick up the tab on his own. He had the resources. He would go it alone, if necessary, and pay an additional $20 to $25 million on top of the $7 million he already had invested.

But Monfort, Coors and Benton wanted in. There was little hesitation. They trusted McMorris, had known him for years to be a good corporate neighbor. Better yet, he was a Coloradan who ran in the same business and social circles as they did. With McMorris, they knew they were going in with one of their own.

And, being good businesspeople, they knew this, too: The Rockies had been given a license to print money. In the beginning, the conventional wisdom was that the Rockies would be swimming in red ink, shackled by the $95-million expansion fee, the $20 to $30 million in start-up costs and an inability to collect on the $14 million every team received from the national TV contract. (The existing twenty-six teams had made it a condition of admission that the Marlins and Rockies not share in the 1993 revenues from CBS and ESPN.) But as time went on, the season-ticket commitments continued to roll in. The local television and radio contracts, which had already been negotiated, were better than anybody could have imagined. The merchandise, which Antonucci helped to design and market, was selling all over the

THE SUBMERGED WHALE 153

country. For all their shortcomings, the Youngstown group had set the table for a successful business venture.

This was not speculative money, and the Coloradans couldn't invest fast enough.

"It was clear this thing was going to work," said McMorris. "I can still remember when Jacobs called me from New York and my wife, Mary, and I got to thinking about how we were going to take care of the problem. And so we drove to Greeley to talk to Charley [Monfort], and there he was, him and Victoria water-skiing on the lake in their backyard, just like any good, all-American family. I told Charley what was going on, and it took him all of probably three minutes to say, 'I'm in.' "

Coors quickly followed suit.

As it turned out, Monus's problem was not his alone. It also affected his longtime friend. "I've been hurt badly," Antonucci said shortly after the announcement of Monus's difficulties. "I had a lot of money tied up in Phar-Mor stock. Now, this happens, people start calling on loans. I had no choice. I had to give up a huge chunk of my Rockies investment. The thing that hurts is I uprooted my family to move here, we've spent all this time, energy and money to get this thing off the ground, and now this happens."

Ultimately, the Monus affair left a $20-million hole for the Rockies' investors, half of which was covered by McMorris, the other half picked up by Monfort and Benton. Coors, which had added its $15-million bid for stadium-naming rights to the $15 million it had already invested in the ownership consortium, held steady.

You can't harpoon a submerged whale.

McMorris was coming to the surface.

Now he had to figure out some way to keep the peace. Monus was gone, left to worry about his own emerging scandal. But there was still Antonucci, whose financial stake had been reduced to next to nothing. He had been the front man, the team spokesman in league meetings and the like. And there was Ehrhart, who had almost nothing invested. He had been there from the very beginning, putting together an ownership group when it appeared the Denver bid was heading for the toilet. But he had involved himself in a dirty little in-house war with Antonucci, privately calling a handful of local Denver reporters and promising to dish off-the-record dirt on Antonucci in exchange for support in his quest to become team CEO. McMorris could have bought the pair out and started anew at that moment, but he reiterated his desire to stay in the background and attend to the business of trucking, not baseball.

In a carefully staged press conference on August 6, McMorris announced that Antonucci would be retained as the CEO of the club, running the daily operations and representing the club in league affairs. Ehrhart would be shoved, quite literally, out the door, moved to another office to help in the construction of Coors Field. Everybody put on a happy face and said it was a workable relationship.

"The recent disruptions," McMorris said at that press conference, "are a thing of the past."

It didn't take long to unravel.

THE TRUCKER DID NOT want to be identified.

"When we were reading in the papers that he [McMorris] wasn't sure how much of a role he'd want in running the Rockies, we were all laughing," he told the *Rocky Mountain News*. "He wants to be recognized. He likes power. He likes to have control. Jerry's never going to be part of something that he isn't going to control."

McMorris scoffed at the suggestion. "I'm involved in a lot of business ventures where I'm not hands-on," he said.

It was clear, though, that the business relationship at the top of the Rockies' corporate pyramid was not going to work. The monied interests were left in the background; the guy running the show, Antonucci, had just a fraction of his original financial stake still invested. Meanwhile, McMorris and the other Colorado investors were beginning to get calls from other members of the local business community. Antonucci, they said, was strong-arming them, telling them that if they didn't advertise, Phar-Mor or Superior might quit stocking their products. Antonucci, for his part, denied the accusations.

"The negotiating style that was employed was, well, many people said to me it was extremely heavy-handed," said Mc-Morris. "I had a lot of phone calls and letters from people. And I thought, 'I had no idea how tough they had been in their dealings with people in this community.' I mean, these were business-people I had known over the years."

McMorris was becoming increasingly uncomfortable with the management arrangement. Privately, representatives from Major League Baseball were telling McMorris that as the largest inves-tor, it was important for him, not Antonucci, to be the team spokesman in league matters. Local businesspeople were calling McMorris and the other Colorado partners, complaining about Antonucci. He felt like he was putting out small brushfires in every corner of the club's offices. Gradually he began to realize that he would have to delegate more responsibilities at the truck-ing company and give more time to baseball.

It had to be done.

"Streamlining," McMorris called it at a hastily arranged press conference on January 26, 1993.

Antonucci was fired. Ehrhart was fired. McMorris ascended to the top of the corporate pyramid as chairman, president and CEO of the Colorado Rockies. This was the ownership group Governor Romer and Major League Baseball had wanted from the very beginning—locally based, financially stable and well respected within the community.

It just took a while to get there.

The submerged whale had come to the surface.

"ONE OF THE GIRLS in the office said this to me the other day," McMorris was saying. "She said, 'When you were a kid, what did you do? You played with those toy trucks and you played baseball. Well, that's what you're doing as an adult. Trucks and baseball. I guess you're a lucky man.' And she was right."

McMorris learned a lot about trucks as a youth—moving vans, specifically. His father was also a trucking-company executive, and he moved the family around. "Let's see," McMorris said, gazing into thin air. "Born in Rock Island, Illinois. Moved to Waterloo, Iowa, to Denver, to Omaha, to St. Paul, to Cleveland and back to Denver." McMorris eventually finished high school in Denver and, at the age of 19, borrowed $7,500 from his father and bought Westway Motor Freight, a business that consisted of three trucks that ran between Denver and Golden. Three decades later, he had built and nurtured that investment into Northwest Transport Service, Inc.

McMorris soon developed a reputation as a tough but fair businessman. He is, by his own admission, "very calculating," prone to sitting back, letting the other guy speak first and then showing his hand. It is said that he is like his father: a perfectionist, a fellow who keeps his emotions in check, who wants things done just right.

"He is a hell of a businessman, no doubt about it," Rich Rodriguez, terminal manager of RAC Transport, a competitor of Northwest, told the *Rocky Mountain News*. "He is hands-on. He gets in the middle of everything. He follows up. I've seen him in some of the smallest meetings, where he shows up personally. . . . That's probably what makes his company work. The whole thing is, he's very much involved."

McMorris walked the fine line between involvement and meddling when he flew to Los Angeles in the midst of the Roadtrip to Hell. He could sense Baylor's growing frustration with a team that was populated by a bunch of older players who Baylor knew, in his heart, could no longer do the job. McMorris sat in the manager's office and listened as Baylor vented his spleen. Dale Murphy, he said, was finished. Bryn Smith couldn't get anybody out. Couldn't Gebhard do something? Baylor wanted youth, wanted to call up players from the minor leagues. Gebhard was hesitant. McMorris listened, left and promised to step into the fray gently.

It didn't take long before Murphy and Smith were gone, and the kids were brought in from Colorado Springs.

At the same time, a number of the team's less prominent partners were grumbling about McMorris and his treatment of them. "The way he acts toward us, you'd think the whole team was owned by him, Monfort, Benton and Coors," said one partner. "It's like we don't exist. The guy's personality has really changed over the course of a year, year and a half. He's really fallen in love with his role, with talking to the media and being a star. It's really too bad."

For the most part, though, his high profile and accessibility rendered him something of a Teflon owner. The cries of dissent were minimal and muted. He could do little wrong.

"The business of baseball is not dissimilar from the trucking business because they're both people businesses," he said. "You treat your players and employees right. You need to be straight up. My philosophy is simple: 'All we've got to do is what we say we're going to do.' You've got to understand that I've spent countless hours dealing with the Teamsters, so I know what it means to deal with the union and to look a man in the eye and do what you say you're going to do. It's kind of funny, but Richard Ravitch [the head of the Player Relations Committee, the owners' representative in labor negotiations] told me I'm the only owner of the 28 who has ever directly negotiated a contract. Some have done it from a distance, but I'm the only one who's sat across the table with the head of the Teamsters and hammered out an agreement.

"I'll never forget one owner's meeting, someone said, 'Before long, [union chief Donald] Fehr will be calling you at home.' And I said, 'Well, what's wrong with that? That's the kind of relationship I have with the Teamsters.' We're not adversaries. We're either going to get there together or we're going to fail together. That's how the world functions."

It was one reason the submerged whale surfaced as an influential player in ownership circles. It didn't take long before McMorris was named to the prestigious Player Relations Committee, and he was part of a group dedicated to convincing Congress that baseball's antitrust exemption was both necessary and deserved. He was also flexing some muscle by pushing the candidacy of United States Olympic Committee Chairman Bill Hybl for commissioner, and by clamoring for Denver to host the 1996 All-Star Game.

As the summer months grew near, the Rockies had begun to show some progress, in large measure because of the influx of former minor-leaguers. But McMorris believed this, too: The team hadn't spent enough money on scouting and players and everything else necessary for a first-rate organization. Antonucci had established what McMorris termed "a tight budget," and McMorris had operated within those parameters. "I think John would be the first to say that the bulk of his time was spent trying to put money together," said McMorris. "So, you put that together with a lack of focus and the upheaval with the ownership situation, this ownership went through a hell of a lot in the last year or so."

As the season grew longer, he knew the budget would have to be expanded. The team was making more money than anyone ever could have imagined; there was no way he could justify a small-market budget in this atmosphere.

"When John was here, he would tell everybody, 'Look, the Marlins way overdid it with scouts, and we're doing it just right,'" McMorris said. "I just felt I had to give Geb what he thought he needed to succeed."

Three months into the season, the Rockies added a bullpen coach, Bruce Matthews, and approved the additions of full-time major-league scouts, a strength coach and an additional full-season Class A minor-league team. The spending, though, would not end there.

"We're going to spend a lot more money next year," McMorris said, referring to the player payroll. "It could be double to two and a half times—there isn't any magic number. And we're going to be active in the free-agent market. We're not going to throw money into the street. I remember talking to [Angels owner] Gene Autry at one meeting, and he said the worst thing that happened to them is they had all that success the first few years the franchise was operating, and they stopped emphasizing the minor leagues and player development and started thinking about the short term. We can't do that. But we also know these fans deserve a better product.''

McMorris looked out the window, then reached for a baseball bat signed by some local politicians on the day Denver was awarded major-league baseball. "Been a helluva year, hasn't it?" he asked.

In the space of two years, the Rockies' original partners were history. And here was McMorris, reclining comfortably in his plush leather couch, sitting in stocking feet and reveling in his new role. Soon he would be heading to Mile High, to sit right behind his team's dugout, visible as any owner in baseball. The Rockies were heading into the All-Star break on a nice little roll, playing winning baseball, drawing more fans than any team in the long history of baseball, making more money than anyone could have expected.

13

Room-check Numbers and Other Tales

REPORTERS gathered outside the Rockies' clubhouse deep in the bowels of Wrigley Field and waited for the doors to open. Typical day, typical game, another loss, this one to the Cubs in the second game after the All-Star break.

"It's gonna be a while, guys," Mike Swanson said of the delay. "We've got a few things happening."

Moments later, Darren Holmes bolted from the clubhouse with a suitcase in hand. A reporter tapped him on the shoulder. "She died this morning," he said of his grandmother. He was leaving for the funeral and would rejoin the team three days later in Fort Lauderdale.

Less than a minute later, Jerald Clark emerged from the clubhouse carrying a bat. He was looking for a batting tee and a cage where he could take a few swings to work out some frustration. "I do this when I'm pissed off," he said. Clark had not played that day and would not be playing very much thereafter. He had been largely unproductive at the bat during the first half of the season, and now Baylor had decided to call up second-base phenom Roberto Mejia from the minors and try Eric Young, the former second baseman, in Clark's spot in left field.

After 10 minutes, the doors opened again. Keith Shepherd, a long reliever who had pitched well after being called up from the Springs only to falter badly in his last seven appearances, had his bag packed. "Hey, Geb," he said, shaking Gebhard's hand. "Thanks for the opportunity. You guys stayed with me longer than I deserved. I appreciate that." Gebhard smiled. "You'll be back," he said paternally.

In the manager's office, Baylor was laying out the details of the latest maneuver, a trade that sent Butch Henry, whom they had once hoped would help anchor a young staff, to Montreal for Kent Bottenfield, the pitcher who had lost to the Rockies in the home opener in Denver.

Welcome to expansion baseball.

What was it Casey used to say? "I've got one team coming, one team going and one team here."

The only constant with the Rockies was change. The Colorado Springs shuttle seemed to be running every hour on the hour. New faces, new names . . . new team, in a state of perpetual flux.

"Check it out, fellas," Swanson said to the assembled reporters. "This last trade we made makes 56 moves we've made this year. And we made the trade on July 16th, which is 52 years to the day that Joe DiMaggio hit in his 56th consecutive game. Is that weird?"

Better question: Would DiMaggio consider suiting up?

To be fair, though, the Rockies were turning things around. After their horrendous 16-40 start, they had finished the first half of the season with a nice run of 17 wins and 14 losses. No longer were the Marlins the only respectable expansion team. By the All-Star break, the Rockies, who were 33-54, had not only pulled within four games of the Fish but had opened a nice edge on the News York Mets and moved up to sixth place in the National League Western Division, one spot ahead of the downsizing San Diego Padres, who had begun unloading their high-salaried players.

The pitching was improving, the ERA—"Don't use that acronym around me," Bear said—finally dipped below 6.00. Galarraga was getting offensive support from Hayes and Bichette, both of whom were having career years, and the Mile High phobia had been diminished, the Rockies having finally learned how to win on their home turf.

On the flip side, though, the Rockies had come to rely too much on user-friendly Mile High to pad their offensive stats. Like the Broncos and the Nuggets, the Rockies were one team at home and another on the road. More, the second half began ominously, with the Cubs sweeping four straight from the punchless Rockies.

"Look at these numbers," Baylor said as the team left Chicago and arrived in Fort Lauderdale for a three-game set with the Marlins. ".220. .180. Guys hitting .320 at home and shit on the road."

By July 17, Baylor had all the statistical evidence he needed. The Rockies were hitting .307 and scoring 5.8 runs in 46 games at home and just .231 and 3.1 runs in 43 road games. He needed to look no further than Dante Bichette (.390 at home versus .213 on the road) or Vinny Castilla (.333 versus .189) or Jayhawk Owens (.375 versus .130).

"I'll tell you what these numbers are: room-check numbers." Baylor flashed a mischievous grin; the numbers suggested that some of the fellows were not getting their proper rest on the road —hence, room checks. "Don't think I won't do it. Or haven't done it. [Earl] Weaver used to do it. Damned right, he did."

He shook his head and peered at the home-and-away disparities. "If I'm a player, these numbers are alarming," he said. "I don't want to turn this into a joke, but I can remember Earl once, he went to the nine guys who were playing, put numbers in a hat and had them pull numbers. Boog Powell batted leadoff. I don't want to do that, but I might."

The important thing, though, was that the Rockies were no longer a laughingstock. They had become competitive, the primary reason being the influx of hungry, young players from the minor leagues—the move Baylor had wanted to make weeks earlier.

Chris Jones, a journeyman who signed with the team as a free agent, came on and made an immediate mark in the outfield, wearing his trademark scowl and banging out several key hits, particularly in the late innings. Jones became an immediate Colorado fan favorite on July 11 in St. Louis when he ran balls-out on a routine pop fly that fell between fielders; Jones, incredibly, ended up on third because of his hustle. "The disturbing thing is that guys like that who hustle stand out like sore thumbs," said Baylor. "You just don't see that kind of thing much anymore."

Armando Reynoso saved a failing pitching staff, winning where no other Rockies pitcher dared to tread—Mile High Stadium. By the mid-season break, he was the unquestioned staff ace, its heart and soul, sporting a 7-4 record with a 3.03 ERA.

This was a staff that had been completely overhauled since the first week of the season. Not one of their opening-week starters was still in the rotation. Nied was on the disabled list. Henry had been demoted to Colorado Springs before being traded to the Expos. Smith had been released. Ruffin was laboring in long relief. And Ashby was still waiting for the light to come on down in the Springs, hoping to be resurrected.

Jayhawk Owens, who had come from the Minnesota Twins in the expansion draft, arrived from Triple A and not only changed his name but changed the face of the Rockies' catching situation. When Joe Girardi was injured, moving to the disabled list on June 5 to have the hamate bone removed from his hand, Sheaffer shouldered most of the burden. But by July, Sheaffer was flagging. Owens, who brought a younger man's vitality and a smoldering intensity to the park, looked very much at home.

"Somebody told me you really don't mind if people call you Jayhawk," Swanson, the team publicist, said to him one day.

Owens's real name is Claude Jayhawk Owens. He is half Cherokee Indian. Since grade school, he had been known simply as "J.," not Jay. Just J.—J period. Kids have a strange tendency to seize on names like Claude or Jayhawk.

"Yeah, Jayhawk is fine," Owens said. "Go with Jayhawk. Just don't call me Claude."

One name had stayed with Baylor since the beginning of

spring training: Roberto Mejia. But Gebhard insisted that Mejia, a 20-year-old second baseman and the spring-training wunder-kind, needed more time and at-bats in the minors and prevailed upon Baylor to start him in Colorado Springs. At mid-season, though, Baylor got his wish: Mejia joined the team right after the break, joining the club in Chicago. "It just drips off that kid," Baylor said. "The way he plays, the way he carries himself. You can just see it."

"Welcome aboard, Roberto," Gebhard said when the pair met in the Chicago Westin lobby. Galarraga, standing nearby, did the translating. Mejia looked every bit like a little boy in a big city.

"He was so excited, he was already sweating when he came down from his room," Gebhard said later.

And then there was Curtis Leskanic, a wonderful eccentric who had started the season on loan to the Padres Double A team. (The Rockies did not yet have a Double A team.) Leskanic was everybody's favorite from the day he arrived at training camp, wide-eyed and slightly crazy, reveling in the most mundane drills, even turning the sliding drill into a day at an amusement park.

"I love that kid," Bear said before Leskanic was summoned to the Rockies. "He's a throwback. He just loves the game, loves coming to the ballpark every day and playing baseball. Of all the guys we've got, he's my favorite. And someday, he's gonna be a helluva pitcher."

Curtis Leskanic.

Where do you start?

"He's crazy," Young said. "But good crazy."

"He's from another planet," said Baylor, who regarded him as a mischievous child.

He was Dennis the Menace in pinstripes, forever bounding about the world of major-league baseball on pigeon toes, looking around every corner for a new secret. Baseball doesn't get many like him anymore; too many athletes seem to look at the game as hard labor. The childish joy gives way to sober-minded business realities. Numbers, man, gotta get my numbers, gotta take 'em to arbitration, get the money while I can. Leskanic seemed oblivious to it all. "Damn, man, I was making like a thousand every two weeks in Triple A, now it's five grand," he said. "Only thing is, I'm not sure I like being in this new tax bracket." He was a little boy in his backyard in Homestead, a tough working-class town near Pittsburgh, playing whiffle ball with his buddies. It was a big adventure.

During one freewheeling stream-of-semiconsciousness interview, Leskanic revealed the following:

• He shaves his arms and legs—does them every two to three weeks. He was shaving a long time before Andre Agassi found himself alone with a twin-edge. He does it for comfort, and he does it in the interest of aerodynamics, claiming a shaved right arm adds two to three miles per hour to his already formidable fastball. "When you've just shaved your legs and put on a pair of jeans—ooh!—there's nothing like it. It's so, you know, liberating."

And it's something the whole family can do—together.

"My wife, Susan, and I take baths together and shave each other's legs. A little candlelight. Some champagne. Very romantic. It's really improved my home life."

We're so happy.

Did we mention that while Leskanic toiled at Louisiana State University, his teammates once shaved off half of one eyebrow?

• He once set his 125-pound Rottweiler, Roxy, on fire with a lighter. But just for a second. There was no fillet of Fido.

"Well, one day, I was just goofing around, trying to scare Susan by playing with a Bic lighter near the dog," said Leskanic. "I didn't mean to set him on fire, but I guess I got too close, next thing you know . . ." The dog was fine, if perhaps a little traumatized. "He's forgiven me," said Leskanic. "I can see it in his eyes."

Other stuff a person must know about Leskanic: He is a JFK assassination–theory junkie, though his contention that it was Colonel Mustard with a candlestick in the conservatory is a bit far-fetched. He lives for The Doors, and will break into song, specifically "The End," with absolutely no provocation. "That Jim Morrison is amazing," he said. "He's also very dead."

Leskanic was nicknamed "Psycho" when he arrived in college because his baseball coach thought he was too timid. "Before long, I began dipping, spitting and dribbling juice on my chin," he said. "When I went home at break, my mom looked at me with this goatee and this look in my eye, she thought, 'What's happened to my son?' "

They are still asking that question.

"Kid has more fun than anybody out there," said Bear. "He just kind of draws you to him."

His wife, Susan, is a nursing student who is finishing up her degree at LSU. She is specializing in anesthesia. Curtis might be a good place to start.

After starting the season in Double-A ball, he moved up to Triple-A Colorado Springs on May 21. One month later, he was in the bullpen, warming up for a future start, when he took a closer look at the baseball. It wasn't the usual Pacific Coast League ball; it was a National League ball, with Bill White's signature and everything.

"What's the deal with the ball?" Leskanic asked as he turned to Springs pitching coach Frank Funk.

The coach just smiled.

"No, really, what's this about?" he asked again. Slowly, it began to dawn on Leskanic that he was taking his twin-edged razor and his Doors to The Show. If you thought the man was a bit high-strung as a minor-leaguer . . .

"My feet haven't touched the ground yet," Leskanic told Denver reporters as he arrived in San Francisco to start his first major-league game. First thing, though, he called home to tell his folks the good news.

"Well," his dad said, "now, don't be disappointed if they hit you around a little bit because that's a great hitting team. Who do they have? Will Clark. Barry Bonds. Matt Williams. That's some lineup."

Leskanic shook his head. "That's *not* what I needed to hear," he said later. "I'm nervous enough without calling home and having my folks tell me I'm going to get knocked around the yard. I didn't sleep for two days."

Baylor, whose presence suggests supreme authority and quiet dignity, couldn't help but laugh at Leskanic's skittishness. The kid was a bundle of frayed nerve endings. By game time, Psycho admitted, "I'm so nervous, my balls are shaking." But he was philosophical, too, as he approached his major-league debut. "I know my roots," he told reporters. "Just because I'm in the big leagues, I'm not going to go out and buy a gold-plated razor [to shave the arm]. I'm going to keep my old rusty one. That's what got me here."

So, how did his debut unfold? His first pitch to Giants leadoff hitter Darren Lewis was in the dirt. The second pitch hit Lewis in the ribs.

"I was just trying to throw the ball 115 miles an hour in the first inning," Leskanic admitted. "I honestly couldn't feel the ball in my hand. My first two pitches I thought were going halfway to the plate. I thought they were going 40 feet."

By now his heart was beating out of his chest. "My first pitch missed by four feet," Leskanic said, "and my second pitch missed by three feet." He walked the second batter, Mike Benjamin, on four straight balls. Baylor sprinted from the dugout to have a chat with his hyperactive, hyperventilating pitcher.

"Well, you know you have to make them hit the ball to get outs," Baylor said.

"Yeah," Leskanic answered.

"Well, make them hit the ball," Baylor said.

He promptly went to a 3-0 count on Will Clark—this made nine straight pitches that were strangers to the strike zone—before Clark singled. Leskanic's balls were still shaking. But he escaped the inning by giving up just one run, and settled down nicely therafter. The Rockies lost, 5–0, but Leskanic went seven strong innings. Afterward, he so enthralled reporters with his freshness and honesty, one San Francisco writer took the time to call Leskanic the next day to tell him how delightful it was to interview him.

The first-inning jitters became a trend. If not for those first innings, Leskanic would be a poor-man's Roger Clemens. Well, almost. "Only guy I've ever seen like him was Steve Dalkowski," said Baylor of the former flamethrowing Orioles minor-leaguer. "We'd have to warm him up two times before he pitched. He'd be in the bullpen throwing 109 miles an hour, but he had no idea where the ball was going. By the time the game started, he was down to 102. That's what we're going to do with this guy."

The young players, such as Leskanic, Mejia and Owens, brought to the team a vitality, an energy that was sorely missing. The veterans generally figured, "This is an expansion team, so I should be playing regularly." When they sat, they moped. The kids made the difference.

"Not enough players are totally committed to the game," Baylor said. "The players don't realize it's a privilege to play in the big leagues. It's nobody's given right. I'm always getting complaints from players if they're not playing. Everyone wants to play. And especially because this is an expansion club they feel they should be everyday players. They never stop and think, and realize if they were everyday players, they wouldn't have been in the expansion draft. Players are a poor judge of talent. Even when they're on an expansion team they grade themselves a lot higher than management grades them.

"You go look in that room, there's only one guy [Holmes] who has a contract next year, so the intensity level *should* be there. These aren't guys who have three- or four-year contracts."

This was a familiar lament from Baylor, who, like most former players, viewed the current crop with a somewhat jaundiced eye. Baylor's feeling was this: These were players on the fringe of a major-league experience; these were guys who needed to do the little things, the extra work necessary to make a mark—and yet, here they were, acting as though baseball owed them something. If the players didn't particularly enjoy Baylor's harping, the beat writers appreciated his honesty. His forthrightness was often misjudged as a lack of patience, but how could he sugarcoat the obvious, defend the indefensible?

Baylor did not scream about lack of ability. He screamed

about lack of focus, lack of desire, lack of professionalism. "Every once in a while, I'll put negative articles on the board," he said. "Like the one where the kid in Cincinnati said we were Triple A. The one where John Franco said the Mets could fatten up on us and the Marlins. The one where Joe Torre said to win the division, a team would have to beat up on the expansion teams. I mean, I care. I see that, I get fuckin' angry. Problem is, the manager cares, but they don't care."

Jerald Clark, for one, was an odd man out. The Rockies were trying to deal him, but he wasn't the hottest commodity. Meanwhile, his frustration was building. He didn't want to gripe about his lack of playing time, but he didn't want to be one of those guys who kicks back and meekly accepts his station in life, either. And so he began a routine, at least on nights when he didn't play, leaving the clubhouse spread behind, grabbing a bat and a bag of baseballs and retiring to a batting cage near the clubhouse. Some nights, he would blast balls off a tee. One night in Miami, he asked a Marlins intern, wearing his good shoes and a tie, to toss baseballs softly from the side. There he would stand, beads of perspiration dripping from his face, smacking one ball after another off the tee late into the steamy stillness of the evening.

"Nnnggh!" he grunted. "Nnnggh! Nnnggh!" One swing after another, one ball after another. Fifteen minutes, and then more. Breathing deeply. "Something's gone haywire," he said as he punished baseballs into the net. "Just before I attack the ball, man, something goes haywire." Weak ground ball . . . weak ground ball. "God, I stink!" he screamed. "Just gonna swing till I turn blue in the face. Maybe green."

He stood there, wiping the perspiration away, hacking away like a man with a machete lost in the high weeds. Meanwhile, his teammates sat back in the calm and cool of the clubhouse, picking away at the postgame buffet, enjoying a beer. He was trying. But he was dying, too. He had lost his job in left field. He would win it back through sheer force of will and hard work.

"Nnnggh!" he grunted.

Clark claimed he was working on something, mechanics, coming through the ball, anything. But this was his catharsis, all the frustration at himself and frustration with management vented on that damn little baseball. This had been the story of his entire career: incredibly hot for a stretch, then completely unproductive for another. At the moment, he was in the throes of a 4-for-31 slump, and Baylor was pushing him out in favor of Young.

"That's the thing, man, is I don't know when those streaks will come," he said. "Every time I go out, I say, 'This is the day. This is the one.' " He shook his head. "I just wish it would get here. Thing is, I can't quit. If I don't come out here and hit, try to do something to get myself started, I feel like I'm throwing in the towel."

He paused. "I don't know, maybe it would be better if I gave this a rest, just kicked back and didn't let it get to me. But I'm not an everyday player anymore. So I'm gonna keep swinging. I mean, I understand why I'm not playing every day anymore. I don't like it, don't like it a bit. But it's always been that way with me. Hey, I got some ABs. But I guess compared to Cat, Charlie and Dante and their numbers, mine weren't good enough."

Clark was in a public-relations no-man's land. He didn't want to grouse or openly question Baylor's judgment, activities that had become something of a cottage industry among the unhappy players. They were sick and tired of the constant lineup changes. Signs of Clark's discontent seeped through. "From what I've been told, I had a real chance in the first half of the season," he said. "Look, I don't want to be a bad seed," he said. "I've just got to suck it up. If they trade me, fine. But I've seen guys who ask for a trade, sometimes it works out and sometimes it doesn't. So, who's to say? Right now, though, you get in there one game, get four ABs, you don't produce, boom, you're out of there. And then you really start to press."

He kept blasting away, the anger slowly draining from his body.

"I wish I had the heavy bag," he said. "Maybe I can bring one on the road. Then I'd really be able to unleash on it. This is better than doing it verbally. I get it out of my system, I feel better and I can sleep."

Clark was not alone in his diminished status. Alex Cole, the

Opening Day center fielder, had been reduced to a spot player, making only occasional starts in center field; Baylor was tiring of his curious baserunning skills and his inability to pull the ball with authority. Boston, who was given the chance to play every day for a stretch, lapsed into his usual state of ennui, happy enough to be a fourth or fifth outfielder and collect his sizable paycheck and enjoy the life of a major-leaguer.

Meanwhile, Young was making yet another transition; he had begun in the outfield, but scouts told him the only way he would play would be if he learned second base. So, he became a second baseman, a pedestrian one at that, only to have Baylor tell him his future was in the outfield.

"Look at that," said Young.

What?

"The glove, man," he said. "My new outfielder's glove. Looks kinda big, doesn't it?"

Yeah.

"I'm the new left fielder," he said, shrugging. "Every day it's something new around here."

Young was disappointed by the move, but he put a good face on it—as usual. He was not among the legion of clubhouse grousers, a diligent worker with a ready smile and a personality that inspired one local Denver TV station to begin a feature called "Young Gun," which featured Young's reports. "Just as long as I get to play," he said. "I knew it was just a matter of time before Mejia came in. I could read the writing on the wall when the Rockies took both of us in the expansion draft."

Otis, the team's outfield instructor as well as its batting coach, rolled his eyes as he spoke about Young's return to the outfield.

"They think they can just throw him out there, like playing outfield is easy," he said. "This is going to be a project. I not only have to get him to play the outfield but to think like an outfielder—playing in different stadiums, positioning, dealing with different things. You don't just go out there and catch fly balls. We'll start first thing tomorrow, first the basics, shagging flies, then move him in and let him catch the balls hit over his head."

Even Baylor seemed a bit leery about the mid-season adjustments. But he figured this, too: Clark wasn't the long-term answer out there. They weren't in a pennant race. Why not let Young, a speedster, relearn left field? "I hate to throw him out there for the first time in three years, especially in Wrigley," Baylor said as the Rockies and Cubs did battle in that first series after the All-Star break. "I don't want him to be embarrassed."

Of course, he was on July 18 in only his second start in left field for the Rockies. In the fourth inning of the game against the Cubs, Young broke back on a harmless, wind-blown Ryne Sandberg fly ball, only to realize the error of his ways, come full-throttle back toward the infield, only to see the ball plop helplessly in front of him for a leadoff double.

"Left field is not a good situation right now," Baylor said grimly.

It wasn't going to be easy. But Baylor wasn't going to stick with the status woe.

"Did I hear right? Fifty-six changes?" Owens asked one day. "That's got to be a record, right?"

Changes? Around the horn:

First base: Galarraga was still a staple there after returning from the disabled list in late May. His average, which had hovered near .400 for most of the season, finally fell below that mark just before the All-Star break, but Cat could have cared less. He was too busy reveling in his redemption. He soaked up his three days at the All-Star Game in Baltimore, utterly unconcerned that he had not been voted to start by the fans, unconcerned that he had not been named by manager Bobby Cox to start as the designated hitter. (Mark Grace got the nod.) He was hitting a lusty .391 after a minor slump and still could not have been happier.

Second base: Mejia was not brought up to sit on the bench. He was going to be the second baseman, given a chance to sink or swim.

Shortstop: Castilla, a Braves farmhand chosen in the expansion draft, had pretty much solidified the position with decent glove work and a live bat, at least at home. He also owned one of the all-time great statistical disparities—a terror at home and a cipher on the road. In the meantime, Benavides, who had lost his job earlier in the season, was rediscovering his game and becoming more confident playing on Mile High's slowly improving infield. By mid-season, Baylor was considering an unusual platoon system: Benavides on the road, Castilla at home.

Third base: Charlie Hayes was firmly entrenched at the position. Rockies officials quietly wondered about his level of intensity and his weight, but his numbers continued to speak volumes. He was having a career year, but his exploits were being lost in the shuffle. A guy named Galarraga had just a little bit to do with that.

Catcher: Girardi remained on the shelf after his hand surgery in June and would not return until August 11. In his stead, Sheaffer initially was the man, only to give way to the younger Owens, who was so impressive, he made possible a later trade in which the Rockies dealt minor-league catching prospect Brad Ausmus.

Outfield: In left field, there were two players. Clark was becoming increasingly frustrated by a lack of playing time, but there was only one way Young could learn the position: by playing. Jones continued to impress in center field, thus diminishing Cole's time at the position. And in right field, Bichette was another boom-or-bust player who was great at home and lost on the road. More curious, still, was his sudden difficulty in playing the position; he regularly took the most circuitous route to fly balls, turning routine plays into ESPN highlights.

As for the pitching, the conundrum was best expressed by Bear: "I've got high blood pressure," he said. "If I take my blood-pressure pills, I can't drink. And if I don't drink . . ."

BY THE TIME the Rockies arrived in Florida to play their last three games of the season series with the Marlins on July 19, 20 and 21, the conventional wisdom was that the Marlins were the vastly superior team. Most baseball people left the expansion draft figuring the Rockies would be the superior club in the first year or two, then the Marlins' youth would make them the better team down the road. But the Marlins were surprising everybody, including themselves, breaking out to a 30-31 record. By the time the 33-58 Rockies came to town, the Marlins had swooned to 38-53, mired in a slump but still talking loudly about breaking the expansion wins mark.

The Rockies derived their only satisfaction from this: They led the season series, six games to three, meaning the worst they could do was to walk away with a tie.

What was on the line?

More than pride.

More than bragging rights.

It was the semicoveted "Surf 'n' Turf" Award, a lithograph commissioned by the Marlins' front-office brain trust that featured a cartoon mountain and marlin engaging in mortal battle. "Okay, fine," said Marlins executive Don Smiley. "So it's not Picasso."

As they say, "It's the thought that counts."

The winner of the season series would receive the Surf 'n' Turf, to have and to cherish, for an entire off-season. And, indeed, the Marlins and Rockies embarked on a three-game series that was played with the intensity you might expect from two teams intent on procuring this priceless piece of, um, art.

"There's really no rivalry," said Baylor.

Perhaps not for Baylor, but Galarraga was still carrying a chip on his shoulder. It was one thing for Marlins general manager David Dombrowski to have traded Cat out of Montreal in 1991 when he was the Expos' general manger; but Dombrowski, like so many others in baseball, had become convinced that Galarraga was finished, and opted to bypass him during his time as a free agent. Cat had wanted badly to come to South Florida; he had a home there, in West Palm Beach, and he would have been close to the area's sizable Hispanic population, not to mention his home country of Venezuela. In fact, Galarraga spent the hours before each Marlins game sitting around the pool deck of the Fort Lauderdale Marriott Marina being interviewed by three different Venezuelan TV show reporters.

"Not short interviews," Galarraga said. "One hour, each."

He was still a story in any language. His quest for .400 was falling on hard times, but he arrived in Florida hitting a robust .382. And there was always that burning desire to stick it to Dombrowski for not signing him. Dombrowski had received reports from Bill Scherrer, one of his scouts in Latin America, that Galarraga had not returned to his old form. Instead, the Marlins lavished big dollars on Orestes Destrade, a South Floridian with Cuban roots who had torn up the Japanese League.

The only one who felt lousy after the first game was Baylor, who was still playing musical chairs with a lineup that was punchless on the road. The Rockies lost, 3–1, once again turning the pitcher, in this case Ryan Bowen, into a Cy Young reincarnate, swinging at pitches that were not only out of the strike zone but outside the zip code. Baylor groused, "Our only run batted in comes from our pitcher"—Kent Bottenfield, who was making his first start for Colorado.

Then, outside the manager's office, Baylor could hear the harsh tones of Peter Durso, the Rockies' high-strung traveling secretary. "Gorilla cocksuckers!!" he screamed. "Bunch of fucking gorilla cocksuckers. Security assholes. I can't even get in my own fucking clubhouse. Gorilla cocksuckers!!"

Baylor smiled. "Peter's here," he said, stifling a laugh.

The next night, the folks in the clubhouse were in a somewhat better mood—even Durso, who was more explosive than one of Vince Coleman's firecrackers. The Rockies won, 6–3, thus ensuring themselves the advantage in the season series and the Surf 'n' Turf. Galarraga messed up Dombrowski's day with a two-run homer and a brilliant defensive play while Bichette, another home-grown player, from Palm Beach Gardens, hit a three-run homer. The Rockies also got some fine relief work from Reed and Holmes, who deserved to share in the moment. Both had been wretched early in the season, booed off the mound at Mile High, and both had gone to the minors to get their arms, and heads, back together. Holmes had been demoted on May 5, only to return on May 17. Reed had had a longer stint, departing on May 12 and returning on June 14. Now here they sat, Reed sipping a beer, Holmes an O'Doul's, remembering those strange days, re-alizing they needed to go back and start anew. Funny, but it wasn't really so long ago that Reed and Holmes were making that long hour-and-a-half drive, every day, from their homes in Den-ver to Colorado Springs.

"Getting home at 1 A.M., leaving the next morning at 10 or 11," said Reed. "That's reason enough to want to stay right here."

They needed to work on their mechanics. They needed to work on their confidence. They needed, simply, to get away, find a safe haven and crowds of 10,000 or so where they could work on things, experiment, blow a couple of Triple-A guys away and rebuild their psyches.

Holmes sat in front of his locker immersed in his own thoughts. The time in Triple A crossed his mind, but on this occasion he was thinking of his grandmother, who had passed away just one week earlier.

"She was out there with me today," he said quietly. "It's funny, I'm not sure she ever really saw me pitch. My grandfather told me they would have the game on, I'd come in to pitch and she would go to the bedroom and pray."

From the relative calm of the clubhouse came a high-pitched squeal. "We wooooon! We woooon! Aggggghhhh!!!" cried Bos-ton.

One day later, the Marlins would close the gap in the season series, winning the game, 6–4, but the Surf 'n' Turf belonged to the Rockies. And were they proud. . . .

"Lemme see that thing," Baylor said as Swanson gingerly carried the lithograph and placed it on his desk.

Baylor peeled back the brown wrapper and gazed at the pic-ture. Then he held it up, like an Emmy. "I thank you for this award, and I dedicate it to the $95 million we paid," he said, smiling.

Then he added, "I'll give this to Geb and let him hang it in his office."

"But I thought you and Geb were getting along," a reporter joked.

Someone wondered who might be responsible for transporting the monstrosity. Swanson raised his hand. "The guys will probably be eating pizza off it," he said.

The final tally: The Rockies had beaten the Marlins in season series, team offense, crowds—they beat everybody in crowds—and marketing, where the Rockies had ascended to first place, the Marlins fourth. The Marlins had the edge in overall record, starting pitching, relief pitching, defense and, some would say, overall organization.

But only time would tell.

14

Big Deals

KY SOX STADIUM is a mere sixty miles south of Denver, a wind-blown little park that sits on a grassy knoll outside Colorado Springs. It is your basic Triple-A ballpark, filled with gimmicks, including a hot tub in which four folks can soak and drink champagne while watching the game, and outfield signs with messages like: FREE SPINAL EXAM: HEUSER CHIROPRACTIC. On a strangely chilly evening in early August, the primary draw was supposed to be a promotion for Baby Dolls, a local strip joint that promises "the finest in adult entertainment," and a frigid bikini contest.

"I've been there," one press-box critic admitted. "Yeesh. Nasty."

But reporters did not make the easy trek down I-25 to see scantily clad bimbettes parade on top of a dugout. (Well, they said they didn't . . .) Nor did Paul Egins, the Rockies' assistant director of scouting, who grabbed a seat behind home plate, pulled out his clipboard and plugged in a Juggs Gun.

They were here to see Bruce Hurst, the once-formidable left-handed pitcher, who had been obtained just days earlier in the Rockies' first-ever blockbuster trade. The Rockies traded Brad Ausmus, their top catching prospect, along with pitchers Doug Bochtler and Andy Ashby to the budget-cutting Padres for solid right-handed starting pitcher Greg Harris and Hurst, who was attempting a last-ditch comeback.

The acquisition of Harris made more than enough sense; here was one of the league's most consistent pitchers, a guy who gave you innings and a solid 12 to 14 victories a year. Every pennant contender wanted Harris for their stretch drives, but Gebhard was not swayed. His was a pitching staff that needed stability and innings, and the Rockies, whose coffers were now bulging, were willing to pay that price.

But Hurst?

He was 35. He was coming off major arm surgery. He was poised to make $2.75 million for the 1994 season. He was everything an expansion team didn't need. Or was he? The Rockies figured it this way: Harris was the unquestioned key to the deal. He was 29 years old and wouldn't be a free agent until the close of the 1994 season. But Hurst was a worthwhile gamble. The Padres agreed to pay his fat salary until September 1 or his first Rockies start, whichever came first. And Hurst's contract, which called for $3 million in 1993, had a $400,000 buyout.

"That was a gamble we thought we needed to take and were ready to take," said McMorris, who was front and center at the press conference to announce the deal. "If he can't pitch, we buy him out, and it's over. If we're not willing to take those kind of chances with the support we have, we don't deserve to be in this business."

The trade was a big hit among the Denver fans, who longed for something resembling starting pitching. And the Rockies made sure to tell the fans that they were the ones who had made the deal possible, taking out ads in both Denver dailies to trumpet the deal and the fact that the huge attendance numbers gave the Rockies the financial clout necessary to make the deal.

On the other hand, there were increasing rumblings inside the Rockies' offices that the deal had McMorris's paw prints all over it. The submerged whale had struck. One Rockies executive cynically asked a reporter, "Did you hear about Jerry's deal?" Another Rockies front-office member said, "McMorris put big pressure on Geb to do a deal. The guy's personality has really changed."

A few days after the trade, McMorris—not Gebhard—revealed that the Rockies had hoped to trade Mejia and prospects to San Diego for Fred McGriff, and then make the Harris-Hurst trade. All of this signaled an apparent sea change in team philosophy. What happened to building with youth, with prospects? The Rockies argued that Ausmus, the catcher they dealt, was strong defensively but overmatched with the bat. They argued that Bochtler, one of the pitchers, was nothing terribly special, and that Ashby, while promising, had been a mystery and a disappointment.

Gebhard looked at it this way, too: With shaky pitching at the major-league level, the Rockies had to rush prospects from the minor leagues, kids who weren't necessarily ready but were needed to fill a spot. With Harris and a healthy Hurst, the Rockies could let kids like Leskanic, Painter and others grow up down on the farm.

And then there was this issue: How many free-agent pitchers would want to come to Denver, even after they moved into Coors Field? Their ERAs would likely balloon. Their numbers would suffer. You need numbers at contract time. Gebhard considered that, and considered the lack of available free-agent arms that might be available in the off-season.

"You owe me a kiss," McMorris told public-relations assistant Karin Bearnarth the day of the deal.

She looked at him quizzically.

"I just added 10 years to your father's life," he said, referring to Bearnarth's father, the team's beleaguered pitching coach.

If nothing else, McMorris's heart was in the right place. He might have banked the proceeds from the remarkable first-year attendance and kept the budget lean and mean by saying, "Well, expansion teams don't trade for folks like Harris and Hurst." But in an age of Padres-like cost-cutting, here was an owner who wanted desperately to win and be accountable to the multitudes. Whether or not the moves made any sense, only time would tell.

"We've been looking to improve the team," said McMorris. "The tremendous support of the fans has made it possible to speed the process up of getting competitive. We know we have to get competitive before we can contend. We have to be a contender before we win a pennant. We're not done. For an expansion team in last place to be out acting like a contender, trying to trade for players that only teams trying to win a pennant were going after, is also unprecedented in baseball, to my knowledge."

Meanwhile, Hurst had some more work to do on a wind-blown evening on the high prairie. It was not a perfect night for the rehabilitation of a surgically repaired shoulder; a cold front had come through, dropping rain on the Springs, leaving high, gray clouds and unseasonably cool temperatures. As Hurst warmed up, Egins settled in behind the backstop.

"We just want him to throw 60 pitches, tops," Egins said, buttoning up his coat against the chill. "I'll look for a couple of things. I want to see if his fastball is moving. Velocity doesn't matter, especially for a finesse pitcher like Hurst. I want to see the deception on his change-up. Are guys being fooled by his arm motion? And I'd like to see him break off a few good curveballs. This is the longest he's gone since he began his rehab, so we want to see how he reacts. After this, we'll give him one more rehab game, then we'll think about getting him up to the big club."

Hurst, a left-hander, is one of those guys of whom it is said, "He knows how to pitch." The minor leagues, and even the majors, are littered by legions of strong-armed power pitchers who know how to throw, but haven't the vaguest idea how to pitch. The craft is steeped in the art of deception. Flamethrowers can bring it 95 miles per hour, but the hitters sit and they wait and they tee off. Hurst, conversely, had staked his career on the quiet economy of pitches, moving the ball in and out, up and down, changing speeds, keeping the hitter off balance. Baylor saw it when they were Boston Red Sox teammates; here was a rare bird, a left-hander who not only survived but excelled in Fenway Park, a noted right-handed hitter's ballpark. Hurst had won 10 or more games for 10 consecutive years, the longest streak in the majors, heading into the 1993 season.

The game began. The Juggs Gun read, "81."

Eighty-one miles per hour. High school pitchers can get it up to 81. For Hurst, though, it was all he needed. The second pitch read, "74." The Tucson Toros hitter swung and missed.

Painter, who was in the stands watching Hurst work, shook his head. "Don't have to throw 95 to get people out, do you?" he said. Burke, the hard-throwing Denver-born pitcher, looked up from his pitch chart and nodded in agreement.

Hurst breezed through five innings with a dearth of pitches, just 49, getting ahead in the count, keeping the ball dancing around the strike zone, coaxing double-play balls and weak swings. Pitching is like real estate. Everything is location, location, location. "When I call Geb with this report, velocity won't be something we'll really discuss all that much," said Egins. "Even when he was healthy, he rarely threw more than about 85. If you know how to pitch, and this guy does, speed doesn't matter."

This was another important step in Hurst's comeback. He started twice for the Padres early in the season and struggled badly. Since then, he had pitched simulated games and started in the minor leagues, attempting to rebuild strength in his shoulder. "All our reports we have is we think he is close to coming off the disabled list," Gebhard said at the time of the trade.

Afterward, Hurst stood in front of his locker, zipping up a green Izod jacket, patiently answering questions. How'd he feel? What was he looking for? You couldn't knock the smile off his face. "This is the longest I've gone in a long time," he said. "The question isn't how I feel now, but how I feel five days from now when I throw again."

These were frightening times for Hurst, but his manner never betrayed any fear. He was 35 years old, and he was looking at the possible end of his wildly successful career. Hurst shrugged. "I know what the possibilities are," he said. "I know if this doesn't work out, I'll have to move on. If that's the case, so be it. Honestly, it doesn't frighten me at all. I know how hard I've worked to come back. It hasn't been fun coming in every day, working in the trainer's room and not being able to play. But if this doesn't work out, I'll know I gave myself every chance. Who knows? Maybe I can find work at Hurst's Variety," he said, referring to his family's store back in St. George, Utah.

Hurst's first rehab assignment, at least since he'd come to the Rockies, would prove to be his best. He struggled in subsequent games with the Sky Sox, but Gebhard and his staff saw some encouraging signs. A multimillion-dollar decision would have to be made—whether to keep Hurst or cut him loose for $400,000 —and the Rockies needed to see him pitch in the major leagues, needed to see just how far he had come.

As HURST WAS forging his comeback, Harris and the Rockies were in the throes of their longest and most painful slump. Home cooking? Hell, the boys had ptomaine. They returned to Mile High with a hint of promise, splitting a four-game series with the St. Louis Cardinals, a team that had inexplicable troubles with the Rockies. But the table had been set in the third game of that series on July 25 when Mejia, overzealous in his pursuit of a foul pop fly down the right-field line, ran over Galarraga.

Another injury. Another stint on the disabled list.

Baylor knew he was in deep trouble. The last time Cat was out, the Rockies went an uninspiring 4-13. There was a reasonable sense of foreboding as Baylor contemplated his limited options. He had, indeed, changed his managerial style over time, recognizing he had a team that could sit and wait for the three-run homer—in the style favored by one of Baylor's avatars, Earl Weaver—particularly in home-run-friendly Mile High Stadium. But now, without Galarraga, BaylorBall would have to make a return.

"Yeah, at first we were doing a lot of hitting and running and squeeze plays, things like that," Baylor said. "My feeling now is, we've got to pick our spots. We can't let guys run out of control. At the beginning, we had a lot of bad baserunning and a lot of running into outs. We can't waste a lot of outs, and we came to that realization. I can't sit there and say, 'This is my style, and we're going to run no matter what.' So we've refined what we're trying to do.

"Of course, now with Cat out, it's back to what we were doing, at least to a degree. We've got to find a way to produce runs with Cat out of the lineup. And that's probably going to mean more of an emphasis on the sacrifice bunts and things like that."

The Rockies needed more than BaylorBall, though; they needed a miracle. After the split with St. Louis, the Rockies fell into the deepest abyss of the season, a slump Baylor could sense was going to engulf his team. The Rockies had not only lost Galarraga but also lost any emotional edge they might have held earlier in the season. These were, indeed, the dog days. And the Rockies, bless their expansion souls, played like dogs. It was bad enough that they couldn't pitch or catch the ball, but now Baylor sensed he had players who were mailing it in. Hayes, in particular, drew Baylor's ire. And the manager made good on a threat to bench players who weren't running out ground balls and playing with verve; he even benched Hayes, one of his three best players, for a game. As usual, Hayes did not quite understand: "There are other guys on this team who don't always run out ground balls, but they always point the finger at Charlie," he said. "There are other guys who are overweight, but they always point the finger at Charlie. Maybe they want somebody who's always jumping around and making a big fuss, but that's not the way I play."

Beyond that, Baylor sensed he had guys playing for numbers, for contracts. Winning baseball, which meant hitting to the right side, moving baserunners, doing the little things that don't show up in the box score, the little things you can't take to arbitration, had taken a backseat to selfish baseball.

"I don't know if our guys can't do it or won't do it," said Baylor, "but it just isn't happening."

The losses just kept on coming. The Rockies dropped three straight to the Atlanta Braves, who had now won all 10 of their games against Colorado. They lost three more to the first-place San Francisco Giants, extending the losing streak to seven games. Worse yet, even the umpires seemed to disrespect Baylor and the Rockies. During the final game of the Braves series on July 28, home-plate umpire Charlie Williams blew a call that should have given the Rockies a game-tying run. The next morning, the newspapers were filled with incendiary quotes from Baylor, who ripped Williams for his decision. Ordinarily, the tiff would have ended there; nine times out of 10, an umpiring crew will leave town after a series. But on this occasion, Williams's group remained in Denver for the following Giants series.

The fun began before the July 30 game ever started.

"I went out there like everything was over with," Baylor told reporters about his customary pregame trip to home plate with the lineup card. "If it wasn't, I'd send someone else out there to do my cowardly work. I said hello to the umpires. I exchanged lineup cards with Joe West. I shook hands with Bobby Bonds," he said, referring to the home-plate umpire and the Giants' coach.

Williams called Baylor over and asked to see his lineup card.

"He wads it up and throws it on the ground," Baylor said. "He called me a few names and, new manager or not, I'm not going to be intimidated by an umpire. He baited me."

Williams admitted to taking Baylor to task for trashing him in the newspapers. "He's glad I didn't tear it up and eat it," Williams told Jack Etkin of the *Rocky Mountain News*. "I wadded it up. That's what I felt about him. . . . I'm an umpire. I work out on that field. I make judgment calls. All of us do all night long from start to finish. I didn't go into the newspaper and say anything about anybody on that field."

Baylor and Williams promptly went toe-to-toe before Williams tossed Baylor from the game—before it ever started.

One day later, Gebhard called the two warring factions together and forged a ceasefire. Baylor relented and said he wouldn't report Williams to the league office. Williams relented and said he wouldn't report Baylor to the league office.

The era of good feeling did not, however, produce anything

resembling a victory. The dog days were a flea-bitten mutt. Seven straight losses, and the Cat-less Rockies were preparing for a 14-day, 14-game road swing—the Road Trip to Hell II.

"This is a scary situation now," said Baylor. "Fourteen days on the road? Shit. That's tough."

The Rockies actually looked forward to a return to Cincinnati, especially a date with Roper, the young pitcher who had said earlier in the season that the Rockies were worse than some Triple-A teams he had faced. Roper, naturally, had spent the better part of the past few months claiming that either he was misquoted or his quotes were taken out of context, which was, of course, a sizable crock. And so the Rockies headed to Cincinnati with a stated sense of purpose and fire in their bellies, and were promptly pummeled in four straight games—including a sickly 9–3 loss to Roper in the third game of the series. By this point, Baylor was tiring of the team's listless play. Sheaffer was so angry after the final game of the series, a game that saw Hayes make two errors seemingly borne of disinterest, that he said, "You can tell which guys care and which ones don't."

Baylor himself was still going through the growing pains of a rookie manager. After eight straight losses, the Rockies seemed to have pulled one out against the Reds on August 3 when Bichette hit a two-run ninth-inning home run off Rob Dibble to give the team a 4–3 lead. But in the bottom of the ninth, Baylor opted to pull Holmes with two outs, a man on second and left-handed hitter Hal Morris coming to the plate. Baylor went to Gary Wayne, a lefty pitcher, which would have been the percentage play except that Wayne had been roughed up by lefties all season. Morris singled, the game was tied, and the game was eventually lost in the 10th when Leskanic lost track of the strike zone.

"That's the one I agonized over the most," Baylor said later in the road trip. "That was a game we had."

It was getting brutal. The Road Trip to Hell II was well under way and the Rockies were falling on their hardest times yet. Seven straight had turned into 11 straight with the Cincinnati sweep. Galarraga, their saving grace, was reduced to spending his mornings with team trainer Dave Cilladi, slowly high-stepping through hotel lap pools, strengthening his knee. Baylor was hoping to salvage a little something from this season, notably getting Cat the minimum of 502 plate appearances required to win a batting title. "Hey, I'll bat him leadoff the rest of the season if that's what I have to do," Baylor said. "He may be the biggest leadoff man in baseball history."

The Rockies took their blossoming 11-game losing streak, the longest in the National League, to San Diego for a doubleheader that might have set baseball back five decades. There were errors. There were fundamental blunders. These were the worst teams in the National League West, and for a reason. The Rockies lost the first game of the set to Andy Benes, and they lost the second to Doug Sanders, a kid making his major-league debut. The Rox made seven errors in the two games, and would have been credited with more if the official scorer hadn't been in such a good mood. And again, BaylorBall had run amok. The manager had admittedly reined in the running game by mid-season, especially with Hayes, Galarraga and Bichette producing so well in the middle of the lineup. But with Cat out, Baylor felt impelled to "make things happen." But bad things happened. In the second game of the doubleheader, the Rockies trailed, 5–0, heading into the second inning. With first and third and two outs, Baylor gave Bichette the sign to steal—if he got a good jump. Bichette was easily gunned down at second base. Afterward, the clubhouse was filled with empty shrugs. "Can you tell me what that was about?" one player asked a reporter.

Afterward, Baylor seemed almost resigned to his fate and the nasty 13-game losing streak that had engulfed his team.

"Fellas," he told his players, "at this rate, we're gonna lose 115 games. This has become a matter of pride, personal pride."

Later, much later, Bear offered the most concise appraisal yet of the new and unimproved Rockies. "I hate to say it," he said, grimly. "But the way we're playing now, we look a lot like the '62 Mets."

15

Dog Days

VICTORY, SWEET VICTORY.

The music in the clubhouse blared. Charlie Hayes smoked a celebratory cigarette and smiled as he traded barbs with Daryl Boston. Jerry McMorris, who had been sitting behind the Rockies' dugout at San Diego's Jack Murphy Stadium, prowled the premises, shaking hands, doing interviews. After 13 straight losses, the worst losing streak in the National League in 1993, the Colorado Rockies finally won a game, beating the Padres, 5–2, on August 8. As Baylor deconstructed the rare win for reporters, his wife, Becky, sat in her stadium seat and privately celebrated the momentary respite from the losing. This would be a nice trip up the coast to Los Angeles. Don would be happy, talkative.

Finally.

"He doesn't handle losing well; that's no secret," she said, laughing, running her hand through her blond hair. "He's just so competitive. He's always going over games, talking about what he might have done differently. And lineups—he's always going through new lineups, looking for different combinations."

For all the competitiveness, though, Becky Baylor and the reporters who covered the team noted a subtle change in the manager's demeanor through the course of the season. This was a man who blew up during a sloppy exhibition game in Tempe; now he seemed to be taking everything more in stride. He could lose now and force a bit of gallows humor. Losing wasn't killing him anymore. He wasn't gaining weight, wasn't losing weight, wasn't falling prey to what Becky calls the "Jim Leyland Syndrome," referring to the Pirates' manager, who resembles a chain-smoking corpse by season's end.

"There's a point in time that stands out so clearly in my mind," she said. "It was during the last West Coast trip, when things were going so poorly. And I remember we had an off day between Los Angeles and Houston and Don and I spent time together, and I really saw that day as being climactic, a real emotional turning point for him. And we talked about the losing, at length, and I could see he was coming to the realization, 'I've reached a wall and I can't keep beating my head against it.' He was so distressed in the middle of that trip, and that day off, it's like something changed. And it was great. It really was.

"I think he just reached a level of—how do I say this?—a level of acceptance. I hate to say there was resignation because that sounds defeatist. But maybe an easier acceptance of reality, an acceptance of what he was faced with, that he couldn't control certain things.

"It's kind of funny because we have friends who will call before we come into town and they'll say, 'How's Don? How's he holding up? This must be killing him.' And then we'll get together and they'll say, 'Wow, he looks great.' And he does. Sure, there have been some sleepless nights, but he hasn't let it eat away at him."

In fact, the day before the victory—a rare off day—the Baylors went on a boat trip. The boat didn't capsize. Things were looking up.

"He handles losing a lot better as a manager than he did as a player," she said. "As a player, losing is so tied to individual performance, I think it was very hard for him to leave it at the clubhouse door. After a particularly bad game, he might not speak to anybody the rest of the night. Now, though, I know he's not going to not speak to me. A lot of that, too, is maturation. He was a very young man as a player. Now he's a little older and he takes things more in stride.''

When Baylor took the job, he raised some eyebrows by saying that his major-league managerial debut was more satisfying, more exciting than playing in the seventh game of the World Series. Becky Baylor hears this and nods in easy agreement.

''Absolutely,'' she said. ''You know why? Because as a player, you are firmly in control of your success or lack of success. If you can produce, you'll always have a job in baseball. But as a manager, you're talking about the open market where you don't have any kind of control. And the truth is, the odds are stacked against you if you're a minority candidate or someone with no managerial experience. So, I think in terms of level of achievement, reaching this goal and becoming a manager was more satisfying for him. In a sense, he broke down another barrier.''

That is something Don Baylor has known all his life, since the day he helped integrate his junior high school in Austin. And it is something Becky Baylor knows, too, as a white woman married to a black man. They met in 1979, after Don had separated from his first wife. Becky was working for United Airlines and he was playing for the California Angels. They were together from 1979 to 1982, when Baylor signed with the New York Yankees. The bicoastal commuter relationship became too onerous, and she joined him in New Jersey. By 1986, they were together in Boston, and were married after the 1987 season.

Since then, it has been a wild and mostly wonderful ride, the pair shooting the rapids of racism, stupidity and ignorance together, often with a dark sense of humor. ''Joking about it, that's a daily part of our lives,'' she said. ''Like when we move somewhere and we're looking for temporary housing, I'll tell him, 'Maybe it would be a good idea if I go first to look at houses.' But that's reality. One year, we were trying to get housing [at the Yankees spring-training site near Fort Lauderdale]. And we went through our realtor in New Jersey, who said all we needed was a deposit for the house. So we got down there, then both of us walk into the office, and all of a sudden they say, 'Uh, we're going to need a cashier's check.' When it was just me and the realtor, they were willing to accept a regular check. But once they saw Don, they thought, 'Let's make sure this is guaranteed.' "

Becky can still remember standing on a street in Boston back in 1986 when she flagged down a cab. The car slowed to pick her up, but then the cabbie caught a glimpse of Don and sped off. There are a litany of ugly cabbie stories: The time, again in Boston, when a driver clearly was miffed at their arrangement and played ignorant when the pair told them they wanted to go to Boston's popular North End. They got out of the cab.

"You know what it is? Little daily indignities, things we've learned to live with," she said. "Like when we go to a restaurant, I can remember a number of times when waiters or waitresses would just toss the food on the table. There was another time, we were together walking through a nice crystal shop, and the saleslady was just tailing us, making sure we weren't putting anything in our pockets. Not once did she say, 'Can I help you?'

"Or one time we went to a liquor store, and all of a sudden, the cashier asks to see Don's ID. I mean, he was 40 years old at the time.

"These are things, little things, we deal with every day. People just won't let you forget that you're different. Honestly, if I didn't have people reminding me every day that we're an interracial couple, I would forget about it altogether. But still, it happens. Like one day, we were walking down the street, and a black man saw us together and he said, 'Brother, you should be ashamed of yourself.' Just this year, in Denver, we got a postcard that had Malcolm X on the front, and the person wrote something like, 'How can you be married to a white woman?'

"It's funny to see the difference in the way people treat us when they know he's Don Baylor and when they don't know. When they know, they're far more respectful. But when they don't, then they want a certified check, or they want an ID. It bothers us. Sure. But I'd have to say it still bothers him more than me. Not that I'm any less insulted or indignant, but for him, growing up black, he feels this anger inside. He feels angry that he's made to feel that way. But his attitude has always been, 'I'm not gonna let you get to me.' He was a tough-assed little kid who kicked butt and took names."

Becky grew up in a largely white enclave in Reading, Pennsylvania, but learned about racism in a unique way. Her father, Richard Giles, coached an amateur basketball team that toured the middle Atlantic states during the 1960s. Time and again, restaurants and hotels would shudder at the sight of the multiracial team, often refusing service. When a local fire hall in Reading denied his team service, Giles raised holy hell, including writing a vitriolic letter to the local newspaper. Before long, the Giles household was receiving death threats in the form of letters and calls, including one from the Ku Klux Klan.

"I learned very early about racism and intolerance," Becky said.

Becky graduated high school in 1969 and attended Boston University, but she lasted only two years during those turbulent times. There were student riots, National Guard troops and an almost daily diet of bomb threats, classroom evacuations and protests. "I became disillusioned," she said. Soon she went to work for United Airlines, first as a flight attendant and later on the ground. In 1976, she was transferred to Los Angeles, where she eventually met Baylor.

So . . . guess who's coming to dinner?

"With Sidney Poitier as Don Baylor," Becky said, laughing. "That's kind of the way it was. But you know, in a situation like that, I felt no trepidation, he didn't seem to feel any trepidation, so the only thing you have to worry about are the families. And we were fortunate. My parents had raised us to look at character and not skin color. And his family didn't seem to be bothered at all. When I told my father about 'Don Baylor,' he was a sports fan, so he knew. As long as the families are good about it and you have friends who are supportive and accept you as you are, the little daily indignities are easier to handle."

Becky Baylor knew better than most: A 13-game losing streak was not the worst thing Don Baylor had ever faced. It was not the worst thing the two of them had dealt with together. Not even close. They commisserated during the bad times and celebrated after the victories, rare as those might have been.

"When you have a hurdle like we do, it can do one of two things: It can bring you closer together or it can tear you apart," she said. "Happily, it's had the effect of bringing us closer."

AS THE ROCKIES' western road trip wended its way toward Los Angeles, Jerry Royster was filled with feelings of ambivalence. It had been, up to that point, a personally frustrating season for a man with big ideas and high goals. He had come to Denver as one of baseball's bright, rising stars, considered by many to be prime managerial material, a longtime player who had retired in 1988 and hopped the fast track to managerial status. His name had, in fact, been mentioned in connection with the Los Angeles Dodgers, whose main man, Tommy Lasorda, seemed to be coming to the end of his career. Royster was, by every measure, a Candidate.

But things had gone sour in Denver. Just before the All-Star break, the relationship between Royster and Baylor deteriorated to the point where Royster was moved—or, better yet, demoted—from third-base coach, a position of great responsibility, to first-base coach. He was replaced by Zimmer.

Now he was coming to Los Angeles, the place where he had learned so much of his baseball as a young player, to speak to Dodgers president Peter O'Malley. Not about a job, he insisted. But simply to talk, to trade insights, to speak to each other about family and life in general.

Here was a man who was offered at least four jobs after managing Double-A ball in 1992, a man who had turned down the Texas Rangers' third-base coaching job to come to Denver and be a part of the developmental process. He was widely considered a man with a future. Now he found himself standing unhappily in the first-base coach's box, his career on temporary hold, and contemplating his options.

"It's really hard for me, every game, going out to that first-base coaching box," Royster was saying one morning in Los Angeles. "I really didn't want to go over there. Not at all. There are just too many questions still unanswered. The job is somewhat demeaning. Third base, that's the prestige job among major-league coaching positions. That's the only job where you can really do some things, at least other than the manager and the pitching coach. When I was at third, I had a lot of responsibility: setting the defense, infield instructor, spring-training coordinator. But most of that was taken away when I went to first. . . . Believe me, I wouldn't have taken a job coaching first base if that's what had been offered. What's so disappointing is I'm in this situation, and then I look at some of the guys I managed in the minors and the truth is, I'd rather be developing some of the guys I left who were on the verge of being major-leaguers. I just don't feel like I'm helping this team as much as I could."

What happened? At the time, Baylor told reporters he simply wanted to move Ron Hassey, then the first-base coach, to the dugout where they could work more closely together. He could have then moved Zimmer to first base, but opted instead to put Zimmer at third and move Royster to first. Why not move Zimmer to first? Baylor told Royster he couldn't do that to a man of Zimmer's stature and experience.

Except Royster wasn't buying. He gritted his teeth and publicly characterized the move as "a demotion," fully convinced that the move was made with him, and not Hassey, in mind. He had heard some theories—secondhand. He had heard that Baylor was incensed at some missed signs. He had heard that Baylor was angry that Royster was so chummy with his old Dodgers mates the day after an ugly, bench-clearing brawl earlier in the season. "C'mon," Royster said. "Saying it wasn't a demotion, saying it wasn't aimed at me, well, that's a lot of crap, and everybody knows it."

Royster sat at a table in a downtown Los Angeles hotel café, picking at a stack of buckweat pancakes, and shook his head. It just happened, he was saying, happened with no warning, for no apparent reason. The change came in mid-July; now it was late August, and Baylor still had not given Royster anything the latter deemed a definitive or reasonable explanation for the move.

"All I want is for someone—the manager, the general manager, someone—to say, 'Jerry, this is why we did it,' " he said. "It's impossible to think that that never happened. There's just no communication."

The relationship had begun to show cracks quite early in the season, after just 14 games, when, on April 22 in St. Louis, Royster sent Young around third and attempted to score him in the first inning of a 5–2 loss. Young was thrown out, and after the game Baylor did not hide his displeasure. Then, just two games later, there was the plug-ugly Marlins game, when the Rockies made every blunder a team can make, when Royster defended Cole for attempting to steal third with two outs and Hayes at the plate. Baylor promptly slammed Cole for the mistake and Royster for justifying it.

"The game in St. Louis: big deal," said Royster. "Eric was bang-banged at home plate. How could that play be considered? And yet, it was. It was considered. And again, the only reason I knew about it was because reporters asked me about it. But Donnie never brought me in and talked to me. Again, no communication. If there's a problem, let's talk about it.

"And that Marlins game. Listen, why would that have a bearing on me? I'm not the guy who gave Alex the steal sign. All I was doing after the game was defending our player. If it was a mistake, how big of a mistake was it? The next day, Donnie came to me and said, 'Jerry, if they [the reporters] come to you, send them into my office, because this way, it looks like the two of us are disagreeing.' I said, 'Well, I'm not disagreeing, but I just don't see any reason to ridicule a player for being aggressive, which is what we'd been preaching all spring.' All I was doing was defending our player because that's what I'm supposed to do." He paused. "Well, apparently not."

And then there was the strange saga of the botched squeeze,

which happened—or didn't happen, depending on the source—
on June 20 during a game against San Diego.

"Here's the situation," said Royster. "We've got men on second and third, Galarraga on third and Charlie Hayes at second,
with one out, and they're intentionally walking Jerald Clark. So,
as they're walking him, Donnie gives me the squeeze sign and
points toward first base. So I'm thinking, 'Okay, I know he
doesn't want to squeeze now with the guy being walked, so he
wants to squeeze once Clark gets to first base. He wants to
squeeze with the next batter, Vinny Castilla.' So I gave Vinny the
squeeze sign, the pitch is outside, he swings through the ball, he
misses and the guy at third is out easily.

"So after the inning, I don't know there's a problem, I come
into the dugout and he [Baylor] says, 'Did you give him the
squeeze?' I said yeah and he said, 'Well, I didn't want the squeeze
there. What I was telling you was to get the squeeze sign from
Joe Girardi,' who was standing close to Donnie in the dugout. I
said, 'What do you mean?' He said, 'I gave you the squeeze sign
and pointed at Girardi.' "

Royster smiled and shook his head.

"I'm sorry, but I have never gotten a sign like that in my life.
Never. I mean, I'm all the way across the field, he's pointing in
the direction of first base and I'm supposed to know that I'm
getting the sign from Girardi? A lot of people in that dugout heard
our conversation and they couldn't believe it. They couldn't believe it. So, then, after the game, I asked him again, 'Donnie,
what exactly did you want?' And he said, 'I was trying to tell you
to get the squeeze from Joe because they [the opposition] were
watching me real closely.' That's not something we've ever discussed, getting a sign from someone else in the dugout. Unless
we've talked about it, you can't assume I'm going to know I
should be getting the sign from another player.

"Anyway, at that point, I'm thinking, 'We won the game, no
big deal,' and Donnie said, 'Yeah, well, don't worry about it,' and
yet, I pick up the paper the next day, and he says, 'Well, there
was a misunderstanding.' Why doesn't he just say, 'Well, we

screwed it up, the ball was too far outside for Vinny,' or something like that. He never once said it wasn't my fault. He just left
everybody to assume it was the third-base coach's fault. I don't
know if I was necessarily hung out to dry, but I know this: I
know I wasn't defended in any manner, and on occasions that
never should have become public in the first place."

Baylor and Royster were a pair that should have worked but
didn't. Both were longtime players. Both were students of the
game. Both believed in balls-out, aggressive baseball. Royster's
hiring was, in effect, an act of intuition. Baylor and Royster had
not crossed paths during their major-league careers, but Baylor
knew of Royster and respected his game and his baseball mind,
and hired him after an interview.

But the relationship soured quickly.

As the season wore on, Royster sensed he was no longer a
member of Baylor's inner circle. He and Amos Otis, the batting
instructor, were outsiders while Baylor surrounded himself with
Zimmer, Ron Hassey and Bear. In fact, one week earlier in San
Diego, Baylor was asked how he unwinds after a tough loss. "I'll
go out and discuss the game with Zim and Hass and sometimes
Bear," he said.

Royster heard that and smiled. "What does that tell you?" he
asked.

"It's been a bizarre year for me because our relationship has
deteriorated since the move," he said. "I still get calls from people
around baseball who are shocked what's happened to me. I
mean, if there were signs missed, and I don't think there were,
well, that's so trivial. Tell me, do you think the coaching at third
base was the biggest concern we had during the year? I don't
think so. I don't think it was a problem at all. And yet to do this,
something that's really detrimental to my career, and to do it
without any real explanation, just doesn't make any sense."

In his heart, though, Royster gradually sensed that he and
Baylor would not work. Privately, he told friends he couldn't
understand why the manager had put so much emphasis on winning and "setting new expansion standards" early in the season.

He felt that Baylor was too publicly critical of his players, too impatient with his incessant lineup changes, so critical he was in jeopardy of a full-scale mutiny.

"Our clubhouse is tense, and it probably shouldn't be," said Royster. "I think we all expected it to be Disneyland because of what was happening in the community. There's nothing but joy in those stands. I wish the clubhouse was better, but I think it also has to do with personnel and guys battling for their professional lives. There are so few veterans, so instability has a lot to do with it.

"Really, I feel like winning in spring training was detrimental to us. We tried to say, 'Oh, it's only spring training, don't get caught up in it,' but then we won there, and we came back to Denver and they had this parade and then 80,000 people in the stands, I think we started to lose perspective. It's like we started thinking we were better than we were."

This was a strange position for Royster, who had spent his 16 years as a player and his four years as a minor-league manager known as a moderator, someone who gets in the middle and tries to mitigate conflicts. He was a self-styled child of the sixties, an era that tended to polarize people, to render them dogmatic and inflexible. For Royster, the conflicts of the sixties had the opposite effect: They softened his edges, made him more intent than ever on helping people get along and find the middle ground.

"I was never militant," he said. "Even growing up and living through the riots in Sacramento. I mean, I was right in the middle of the riots. I can still remember the summer of 1969, a bunch of us had finished playing a legion game, and every Sunday, we'd all go to Oak Park and hang out. But this one day, we're riding through the park and there's no one there. Well, the reason was, and we didn't know at the time, was that a policeman had been shot that day and they had cleared out the park. So, the six of us are driving through there, just looking around for people, and next thing we know, oh my God, there are police cars, one behind us and two to the side, right behind us. Well, what happens? The driver, a kid named Herbert Williams, takes off. He didn't have any choice. And knowing what I know now, I'm glad he did. These cops were in full riot gear. They were ready for action, especially after one of their own had been shot.

"So we take off, turn left, make an immediate right, the cops are still too close. So we stop the car, we all run out of there and run into the neighborhood. I remember running up the stairs to the house of one family I knew, and they're in their windows, yelling at me, 'Get down! Get down!' and I hear them firing at the car. Then they blasted up at me—boom!—and I hear the window above me break while I'm down on the front porch. Then I heard sniper fire, real sniper fire, people from the neighborhood firing back. It was like being in the middle of a war.

"And it was so strange, so black and white at the time. I've never been a black and white person. My friends, most of whom were black, some of them were into the black-power movement, H. Rap Brown and Huey Newton, but I never was. I had friends black and white. It really never mattered to me. But that was one amazing summer, the last summer I spent at home before I went on to professional baseball."

The war did follow Royster, though, when he arrived at the Dodgers' A-ball team in Daytona Beach. The draft lottery was still of paramount importance in the lives of young men throughout the country. One night, the entire team gathered in the lobby of the Edgewater Beach Hotel in St. Petersburg after a game to watch the lottery, to drain beers, to ease their angst.

"We already knew that numbers 1 through 125 were definitely going and maybe another 10," said Royster. "I was number 135. But as we sat there after the game, it was very subdued. I can remember the game that night just didn't seem to matter because our lives were about ready to change. It was strange, because we sat there knowing that a couple of guys were definitely going. We had one guy with number 1, two more in the early 100's, a guy who was number 3. About seven guys were definitely going to leave us. We just sat and talked; we had guys saying they were going to Canada, 18-year-olds and 19-year-olds who thought they had it all mapped out, how they were going to avoid going to war."

That night, Royster recalled, one guy just lost it. "Absolutely lost it. He had an emotional breakdown in the lobby of that hotel. And it wasn't something where he was trying to get out of going; he really went crazy, and spent many years in an institution. I can remember calling the manager and telling him we were at the hospital and were checking him in. It was weird; we thought maybe he'd been drinking because he'd just start babbling and not making sense. But that wasn't it. He just went over the edge. I saw him about two years ago, the first time I'd seen him since that night, and I asked him if he remembered that night, and he said he really didn't, but that was part of his therapy.''

Royster's number never did come up that night. "From that day on, the war stopped being an issue in my life," he said. "After that, it was just baseball.''

He was signed by the Dodgers in 1970 as a nondrafted free agent, but never could crack the fabled Los Angeles infield of Ron Cey (third base), Bill Russell (shortstop), Davey Lopes (second) and Steve Garvey (first). In the winter of 1975, he was traded to the Atlanta Braves, where he became a regular for nine seasons. He then bounced around as a useful utility player, willing and able to play infield or outfield, playing two years in San Diego, another with the White Sox and Yankees and finally finishing up back with Atlanta in 1988. He was fully prepared to make the move to the broadcast booth after long discussions with Braves owner and media mogul Ted Turner, and had even taken classes at the Connecticut School of Broadcasting, when Charlie Blaney, the Dodgers' director of minor-league operations, asked if he would be willing to manage in L.A.'s minor-league system. Three times he asked; three times Royster said no. But then the Dodgers found a spot managing the Kissimmee, Florida, club, which would keep Royster close to home, close to his wife and daughter. "Coaching, managing, had never crossed my mind when I was a player," he said. "Never.''

But Royster had early success and rapidly began the climb through the Dodgers' minor-league system. By the time he reached Double-A San Antonio in 1992, he was considered a major-league managerial candidate. But again, he reached a dead end with the Dodgers; he couldn't crack the lineup in the early seventies, and there was no room at Triple A or on the Dodgers' staff for 1993. So, he was told, in not so many words, to look for a major-league coaching job, get experience, preferably in the National League West, the division in which the Dodgers play. "That's why I came here," he said. "And to work with Don and to be part of the developmental process with an expansion team."

By mid-season, all of that had soured. Royster wanted desperately to approach Baylor or even Gebhard, who he believed had played a prime role in his demotion, but held back. "So many good things have happened this season," he said. "It would have been pretty selfish for me to go in and raise a stink about my situation." What was the point, anyway? He was not a part of the brain trust. His body was in Denver, but his heart was a thousand miles away. The Candidate had options, and damned if he wasn't going to exercise them as soon as this strange season ended.

THE LOSING STREAK was history, but the victory in San Diego seemed, at least at the time, little more than a momentary respite. The Rockies still weren't playing well, and they were moving north to play a team that had given them fits, the Los Angeles Dodgers, followed by three more in Houston against the Astros.

But then the unexpected happened: The Rockies turned the thing around and began to win. The Road Trip to Hell II was turning into a comedic romp. Team Schizophrenia, losers of 13 straight, would go on to win six straight games, just one short of the expansion record, and finish out the expedition with a very respectable 7-7 mark—not bad after an 0-6 start.

The trip to Los Angeles was especially satisfying for Baylor, who never had much use for the Dodgers' organization. Some of this went back to his days with the Angels, who viewed the crosstown Dodgers as haughty and arrogant, the city's media darlings. Then, of course, there was the bench-clearing melee earlier in the season that left a bitter taste with both Baylor and Tommy Lasorda. "Now, this," said Baylor, "is a rivalry."

The Rockies got something they never could have envisioned: terrific starting pitching. The kind of starting pitching the Atlanta Braves get nearly every night. They beat the Dodgers, 3–2, on August 9, the first game of the series, on Greg Harris's best start since the trade and Vinny Castilla's RBI sacrifice fly. The latter was something of a newsworthy event: For homeboy Castilla, this was his first road RBI in 96 at-bats.

The pattern continued the next three nights: a 4–2 victory, led by Kent Bottenfield, who already was paying dividends after the trade for Butch Henry; a 3–2 victory, led by Armando Reynoso, who had been in a personal slump. Better yet, the win left the Rockies at 40-74, a half-game ahead of the Mets for the worst record in baseball. And, one day later, the Rockies completed their first road sweep as Willie Blair, his arm sore and overworked, gutted out a 4–1 victory.

"I could get used to this," said Baylor, eyeing a nice bottle of red wine on his desk. "Yes, indeed. Get seven, eight innings of quality pitching, don't have to overwork the bullpen, this is nice."

What he didn't appreciate, though, was Lasorda's postgame tirades, which implied that the Dodgers had beaten themselves. "He just can't give us any credit, can he?" said Baylor, who didn't have to look far for slights, real or imagined. "Why doesn't he say that we pitched some great ball games and they didn't do shit at the plate? Why doesn't he say that? No, he says they threw the ball away. Hell, Vin Scully can't stop talking about it. 'How can the Rockies beat these guys?' Give us some credit."

The rampaging Rockies took their act to Houston one night later, and the magic continued. On August 13, Charlie Hayes came back from his wrist injury and suspension—he accepted his suspension for the L.A. brawl when he hurt his wrist—by hitting an unlikely two-out, three-run homer in the ninth inning to beat the Astros, 5–3. The Rockies had now won six straight, one short of the expansion record set by the 1961 Los Angeles Angels.

That would end the next night, when Pete Harnisch over-whelmed Harris and the Rockies, 9–0. But the road trip could be declared an unmitigated success one day later as the Rockies came back again to beat Houston, 4–3. They had started 0-6. They finished 7-7. They were glancing at the Mets in their rear-view mirror. "That's a helluva hill to climb," said Baylor, packing for the flight back home.

16

"So, Which One Is the Expansion Team?"

IT WASN'T Nine Days That Shook the Baseball World. It wasn't baseball Armageddon. It wasn't the Brawl for It All. Even Don King couldn't have promoted this matchup.

But it mattered, especially to the Rockies.

Seven games in nine days, the Colorado Rockies versus the New York Mets—the battle for the worst record in all of baseball. An expansion team versus a team doing a rather convincing impression of an expansion team. The beloved Rockies versus the beleaguered, bedraggled, bedeviled Mets, a once-proud franchise that operated with a swagger, reduced to a simpering, whimpering collection of nobodies and overpriced veterans who seemed to care less.

Once upon a time, the Mets were Mex (Keith Hernandez) and Nails (Lenny Dykstra) and Kid (Gary Carter), a team both arrogant and unrelentingly good, a team with an attitude. By now, though, the Mets had fallen into the black hole, a team without a clue, going through the paces of yet another horrific season characterized by wretched baseball and even worse behavior. Bobby Bonilla was menacing reporters. Bret Saberhagen was throwing fits and tossing Clorox bleach at journalists. Vince Coleman was throwing low-grade explosives out a car window in the parking lot of Dodger Stadium.

The Rockies still had something to play for—jobs, statistics and even a little revenge. They continually dredged up Mets reliever John Franco's statement from the first week of the season, when he suggested that the Mets could get an early jump on the pennant race by fattening up on the expansion Rockies and Marlins. And they could recall the words of the New York writer Bill Madden, who suggested that the Rockies would be worse than the '62 Mets.

The series began with the Mets at 42-78. The Rockies were 44-77.

The battle for last had been joined.

August 21

"We deserve something for having to watch this," a New York reporter moaned.

"No shit," said another. "The Rockies and Mets. A doubleheader. I'm putting in for double OT."

The two teams found themselves playing at an appropriate venue: Mile High was a pitiful excuse for a field after having hosted two football games, a handful of baseball games and the Pope's visit, all in the space of one week. But, then, these were two pitiful excuses for baseball teams. Of course, the Rockies had an excuse: They were an expansion team.

It wasn't enough that the Rockies won the first game by a 4–3 score. Nope, after the first game, reporters were met near the Mets' clubhouse door by club executive Gerry Hunsicker, who came bearing some more bad news:

"Well, there's been a boating accident," he said glumly. The New York reporters braced themselves; in spring training, Steve Olin and Tim Crews of the Cleveland Indians had been killed in a boating mishap. What else could go wrong with this franchise?

"It's Bret Saberhagen, but we don't think it's serious," he

continued. "He sprained his ankle and required some stitches to close a bad cut. Apparently, he was in his boat and another boat came floating toward his. He then stuck out his foot to try and stop the other boat and he slipped. His foot got sandwiched between the boats. But it just appears to be a superficial cut."

A New York reporter asked, "You're not kidding now, are you?"

Gallows humor at 42-79? Not likely. Not now.

For the Rockies, the bigger news was being made on the field. The game marked the triumphant return of Galarraga to the lineup, his first appearance since July 24. The *Rocky Mountain News* trumpeted his return on its front page, with a huge picture and the caption "The Cat is back."

This was reason for more than celebration, though; it was a time for speculation over Galarraga's strange and oft-interrupted quest for the batting title. His average was still .392, but you couldn't find his name listed among the batting leaders; he lacked the necessary plate appearances. Through much of the season, it was assumed that Galarraga's two stints on the disabled list would prevent his amassing the required 502 plate appearances necessary to qualify for the batting title. But it was discovered that Rule 10.23, a rule never before invoked since it entered the books in 1967, might give Cat the title on a technicality. The rule says, simply, that if a batter is short of the 502 plate appearances, he can be given an 0-for-whatever to reach 502; then, if his average remains the highest in baseball, he can still win the batting title.

"I still haven't figured out exactly why that rule was put in," said Peter Hirdt, a statistician at the Elias Sports Bureau in New York. "But I think it showed great vision and foresight. The bottom line is, if Galarraga can take, say, an 0-for-25 and withstand that and still be the top hitter, he deserves the batting title. I think it's a great rule. You're going to get a lot of debate on this, but it makes good sense to me, and I'm a guy who's very sensitive to things that taint the statistical sanctity of the game."

Galarraga could have cared less how he won the batting title, or if an asterisk was to be affixed. "It makes no difference," he said. "To be the first Venezuelan to win the title means everything to me. There's never been a Venezuelan. That's what means the most."

While there was some debate over the rule itself, there was greater debate in Denver regarding Baylor's use of Galarraga. At the time of his departure onto the disabled list in late July, Baylor had said, half-kidding, that he might make Galarraga the biggest leadoff man in baseball history, all with an eye on getting him the necessary plate appearances. Later, he talked about having Cat bat second, which made no sense competitively—why use your best run producer second?—but would help get at-bats. Baylor was criticized by the bulk of the Denver media and by Hirdt, who said, "That's where you run into trouble, is when you do something that's not in the best interests of winning in order to produce a record. That's something where a commissioner—if we had a commissioner—should step in and say, 'No, this is not in the best interests of the game.' "

By the time Galarraga returned, he was batting one place higher in the lineup, hitting third. That could be justified, what with Hayes and Bichette hitting so well and driving in runs.

In fact, Cat went 0-for-3 in the first-game victory, though he hit the ball hard. "My timing is a little bit off," he said. "But the last time I came off the disabled list, I hit the ball well, so I don't see why it won't happen again. Really, I didn't do too badly for the first time back."

Galarraga did not start the second game of the doubleheader, leaving room to chronicle yet another comeback story: Hurst, who had been shaky during his rehab assignments in the minors, took his 80-mph fastball and his smarts to the mound in game two, and breezed through four innings of shutout baseball. The Rockies led, 6–0, when Hurst threw a 1-0 pitch to Dave Gallagher. He then lowered his head, gestured toward the dugout and stepped off the mound.

"I heard something pop," he said later.

There would be a few more miles to go on the long road back. Hurst left after 49 pitches. He was not, however, downcast after the game. "Let's see how it feels in three, four days," he said. "I heard the pop and felt some stiffness. But this is my spring training, basically. I know how far I've come in one year. I just have a ways to go."

The bullpen came on and kept the Mets out of business. Afterward, Holmes trudged past reporters outside the clubhouse after saving both ends of the doubleheader. He had converted his 12th and 13th straight save opportunities and was now 16 of his last 19. The Mile High boos and the days in Colorado Springs were now a distant memory. "Two Advil," he said, mimicking Nolan Ryan, "and ah could have gone another two innings."

By the way, Galarraga went hitless in one pinch-hit appearance in the second game; he was now hitting .387 to Tony Gwynn's .355.

August 22

Bob Gebhard paced the dugout a few hours before the game. A number was dancing on his lips: "17 and 22," he said. Then he smiled. "But I'm not counting." No, not much. That was the record the Rockies required to reach their own magic number, a record of 63-99. When the season began amid high expectations, the team could think about breaking the expansion record of 70 victories. Now, after a miserable 16-40 start, the idea of going 63-99, of avoiding 100 losses, was especially appealing. The difference between 100 and 99 is much more than just one game; 100 is an ugly round number, evocative of ineptitude or even worse. But 99 losses, well, that bespeaks respectability. Established teams have been known to lose 90-plus games.

The Rockies figured that maybe they could, to paraphrase John Franco, fatten up on the weaklings. Like, uh, the Mets.

On this day, the Rockies moved one step closer, winning the kind of game they had often lost, beating the Mets, 4–3, and sweeping the series. This not only put three full games between themselves and the Mets but moved the Rockies into sixth place, past the San Diego Padres in the NL West. "Hey," said Dante Bichette, "we've even got a chance to catch Florida."

Four in a row. Eleven of their last 14. Break up the Rockies!

Once again, the hero was Freddie Benavides, the slight shortstop who had come to Colorado from Cincinnati in the expansion draft. He homered off Sid Fernandez, his third game-winning hit in four games.

He had been known as a good-field, no-hit player as a backup to the great Barry Larkin in Cincinnati. And he had done little to erase that reputation during the first three quarters of the season, losing his starting job after a bout of ineffectiveness and injury. But Benavides persisted, and eventually found himself in something of a platoon with Vinny Castilla. "Those two guys are one of the best unwritten stories of our year," said Jerry Royster, who, in his day, was part of a platoon known as "Timry Flanster" —a second-base platoon of Royster and Tim Flannery in San Diego.

"It's strange, too, because you think about shortstop, you think about just one guy dominating that position for a long time," said Baylor. "Like Larkin, Ozzie Smith, Cal Ripken. You just put the same guy's name on the lineup card and that's it. We've got an unusual situation. Right now, it's working okay, but I'd like to see one guy win the job. What you have in Castilla is a shortstop only, and Freddie we can move around a few places, spot him at second when we need him."

It was hard not to root for Benavides: He emerged early as one of the most affable guys in the clubhouse, one of the few folks who took the time to remember even the reporters' names. And he offered a valuable service beyond hitting and fielding: As a Mexican-American born in the border town of Laredo, Texas, Benavides often served as an interpreter for Armando Reynoso and Roberto Mejia. "That's something I want to do after my playing days are over," he said. "It's so difficult for Latin players to make the adjustment, I'd like to be involved in the game coaching and using my language skills to help those people."

As the Rockies reveled in the winning streak, Daryl Boston shook his head as he considered the team in the clubhouse across the way. He had been a member of the Mets one year earlier, had been part of the circus. He had been one of the more popular players in the Mets' clubhouse, close friends with Doc Gooden and Vince Coleman, in particular. Boston was the ultimate bachelor, always dressed to the nines, completely enamored of the perks the major-league life provided. He had liked New York, liked hitting the clubs—Nell's, China Club and the other hot spots. Now he saw a team of strangers.

"Shit, man, I don't know even half those guys," he said. "That's their farm team out there. It's kind of a shame, you know? They've still got guys who've been around long enough to know not to quit. But watching them, there isn't any intensity. They've had so many off-the-field things happen, so many disruptions in that clubhouse, I don't see how they can concentrate anymore. The intensity's not there. Definitely. It's obvious."

The Rockies and Mets took a brief respite from one another, the Rockies losing two of three in Philadelphia, where the Phillies were coasting to the NL East crown. The Montreal Expos would make a bit of noise with a late-season run, but the Phils went wire-to-wire with relative ease. Anyway, the Rockies-Phillies series didn't mean anything.

But on August 26, acquaintances were renewed. This was bigger than big, bigger even than Sid Fernandez. Bad versus worse. As the Rockies took the bus up the turnpike to meet the Mets, they learned that the Mets had, that afternoon, been mathematically eliminated from the National League East pennant chase. In late August. The Rockies couldn't brag, though: They were just one game away from mathematical elimination in the National League West.

August 26

Typical day with the Mets.

"Press conference at six in the Jets' locker room," came the announcement. "Regarding Vince Coleman."

Christ. More with Vince Coleman. By this point, the Mets were in an untenable position with their troubled center fielder. He had been a public-relations nightmare from the start, having had run-ins with his former manager, Jeff Torborg, and a coach, Mike Cubbage, not to mention an icy relationship with the New

York media and a propensity for hamstring injuries. But the last misstep had been too much: Coleman had thrown an explosive, an M-80, out of his car and near a crowd in Los Angeles. The Mets had placed him on the baseball equivalent of administrative leave, pending his hearing. They were still paying him, much to their chagrin, but they wanted no part of his presence.

"Yeah, I had dinner with Vince last night at the Shark Club, got some soul food," said Boston, who had befriended Coleman one year earlier in New York. "He knows it's over for him here. I know he wants to play and prove what he can do, but I don't see how that's going to happen. Everybody's painting him to be this terrible guy, but I know him. I know his family. I love the guy. I mean, he can be tough with you guys; he'll tell reporters to get the fuck away from his locker and stuff, but, you know, he just takes too many things to heart. I mean, he wasn't trying to hurt anybody. He knows it was a mistake, and he's sorry about it.

"The question is, why are they doing this to him, but some of the other guys, like Bret Saberhagen, they slap him on the wrist? What Vince did wasn't any different from Saberhagen [who had confessed to spraying bleach on reporters in the lockerroom]. But Saberhagen has had some success over here and the press likes him, so it's a different story."

For Mets co-owner Fred Wilpon, however, there was no gray area. Wilpon appeared at the press conference with the team's legal counsel and the new manager, Dallas Green, and said, quite succinctly, that while the Mets could not "fire" Coleman before his hearing, he would never let Coleman return to the Mets family. Ever. At times, he sounded and looked like a high school principal, telling the press how he met with the team for the first time in 14 years of ownership and told them, "No more screwing around. No more embarrassments. You don't like it, take a walk."

It was an incredible scene. "Sometimes," said Wilpon, "they act like kids." Or worse.

Only one thing went right for the Mets that night: They won for a change, 7–1, behind Gooden. Of course, the Rockies made it rather easy on the Doctor, flailing away early in the count, as was their practice. With this team, the only walks were intentional. Free swinging and . . . missing. The Rockies were not the most patient bunch.

The Mets had crawled to within three and a half games of the mighty Rockies in the race for last. Six people in Queens cared.

"You're asking me if it means something not to finish last?" asked Bobby Bonilla, lowering his head and muttering. "Let me tell you: Finishing last or next to last, dude, it don't mean jack shit. All I know is we didn't finish first. The rest don't mean jack. Maybe it means something for them [the Rockies] not to finish last, but for us, who gives a fuck?"

August 27

This was the place, right here in the corner of the Shea Stadium visitor's dugout, near the catacomblike runway to the clubhouse. This was the place where Don Baylor saw history made, the place where the Curse of the Bambino or Dame Fate or whatever in hell it was took the 1986 World Series away from the star-crossed Boston Red Sox.

"Same spot, right here," Baylor was saying before the game, recalling the 10th inning of Game Six. As he sat, a torrential rain soaked the field. "Me and Tom Seaver, right in this corner. We sat right here for outs one and two and then we moved up toward that step, ready to run out onto the field and celebrate. I like sitting here. I like to torture myself."

On a night when the Rockies and Mets played a game that meant nothing, Baylor found himself reminiscing about a game that meant everything—and perhaps even a little more to the suffering multitudes in New England. October 25, 1986. This was a game for the ages, a drama that crystallized nearly a century of despair for the region's angst-ridden fans.

It had been the culmination of a remarkable week and a half of baseball, as the Red Sox, buoyed by homers from Baylor and then Dave Henderson, came back to beat Baylor's old friend, Gene Mauch, and the California Angels in the American League

Championship Series. From that sublime moment of ecstasy, to this . . .

"Two outs," said Baylor, gazing dreamily toward first base. "They had all the TV cables laid out, they had the champagne chilling in the clubhouse, Bob Costas was running around getting set up in the winner's clubhouse, and I remember they flashed on the scoreboard, 'Congratulations, Boston Red Sox.'

"And then, the Curse of the Bambino strikes."

With a vengeance.

The Sox had scored two runs off Rick Aguilera in the top of the 10th inning, and pitcher Calvin Schiraldi opened the bottom of the inning by retiring Wally Backman and Keith Hernandez on routine fly-ball outs.

And then it happened: Gary Carter singled to left. Pinch hitter Kevin Mitchell singled to center. On an 0-2 pitch, Ray Knight singled to center; Carter scored and Mitchell moved to third.

Bob Stanley replaced Schiraldi and went 2-2 on Mookie Wilson. The Mets batter fouled off two pitches before Stanley's wild pitch scored Mitchell with the tying run. After two more foul balls, Wilson hit his fateful ground ball at Buckner. It was the trickler heard 'round the world. Knight scored. The series was, for all intents and purposes, over.

"After that, things were never the same," said Baylor. "A lot of people were never the same—Schiraldi, Rich Gedman, Buck, Bob Stanley to some degree, and, of course, [manager] John McNamara. Hell, it affected entire families. That whole team was never the same. All winter, that's all people talked about, and there was a lot of whispering and finger pointing, especially about Mac's decision"—to leave Buckner at first base instead of replacing him with Dave Stapleton.

"For that one year, the Red Sox were a team and we did things together. But I could tell when we got to spring training [in 1987] that things weren't right. And we went back to being the Red Sox that people always hear about: the '25 players, 25 cabs' Red Sox. Whatever we had, we lost, because of that game and that series."

Nothing was quite the same when Baylor and the Red Sox

came to spring training in 1987. Bob Stanley and Rich Gedman were still embroiled in a childish "passed ball or wild pitch" debate. Roger Clemens was angry about stories that said he had asked to be removed from Game Six instead of being pulled by McNamara. The issue of World Series shares also followed the club; the Red Sox did not include the Fenway Park grounds crew in a postseason share because they felt that the group had done nothing to help their cause.

The game and the blunder dogged Buckner far into his retirement, ultimately forcing him to move out of New England. "I was just surprised it took him seven years to do it," said Baylor.

And it still follows McNamara, lingering like a bad cold. When he was named manager of the Cleveland Indians in 1990, the second question of his introductory press conference was, "Do you still regret not putting Stapleton in for Buckner?" Baylor remembers having McNamara to his house after Baylor and the 1987 Twins won the World Series. "It was still on his mind," Baylor said, "because he kept bringing it up."

What, Baylor was asked, would he have done in that situation? Do you stick with Buckner, the noble veteran who played so hurt and so heroically? Do you play the percentages, go with Stapleton, a better defensive player? Baylor sidestepped the question by saying that he would draw on the wisdom of his many managerial mentors, Earl Weaver and Tony LaRussa, Chuck Tanner and Gene Mauch. Then it was suggested that some of those managers would have gone by the percentages and some of them would have played it on gut instinct.

"Yeah, that's a tough one," said Baylor. "One of the things about Johnny Mac is he was such a player's guy, he probably thought, 'Buck is my guy and he deserves to be out there.' It's so hard to know when to manage with your head and when to manage with your heart."

As Baylor spoke, the grounds crew pulled the water-logged tarpaulin toward the dugout, sending a torrent of disgusting brown liquid down the steps and into the dugout, nearly soaking Baylor's shoes. This had never been a good place to sit. Never.

A few hours later, Baylor would find himself at the other end of that dugout. The stakes were dramatically diminished, but the results were similar. The Rockies remained punchless, losing to Sid Fernandez and the Mets, 3–2. Where's Billy Buck when you need him?

August 28

"Three-run Johnson," Vinny Castilla cackled. Then he traded high fives with Armando Reynoso, who didn't need any translation. The Rockies pitcher hit his second home run of the season, a three-run homer, and the Rockies finally won a game in New York, 7–5.

And guess who looked like the expansion team? In the fourth inning of a sloppy game, Eddie Murray, the terminally dour Mets first baseman, turned a double-play ball into an adventure, tossing the rock into left field. Before it was over, outfielder Joe Orsulak would airmail his throw a couple of miles over the catcher's head, leading to two unearned Rockies runs.

"All I'm thinking is, 'Keep throwing it around and let Zim keep waving,'" Baylor said afterward. "Routine plays turned into a fiasco." Meanwhile, the Rockies' defense was turning difficult plays into routine ones. Hayes, in particular, finally showed the range that had made him a Gold Glove candidate one year earlier. A happy trend was developing.

August 29

Boston walked around the clubhouse, smoking a cigarette and looking like something the cat dragged in.

"Yeah, well, you've got to know when you can do certain things and when you can't do certain things," he was saying. "I knew Jerald [Clark] would be playing, so, you know . . ." Yeah, you know . . . party. Have a few cocktails. Hit the hot spots, just like the old days in New York. "It's like I told the young guys we had in New York," he said. "Don't come in here thinking you can eat the whole Big Apple in one night. Just take little bites here and there."

Boston looked like he'd been part of a movable feast. But at least he was styling. If his black hightops were no longer allowed —Baylor had outlawed them—then the designs he and Hayes had etched into the sides of their heads were certainly a fashion statement. "My wife saw it on TV," said Hayes. "She left a message for me: Call ASAP."

Hayes was getting grief for more than just his new do, though. Before the game, most of the Rockies convened in their lounge to watch the Little League World Series. In 1977, Hayes had been part of the Hattiesburg, Mississippi, team that lost—naturally— to Taiwan in the final. "I was the pitcher," he remembered. "We beat Dwight Gooden's team in the semis, but they [the Taiwanese] were tough." In this game, Long Beach had a kid standing at second base, the potential winning run—and his name was Charlie Hayes. Ultimately, the younger Hayes would score the game's winning run.

The Taiwanese didn't make the final this time.

By game time, it became sufficiently clear that one of those overaged Taiwanese kids could have tossed a shutout at the Mets. On this day, the Mets barely even went through the motions. They played like a team intent on meeting a date. Lance Painter, the Rockies' lefty who started in the minors, came to the majors, went back to the minors and returned for a second time, was looking like Sandy Koufax.

The final was Rockies, 6–1. It wasn't even that close.

"Lance Painter?" asked Dallas Green, who had taken over for Torborg only to find out the Mets were beyond even divine intervention. "Sometimes the faucet is turned on and sometimes it isn't. Today, we didn't even have it turned half on."

On this day, the Mets deserved all the barbs they saw in some of the more ill-spirited offerings ever on a Banner Day. Down the hallway, though, Painter was being lauded. Like so many of his teammates, he had gone back to Triple A only to return a more confident and accomplished pitcher. As usual, the Rockies needed all the help they could get; Hurst's comeback had been aborted and he had been placed back on the disabled list.

Dallas Green wasn't feeling so hot himself. "We don't know

how to play the game," said Green, who was sitting in his office long after the game, staring off into space. "The thing that kills me is, these guys will have forgotten about this game five minutes after they walk out the door. No, actually, they've already forgotten about it. When I hear Donnie talk about how the game has changed since our days, I know what he's saying. It's really changed, dramatically. You can't discipline guys anymore. Between the agents and the Players Association, what can you do to a guy?

"I hear people say it's all about money, that money is the reason guys act this way. But I think it goes a lot deeper than that. I think it's a societal thing. When I was a kid, we respected our elders, we respected teachers and police officers. That's not the case anymore. There's been this whole breakdown of authority. Maybe that's a reflection on us as parents."

This is what it had come to: Green was reduced to offering treatises on the decline of Western civilization. For the Mets, a split of the series in New York didn't, in Bonilla's inimitable words, mean "jack shit." The Rockies, however, couldn't have been more pleased. They had come to New York to christen their season, only to get beaten twice, only to listen to Franco's ruminations, only to read how they were poised to become the 1962 Mets. And now they had taken five of seven games against the Mets and put some distance between them for the worst record in baseball.

"I kind of enjoy beating these guys," said Joe Girardi with a glint in his eye.

17

A License to Print Money

THE NEWSPAPER clipping has begun to yellow and get dog-eared. It is a story from the business section of *The Denver Post* and it is dated August 4, 1991:

"The new Colorado Rockies baseball team will lose money in its first years of operation, but team owners could hit a financial home run if they can put a winning team on the field before long. The Rockies could lose 'north of $20 million in cash' in the team's first few years, according to Stephen Kurtz, a partner with the Denver accounting firm Shenkin Kurtz Baker and Co. Kurtz serves as chief financial adviser to the team."

Two years later, Rockies officials admit that some of Kurtz's projections were intentionally gloomy. It never hurts to poor-mouth just a little bit at the start, especially when you're entering discussions on a stadium lease for Coors Field, which would open in 1995. But there was a germ of truth in Kurtz's fiscal scenario. At the time, the Rockies were looking at some frightening expenses: $95 million in initiation fees and another $15 million or more in start-up costs. Worse, the club would go through the first year without seeing a penny of the $14 million the team received in 1993 national TV money.

The fiscal forecast was nearly as gloomy as the competitive forecast.

The questions were, How much would they receive from local television? How would they do on a local radio contract? How many fans would fill Mile High Stadium? The *Post* story continued, "One optimistic financial scenario shows the Rockies breaking even by 1995, with revenues and expenses of about $53 million. The scenario assumes fairly high ticket sales and media revenues and relatively low payroll costs."

Fast forward to 1993 . . .

"It's a gold mine," said David Glazier, the Rockies' vice-president of sales and marketing. "An absolute gold mine."

"It's almost like a license to print money," said Bernie Mullin, the team's senior vice-president for business operations. "This is, without question, the most successful first year in the history of professional sports."

How successful?

According to industry and Rockies' sources, the team was poised to earn approximately $60 million its first year. And with expenses at about $35 million, the team figured to turn a remarkable $25-million profit, more than even the most optimistic or foolhardy baseball booster could have imagined. By year's end, the Rockies, a team that was supposed to be shackled by having to play in a "small" market, would rank among baseball's top six teams in terms of profitability. Little wonder, then, that team owner Jerry McMorris was confused over whether to enter a gathering of small-market or large-market owners during an August owners' meeting in Wisconsin where the owners discussed revenue sharing. He ended up in the large-market meeting, a clear signal that the Rockies had, indeed, become an overnight fiscal sensation.

A quick thumbnail sketch of the team's financial ledger:

• *Tickets:* The team would go on to sell around 4.5 million tickets. The average price was $8.25. Take away the 10 percent city tax, and the team took in more than $34 million in ticket revenues alone.

• *Concessions:*   While the Denver Broncos do not get a dime from Mile High Stadium concessions, the Rockies convinced the city early on that they would need some of those revenues to stay afloat. The Rockies worked out a deal to receive 38 percent of the gross concession revenues, or 90 percent of the city's 42 percent take—much to the consternation of the Broncos, who continue to clamor for a renegotiation of their stadium lease. According to sources, the Rockies were looking at a profit of roughly $7.5 million from concessions, and another $2 million (approximately) from game-day program sales.

• *TV:*   Local-television revenues are at the heart of nearly every team's financial success or failure. It is what sets the New York Yankees apart from the Seattle Mariners, why the Los Angeles Dodgers can spend money on free agents and the Pittsburgh Pirates can't. The biggest issue in baseball today is revenue sharing—specifically, how to get the big-market clubs to share some of the local TV booty with the small-market clubs (to create a more even playing field).

When the Rockies came into existence, the gloom was palpable. Denver, with 1.05 million households, ranked as the nineteenth largest media market in the nation. According to a 1991 *Post* story, "If the owners of Major League Baseball's expansion teams in Denver and Miami expect television stations and cable networks to break into feverish bidding for broadcast rights to the games, they may be disappointed. The selections of the sites by the National League . . . triggered euphoria on the streets of both cities but got only a lukewarm response from the TV industry, which is in the throes of its worst recession in 15 years."

Another day, another incorrect projection. The Rockies' net revenue for local TV: around $6 million, a number that ranked them 10th or 11th, behind only the big dogs—the Dodgers, Cubs, Yankees and the like. "What we did was, instead of getting a cash-rights offer, which is the case with most teams, we did a deal where we paid 'X' amount to Channel 2 for the time, then sold our own advertising," said Mullin. "Now, you see this is what Major League Baseball is doing on a national basis with their new contract. When you're in a market where no one will give you what you want, you have to establish your own market value. There's no question: The deal David Glazier and I did is the best for our market size in the country."

• *Radio:* After many rounds of negotiating, the Rockies eventually signed a lucrative deal with KOA radio, a multiyear deal that would pay the team $4 million—plus another quarter-million in sales of network affiliate fees—the first year. This was the opposite of the TV deal; this time, the station paid the Rockies a rights fee and the station sold the advertising themselves. One industry source put the Rockies' radio deal at sixth or seventh in baseball.

• *Merchandising:* You couldn't go anywhere in the country without seeing Rockies paraphernalia—the hats, the shirts, everything and anything with the Rockies' silver, purple and black insignia. By season's end, Rockies merchandise was the best seller in all of major-league baseball. Of course, it doesn't matter, financially, who sells best and who sells worst—all teams share equally in the national merchandising booty. It is estimated that the Rockies earned $2.25 million on the national merchandise sales and another $3 million on local sales from their own stores and catalog. "The founding fathers of the ownership group, when they selected purple, they chose the hot color of the nineties," said Rockies merchandising director Mark Ehrhart, Steve's brother. Carol Coleman of Major League Properties, the game's marketing arm, called the success of Rockies merchandise "pretty amazing."

When it is all tallied up and the Rockies add in another half-million or so for scoreboard signage, game-day advertising and the like, the number—approximately $60 million—is staggering. "Everything has changed since the day we got here," said Gebhard. "Before, we had no idea we were going to be getting 50,000 fans a game and we were conservative about the way we did things. We're still not going to spend money foolishly, but now we have the freedom to do a lot more things.''

The Rockies' financial success is not a one-year wonder, either. While it's unlikely the team will draw 4.5 million its second year at Mile High, the team stands to benefit from added revenue streams from their sweet stadium lease at Coors Field. ''Everyone has called it the best lease in the history of sports,'' said Mullin. ''The concessions deal is one of the best ever negotiated. Once the team moves into Coors Field, then you add the money we'll get from the national TV contract, and it's going to be an even larger number.''

As the attendance numbers kept growing, as all the numbers kept growing, Rockies executives and area baseball proponents could merely shake their heads in wonderment. But Mullin, along with Antonucci, Glazier, Ehrhart, Monus, Jacobs and the rest of the original franchise builders, had a suspicion they might be sitting on something special.

''I really believe, even with all that's happened, that you have to give a lot of credit to Antonucci, Ehrhart, Jacobs and all the people who had those breakfasts every morning at the Brown Palace, putting this thing together,'' said Mullin. ''Those were the people who knew the real strength of this market. All you have to do is look at demographics. The target group for baseball fans is the 18- to 45-year-old group, which is way overrepresented in this area. This is a very young, very active citizenry. Then, I think it helps that the Broncos have helped create a sellout mentality, and that helped drive season-ticket sales to the highest level in major-league baseball. The other factor is the regional nature of the franchise. We're talking about 11 states. For people to drive a number of hours to a sporting event is not unusual in this part of the country. We have statistics that show that more than 25 percent of our season-ticket holders drive 50 miles or more each way to a Rockies game. You won't get that in New York. People won't drive to Philadelphia for a game.

''And then you look at groups that don't attend baseball games in great numbers and those groups are grossly underrepresented in our area. Senior citizens tend not to go. African-Americans tend not to attend in great numbers. But the numbers show that Hispanics do go to baseball games, and Denver has a very sizable and strong Hispanic population. And finally, there was the 30-year wait. Everything just sort of ignited. It took off."

As the season neared its close, the on-field phenomenon had produced a phenomenal off-field windfall. One of the many "experts" left dumbfounded by the team's popularity was Ford Frick, of the famous baseball Fricks, who is managing director of the Denver economic consulting firm of Browne, Bortz and Coddington, which did work for the city's early baseball boosters.

"I think everybody expected a first-season success," said Frick. "But I don't think anyone foresaw, including the owners or anyone else, the strength of this success. We certainly expected it in the early season, a lot of sold-out games and good attendance during the summer months. I thought, you know, maybe three million or something like that. And I thought that would have been very good. This is one of the smallest, if not the smallest, markets in major-league baseball. The stadium is not particularly attractive for baseball. I thought it would wear thin quicker. It's a losing team.

"We did a lot of analyses trying to predict attendance prior to this and really came to the conclusion that the only thing that matters in baseball attendance is a win-loss record. I don't care, if you have a losing team, you can't draw in New York. There wasn't a whole lot of hope for a losing team. So, yeah, I'm very surprised and a little mystified, too.

"I think a lot of it has been serendipitous. I think this team came in a time when Denver really was coming out of a long-term depression, a psychological depression. People were feeling good, they were making a little more money. . . . For the first time in probably eight to ten years, they were optimistic about the future, and along came this silly team. And it was just sort of a rising tide that carried the ship. I don't think there is a whole lot we can learn from this. It's just sort of a unique phenomenon where it caught fire and it was sort of like, gee, we did this right, we won this crazy thing. . . . It caught a wave just as it crested. Who knows if you could ever replicate it?"

Tom Clark of the Greater Denver Chamber of Commerce was in on the ground floor of the first economic-impact study that was done back in 1990. At that time, Clark's group guesstimated that an expansion baseball team would have a $90.5-million impact on the community.

"In the beginning, people were saying, 'This is an economic-development deal,' and we kept saying, 'No, it's not economic development, it's just plain fun, a sports deal,' " said Clark. "Because other franchises had simply not been that successful. Our original projections were based on the Rockies being the most successful expansion team ever with about 1.7 million fans. Now we're looking at 4.5 million fans, so my gut tells me we're looking in the neighborhood of $250 million in economic impact. Now you can say it's an economic-development deal because it's been an economic boon. The way we saw it originally, the economics simply don't work for an expansion team. But the Rockies have rewritten the entire book on it. Let's face it: It's been pretty damned dramatic."

So dramatic that Jerry McMorris, the team's principal owner, began to have second thoughts about the capacity of the club's new park, Coors Field.

When the owners convened for a meeting in Denver in June, he found out his club was the talk, and envy, of baseball. The attendance numbers were staggering, stupefying. Later, McMorris would speak of some "jealousy" among rival owners. Some of them begrudged the Rockies' success; others wondered how they might draw inspiration from their story. And the attendance numbers never waned.

"Our capacity at Coors Field will only be 43,800," McMorris began to think. "Why not increase the capacity and accommodate more fans?" He approached several baseball owners at the meeting and broached the question. The answer kept coming back the same. "Hang tight with 42,000 to 47,000," he was told time and again. "Keep the ballpark intimate. Maintain the value of a season ticket. Make Rockies baseball a tough ticket in town."

It was a sentiment echoed time and again through the expansion process; the Lords of Baseball felt 44,000 or so was the optimal capacity, especially for a market the size of Denver. It was one of many reasons why the establishment did not find 75,000-seat Mile High Stadium suitable for baseball. Too many seats meant too few previous commitments from fans, no compelling reason to buy season tickets. Why would a fan want to commit to 81 games when he knew he could go to the park anytime, any game, and pick up a decent ticket? The Rockies and the rest of baseball knew the primary reason the Rockies sold 28,627 season tickets was because fans wanted to position themselves for a good season ticket in Coors Field.

"What about your park?" McMorris asked H. Wayne Huizenga, his counterpart in Miami.

"I could sell more tickets, but that's not what's best long-term," Huizenga said. His Marlins were playing at 70,000-seat Joe Robbie Stadium, but Huizenga was limiting capacity to 44,000 for baseball.

"I can see that side of the argument," McMorris said. "We don't want to lose the intimacy of the park and we don't want to devalue our tickets. I know you don't build a shopping mall to accommodate Christmas-shopping season. But I look at the tremendous response and interest in the region, and I think what we have is totally unique. Expanding capacity could be good for the fans and for us."

He had the numbers to back up his claim. The Rockies had the greatest single-game attendance record. They were the fastest to one million fans, two million, three million, and would ultimately break the all-time season attendance record. Would 43,800, the current capacity being discussed by the architects, be enough?

There was immediate criticism. The idea behind the smaller capacity was to create an intimate environment, a ballpark rather than a stadium. Some questioned McMorris's motives. Even though the Rockies were willing to pay for any additional seats, they stood to profit handsomely from the added capacity. First, Rockies executives were able to convince the Stadium District to add about 1,200 more seats, to expand to 45,000. But he kept pushing, and by late in the season, he had finally gotten the architects, HOK, to agree to a stadium of 50,000. Actually, he wanted even more, closer to 55,000, but the Stadium District and the architects prevailed.

"I was like a lot of people," said Tom Gleason, deputy director of the Stadium District. "At first, I thought the added seats would undermine the whole notion of an intimate ballpark. But once I saw what the architects were doing, my mind was changed. And I honestly don't think this is about enriching the Rockies. I think I'm as cynical as anybody, but I just think Jerry has been so overwhelmed by attendance, and has heard from so many people who want to come to games and are worried about being shut out, that he feels an obligation to provide these seats."

By September, the new stadium site had been blessed by a Native American group and dinosaur bones had been unearthed. Construction was ready to go. The whole equation had changed. A license to print money? The founding fathers, primarily Antonucci, Monus and Ehrhart, could not enjoy the spoils. But McMorris and his partners were in heaven.

"Our fans," he said one day, "have been very good." And then he broke into a broad smile.

When the franchise was awarded, the Rockies were a highly speculative business venture. By late in their first season, they were the talk not only of baseball but of all professional sports. Some of the success was borne of smarts; some of it was kismet. Either way, the dynamics of Rockies baseball had changed and changed forever. The small-market mind-set could be pitched. Now the Rockies could go toe-to-toe with the big boys, could challenge for high-priced free agents, could speed up the timetable for success. In a time of recession and dwindling TV monies and tax revolts, the Rockies had bucked every trend, defied all conventional wisdom.

18

Sixty-three and Counting

GAME 153. Don Baylor sat behind his desk in the Mile High clubhouse and shook his head in amazement. "What happened to the baseball season?" he wondered as a ceiling fan whirred overhead. "I almost hate to see the season coming to an end. Just 10 games left and we're playing our best baseball. We're playing well, the guys are looking forward to coming to the park every day. When you're getting the crap kicked out of you 18-to-1, it's no fun. But now, every day we come to the park, we feel like we have a chance to win."

The Rockies' inaugural season was coming to a raucous close. There were five games left in the final home stand, with five road games remaining, two in San Francisco and three in Atlanta, right there in the vortex of the pennant race. While so many other teams were going through the September motions, playing for little more than contract numbers, the Rockies were emerging from the dog days of August as one of the better teams in all of baseball.

And a large part of their success could be attributed to Baylor.

His competitive bent might have been an obstacle earlier in the season; some players privately grumbled about his incessant lineup changes. But now he had a team that was fighting hard night in and night out, refusing to quit like so many established teams—read: the Mets—shooting for a number that once seemed unreachable: 63.

Sixty-three victories. As the Rockies prepared for their September 21 game against the San Diego Padres, they were just one game away from number 63 and the guarantee that they would not lose 100 games this first season.

"How about 70?" somebody asked Baylor.

He smiled. "Sixty-three. That's all I want—today," he said. "Then we'll worry about the rest."

Once upon a time, 55 victories seemed like a distant star. The Rockies began the season in the doldrums, standing at 16-40 and showing little hope for improvement. They were not only losing; they were absorbing beatings. The pitching, in particular, was abysmal. But somehow, slowly, the big mess began to take some shape, most dramatically after the team's 13-game losing streak. The pitching staff improved markedly, especially the bullpen: Bruce Ruffin seemed reborn and Steve Reed revitalized in the setup role; Darren Holmes had become an automatic save. Meanwhile, the hitting continued to define the team, more so at Mile High than on the road, the Rockies hitting .346 through the first eight games of the last home stand.

More numbers: The Rockies entered game 153 having won nine of their previous twelve games, and were 26-16, good for a .619 winning percentage, since snapping the 13-game losing streak back on August 8. Moreover, the team had learned to play at home, giving the multitudes their money's worth, going 28-21 after starting the year 7-20 at Mile High. Since that 16-40 start, the Rockies had gone a very respectable, very nonexpansionlike 46-50.

In June, they were being compared to the 1962 Mets. By late September, they were being compared to the best expansion team ever—the 1961 Los Angeles Angels. They had now leapfrogged well past the Mets and Padres and had pulled within a game of the Marlins. The whole season had turned around.

"There's a lot of pride in this room," said Eric Young. "People don't realize that sometimes. They think it's all about money or playing for personal numbers, but these are all guys who came here to make their names and establish themselves as winners. It hurt every guy in here individually when we weren't winning. But now, we're playing great. It's too bad it took most of the season for things to come together, but I think it says something about our team that we didn't quit when so many other teams are packing it in."

All of a sudden, the Rockies were providing good news—and on the field, for a change:

• Andres Galarraga's quest for the batting title had become a civic venture. His name was never found among the batting leaders because he still lacked the necessary plate appearances to qualify. As the Tuesday night game with the Padres commenced, Cat had 460 plate appearances—42 short of the magic number —and at his current pace, he figured to finish with 500 plate appearances, two short of the number necessary to qualify for the batting title. But he was not merely hanging on, hoping to get plate appearances; he was still swinging a surreally hot bat. He came in hitting safely in 17 of 18 games, a .403 average, and had hit .348 in the 31 games since coming off the disabled list. His current magical number? He was hitting .377 to Tony Gwynn's .358.

• Charlie Hayes, the forgotten Rockie whose numbers far exceeded his Q-rating, had just been named National League Player of the Week for hitting .385 with an .808 slugging percentage. He still couldn't find his way into fans' hearts with his lapses into uninspired play, but his offensive statistics, especially at Mile High, continued to impress. "It's the way the media chooses to portray you," Hayes would say over and over again, like a mantra. "I'm not a bad guy, but that's the way the media paints me. It's always been that way and I don't know why. I don't complain, I play hurt, I put up good numbers, but if somebody's going to be criticized, it's going to be Charlie. But it don't bother me. It don't bother me at all.''

No. Not much.

• Joe Girardi, who missed 60 games in June, July and August after his hand surgery, returned with a flourish. Baylor tried something unusual, inserting a slow-footed catcher into the second spot in the lineup, and Girardi responded by hitting .318 in 29 starts at number two.

• The bullpen, which had been primarily responsible for the team's miserable start, had found its niche. Ruffin, who had been teetering on the brink of being released earlier in the season, regained control of his nasty slider and became a left-handed ace. Reed remained murder on right-handed hitters with his submarine delivery. Holmes continued to be one of the team's best comeback stories, converting on 22 straight save opportunities.

• And then there was some of the best news of all—David Nied's return. Nied, who had plummeted to rock bottom and gone on the disabled list in early June, returned nearly three months later to give the Rockies brass hope for the next season. He came back on September 12 in Pittsburgh and gave up just one earned run in three and two-thirds innings, then followed that up with back-to-back five-inning scoreless efforts at home against Los Angeles and San Diego.

Earlier in the home stand, Bob Gebhard and Jerry McMorris received some more good news: Baseball was realigning, with each league splitting into three divisions and sending four teams each to the playoffs. The Rockies made out like bandits, escaping the talent-rich Atlanta Braves and moving into the reconfigured National League West, a division that figured to be, at least in the short term, the weakest in baseball.

Without playing a game, the Rockies had moved up to fourth place in their division, checking into the same division with the San Diego Padres, Los Angeles Dodgers and San Francisco Giants. This was a competitive godsend. The Giants, who were battling for the West crown, were a strong team now but had a woefully weak minor-league system. And there were some questions about the new ownership's financial abilities, particularly with the team stuck in windy, miserable Candlestick Park. The Padres had some decent, young talent, the result of the many cost-cutting trades they had forged during the year, but the team's ownership was notoriously cheap, and wasn't likely to spend money on a player who might put the Padres over the top. The other competitor, the Dodgers, had almost unlimited resources, but in recent years their once-respected farm system had gone on the blink. More, management had done a poor job using its resources, spending boatloads of money on underachieving free agents like Darryl Strawberry and Eric Davis.

This left the Rockies in an enviable position and with a chance to compete for a divisional title much sooner than anybody could have expected. Their farm system was still just a year old and quite underdeveloped, but the business success of the team had left them with a war chest they could never have envisioned. "It's going to be interesting, a couple of years from now, we're going to be in that position, not quite in the pennant race but not quite out of it either, when we're going to have to decide whether to make that move that gets us over the top," said Gebhard. "We still have to approach this with a seven-team-division mind-set. We can't let ourselves be rushed. But there's no question, we're closer now than we were before realignment. I've talked to Jerry McMorris about this. I know he's very competitive and there's going to be pressure from him, from the fans and from the media, and they're going to want to know, 'Why isn't Gebhard doing something?' That's where we're going to have to be patient."

For all the good news afield, the best was still in the orange-and-blue stands of Mile High Stadium. Four days earlier, on September 17, the Rocky Mountain region's multitudes set the all-time single-season attendance record, a mark set just one year earlier by the world-champion Toronto Blue Jays. On that day, the Rockies went past Toronto and settled in at 4,054,587 fans, eclipsing Toronto's record of 4,028,318.

By September 21, publicist Mike Swanson was stretching the bounds of creativity as he attempted to lend some perspective to the team's remarkable drawing power:

"Tomorrow, the Rox should pass its 30th state in population when the club surpasses Louisiana's total of 4,287,000," he wrote in the game notes. "The Rockies are the only team in baseball to have more fans come to their games than the total that live in their state. The season total entering tonight stands at 4,209,984, which is 739,984 higher than Colorado's population in the 1990 census. The next closest attendance figure to its state's general population is Baltimore's 3,230,985, which is 1,677,014 less than the resident total for Maryland." Over the next few days, Swanson would break out the world atlas and enumerate the countries' populations that the Rockies had beaten. Look out, Moldova . . .

The only discordant notes: Dante Bichette's personal-best season had been cut short four days earlier in a game against Houston by a Doug Jones pitch that cracked a bone in his hand. He had quickly established himself as a Rockies regular and fan favorite in right field, brandishing his distinctive crow-hop and a rifle arm. When the Rockies asked a focus group of young and mostly female fans why they sat in the south stands, out behind right field, they answered, "Because Dante has a nice butt." His offensive numbers were not shabby, either, finishing up with a .310 average, 21 homers, 89 RBIs and 43 doubles.

The other problem area: Pitcher Greg Harris, who had been acquired from the Padres and was expected to excel as the team's staff ace, was struggling. By late September, Mile High's fans were booing him with unusual vigor. "I don't blame them," said Harris, who was more critical of himself than any leather-lunged fan. Rockies officials worried about Harris, but reminded themselves that he had pitched more than 360 innings when you added in his winter-ball efforts. For now, they would slough it off on a tired arm.

But compared to the early-season follies, when double-digit losses were the norm, life in expansionland was a veritable baseball Shangri-la. "I hate to think it's almost time to go back home," Baylor was saying, filling out the lineup card for game 153. "We were just getting things going. It's funny to talk about spring training and Opening Day because it all seems so long ago. But it also seems like it just happened yesterday, too.''

THIS WAS THE strangest chase for a batting title anyone could ever remember. Galarraga was leading the National League in hitting, but he was always, in a way, trailing. He led Tony Gwynn by 19 points as the Rockies and Padres did battle on September 21, but he trailed in his quest to get 502 plate appearances. Galarraga could still win the title, even if he came up short of 502, by absorbing whatever oh-fer was necessary to reach the magic number.

''I never knew about the rule until somebody mentioned it to me about two months ago,'' said Baylor. ''But that's what makes what Cat's doing so special. A lot of guys, if they're in a batting race, I've seen them duck it. They won't play against certain pitchers who they have trouble with. I've seen that happen. But Cat can't sit out against anybody. He not only has to play and get at-bats, but he has to keep hitting. The pressure is there for him every single day. He's got to stay healthy and he's got to hit. Even if he has the big lead in batting average, he doesn't know if he's going to come up short in plate appearances. He doesn't know what kind of 0-for-whatever he's gonna have to take at the end of the year, if he has to take any at all. Right now, it doesn't look like he'll have to take more than an 0-for-4 or something in that area. But he's been injured twice, and he keeps stretching it for those triples. You think back to one day earlier, he takes a pitch off the hand, he breaks it and his season is over, and there goes the batting title.''

There was some effort throughout the league to disparage Galarraga's title pursuit. ''He's playing in a hitter's paradise,'' went the argument. ''Altitude, the huge field, it's a tainted mark. Plus, he may have to win the thing on a rules technicality.'' One manager, San Diego's Jim Riggleman, had publicly questioned the Galarraga candidacy; it wasn't until the Padres returned to town that Riggleman apologized for his remarks.

Baylor, for one, was tired of having to defend Galarraga's magical season. "He's just pounding the ball," said the manager. "Ever since starting 0-for-12 in spring training, I mean, he's just never quit hitting. He hits, he goes on the disabled list, he comes off and keeps hitting. And they haven't been cheap hits. He certainly hasn't had any leg hits. He's just having one of those years.

"I keep hearing about our ballpark. But how about guys who win the title playing on Astroturf? You look at the guys in Atlanta —David Justice, Ron Gant, Fred McGriff—they play in the 'Launching Pad' [Atlanta's Fulton County Stadium] and nobody says there should be an asterisk next to their home-run marks. Compare Oakland versus Boston and those ballparks. Every foul ball in Oakland is going to be caught; in Boston, the ball goes in the stands and Wade Boggs has another chance for a base hit. Does that mean you should diminish Boggs's batting titles?"

Baylor and Galarraga could also point to this handy statistic: While Cat was feasting at Mile High, hitting a robust .402 there, he was also hitting .344 on the road—no altitude, no short left-field porches, no giant outfields.

As for Cat himself, he seemed alternately oblivious and buoyant about the chase for the title. Pressure? Yeah, there was pressure—pressure to be the first expansion player to win a title, pressure to become the first Venezuelan batting champion. The latter was terribly important to Galarraga, who knew that most of the other baseball-player–producing Latin countries had produced batting champions. But Galarraga seemed to be handling all the media attention and all the off-field promotions with quiet equanimity. "At times, it makes me crazy, phone calls all the time," he said. "Because I'm not only doing this for myself and the people here, but I'm doing this for Venezuela. I keep getting calls and letters from Venezuela, people in the media calling. It's hard because I don't like to say no to anybody."

Cat's chase had become front-page news back home in Venezuela. During an earlier trip to Florida, Galarraga had done three back-to-back-to-back one-hour TV interviews with Venezuelan crews. And as the Rockies came home for the final 13-game home stand, Venezuelan TV and newspaper personnel were on hand. It was during the last home stand that Galarraga had asked the Rockies to refrain from playing the theme from *The Pink Panther* before he stepped into the batter's box, and instead play a Venezuelan song, "Bottate la Bola," which means "Hit the ball" and is a song played during the winter leagues after a hitter smacks a home run.

Galarraga's unprecedented batting quest provided Venezuelans with more than an opportunity to swell with national pride; it provided a diversion, a beacon of good news in a country that had been beset by mostly bad news in recent years. In a story commissioned by *The Denver Post,* writer John Commins, an editor with *The Daily Journal,* an English-language newspaper in Caracas, described how Cat's exploits had helped to lift the sagging spirits of a once-vibrant nation.

"There isn't much to cheer about in Venezuela these days, unless you follow the exploits of El Gato. The country is awash in political scandal and economic hardship.

"Twice in a year and a half Venezuelans have weathered coup attempts as well as a 30-day period this spring in which three different presidents served following the constitutional ouster of President Carlos Andres Perez, who was removed from office after being indicted on corruption charges.

"The citizens of this oil-rich nation, many of whom just 10 years ago led a lifestyle that was the envy of South America, now face an 'official' annual inflation rate of about 35 percent. Some Latin economists say it's unofficially closer to 50 percent.

"The country is in decay.

"By conservative estimates, at least half the nation lives in poverty. The cars in the street get older. The potholes get bigger. The crime rate skyrockets. The murders are numerous and are depicted on the back pages of the newspapers on Mondays.

"A presidential election is set for December. With the new administration it is inevitable that severe measures will be implemented. And there is widespread speculation that oil prices will continue to fall, further depleting the government's chief source of revenue.

"But as in other countries, Venezuelans use sports to escape the gloom and doom of politics. . . ."

Galarraga could not escape the heightening sense that he was doing something not only for himself but for his entire nation. But somehow, he seemed largely immune to the pressures. Every day seemed the same: Do something for the Rockies' promotions people, answer the enlarging stack of fan mail, do a couple of interviews and put up another 3-for-5 night.

"I can guarantee you he's more aware of it now than a month ago," said Baylor. "For a while, I'm not sure it was in the front of his mind. But now he's down to the final 10 games. If Tony Gwynn doesn't come back from his physical problems, maybe he feels some relief. But Gwynn is talking now about coming back the last week of the season, so now Gwynn's not a ghost anymore."

Gwynn, who was stuck at .358, had not played since September 5. He had required arthroscopic knee surgery on September 12, but had resumed batting practice and was talking about a final push the last week of the season. "If that happens, and Gwynn is hot, then Cat has to think about the subtraction," said Baylor. "But I'll tell you this: Gwynn better fall out of bed hitting the baseball. He's got to get four, five hits that last week. And that's not an easy thing to do."

Certainly, Galarraga was not giving up any ground. He came to bat in the first inning of the September 21 game and hit a harmless nubber down the third-base line, one of the few balls he hadn't smacked in recent weeks. This led to another rare occurrence: a leg base hit.

One-for-one.

An inning later, Galarraga was back at the plate with the bases loaded. He ripped a Todd Worrell pitch to left field for a run-scoring single.

Two-for-two.

In the fourth inning of a typically wild Mile High game, Galarraga stepped up with one out and nobody on. He thrashed a double to the left-center-field wall.

Three-for-three.

The Rockies led, 8–4, entering the bottom of the sixth, a time in the game when Baylor might, in the past, have given Cat the rest of the night off. But he was swinging the bat so well, getting those much-needed plate appearances. The first pitch from Andy Mauser was a high room-service fastball. Galarraga turned on it, but hit a bullet one-hopper right at the shortstop, who threw him out easily.

Three-for-four.

He wasn't finished. Cat was at bat in the bottom of the eighth inning, the Rockies still leading, 8–4, in an interminable, sloppy game. Padres relief pitcher Gene Harris tried to sneak a fastball past Galarraga on the outside corner. He swung late, but the ball went screaming past the first-base bag and down the right-field line for a double.

Four-for-five.

The hits—and errors and wild pitches—just kept on coming. Galarraga came up yet again in the seven-run eighth inning, lining out sharply to the second baseman.

Four-for-six.

The batting title, and those 502 plate appearances, seemed more accessible than ever. His updated number was .381, 23 points ahead of Gwynn, who sat on the opposing bench and resigned himself to the inevitable. "It's his to lose," Gwynn said later. "I just don't know if I can come back."

Even more, with the 15–4 victory over the Padres, the Rockies won their 63rd game, guaranteeing they would avoid a 100-loss season. They also moved percentage points ahead of the Marlins—the Rockies at 63-90, the Marlins at 62-89. The last time the Rockies had led the Marlins in the standings was on April 25, and the Rockies were 6-10 compared to Florida's 6-11. That was almost five months ago. Now the Rockies were back on top.

Sixty-three. That was the Rockies' magic number.

"Huge, this is huge," said Bear, smiling broadly. "Because of all the negative comments and all that crap. Sixty-three became our unspoken goal. Of course, lately, it hasn't been so unspoken. Almost every night, we would look at one another after a win and go like this." Bear presented his hands, 10 fingers extended, then subtracted one after another after another. They had reached 63. This was an accomplishment.

"I can look back at my book of crossword puzzles and look at the day when I wrote down 15-37 in the margins," he said. "Those crosswords were my way of keeping my sanity. Now I can put 63-90. Always, deep down, I thought it was going to get better. It had to, didn't it?"

THE FORECASTERS called for a wretched day when the Rockies played their final home game of the 1993 season, just as they had for Opening Day at Mile High. Once again, they were wrong. September 26 dawned warm and sunny, a perfect, pristine autumn day in the Rockies. And, as was the case on Opening Day, the fans arrived ridiculously early, hoping to soak up as much atmosphere and baseball as they possibly could before winter stole their team away.

"I say we forget the baseball game and just have a giant autograph session," Joe Girardi was telling teammates as they stretched before the game. "That's what these people would prefer, anyway."

The kids, the autograph hounds, were leaning over the railing some two hours before game time, loudly beseeching their heroes for autographs. "Dan-tayyyy! Dan-tayyyy!" they screamed. "Cat, please, just sign this ball. Cat, oh, please, Cat!!!"

On this day, the love affair would be fully consummated. On this day, there were the final, dying echoes of a civic primal scream that had lasted since the day the Rockies arrived in Denver back in early April. One more chance to watch Cat. One more day to pay homage to Armando Reynoso, who saved a floundering pitching staff in mid-season. One more day to sit in the sun and consume a hot dog and revel in the fact that the Rocky Mountain region was now major-league.

"Yo, EY, you going deep today?" Freddie Benavides asked Eric Young. The Rockies' second-baseman-turned-outfielder smiled. "Yeah, EY's going downtown," said Chris Jones. Young and everybody else knew: He had not hit a home run since Opening Day in Denver. He had gone more than 500 plate appearances without going deep. By now the media was giving him a good-natured hard time about his power outage, not to mention his teammates and his unofficial fan club out in the left-field bleachers. "They've been telling me now for a couple of weeks," Young said before the game. "They've been saying, 'EY, you hit one Opening Day and you owe us one the last day.' "

Young is not, by any stretch, a home-run hitter. In fact, the Rockies' management felt that Young's home run in the first game in Denver was the worst thing that could have happened to this spray hitter; suddenly, he thought he was Babe Ruth, overswinging, going after high fastballs. During batting practice, Amos Otis would make sure to keep him from the home-run–hitting mind-set; every time EY would go deep in BP, Otis would tell him either to bunt or to hit the next pitch to the opposite field.

But on this day, Young could not resist. He bounded into the clubhouse late in the morning and told the world he was going to hit a home run. "Damn right he did," said Otis. "First thing he said to me today. I said, 'Yeah, right, just get a couple of hits, okay?' "

Baylor didn't want to hear about it. "He knows better than to talk that kind of nonsense around me," he said with a devilish grin.

An Eric Young home run? That would be just a little too Disney-esque, a bit too contrived. But, then, the whole Rockies season had been something of a storybook. First, there were the fans, who, on this final home date, topped out the attendance record at a ridiculous and thoroughly astounding number: 4,483,350. "It would have been four and a half million if not for the two rainouts," McMorris lamented. But as the season neared its exclamatory conclusion, the fans were not the only story. By now, their ardor and loyalty had been rewarded by a team that was playing some of the best baseball this side of the Atlanta Braves.

The final home game proved little more than a continuation of a trend that had begun the day after the hellish 13-game losing streak had been snapped. The Cincinnati Reds scored in the first inning, but the Rockies responded in the third when Galarraga (of course) hit a two-run homer and took the requisite curtain call. The Rockies continued to pour it in and led, 7–2, moving into the bottom of the fifth.

That's when Young, the man who hit the Opening Day homer that was so redolent with possibility, stepped to the plate against Reds reliever Johnny Ruffin. The count moved to two balls and one strike when Young eyed a high fastball. He hit a fly ball that instantly appeared doomed for the foul territory in left. Young stood at home plate, not to admire his handiwork but to watch his shot settle harmlessly in the stands. "I kept thinking, 'Run, EY,' " said Baylor. Otis kept muttering, "Who does he think he is, standing there like that? Babe Ruth?" Slowly, the ball began fading back toward fair territory. Young was beginning to get an idea. The stadium erupted in cheers. "Got over the fence by at least two rows, didn't it?" he said later.

Home run.

One on Opening Day and one on the last day. A dream season now had a perfect symmetry. National League president Bill White had been in the Mile High stands on the first day and he had been there on the last day. Don Zimmer, who had replaced the still-airborne Royster the first day, stood in the third-base coaching box on the last day, once again waving Young in. "EY only hits homers when there are crowds of 70,000 or more," chided reliever Bruce Ruffin.

But there was more. In the seventh inning, with the Rockies leading, 8–5, Young came up again against Cincinnati's Scott Service. This time the ball settled easily into the left-center-field stands. "I knew it was gone when I hit it," Young said, sounding like your basic home-run hitter. Baylor was more bemused than anything. "EY hitting two homers in a ball game," he said. "You might have seen it for the last time in your life."

By the time it was over, the game proved better than an

autograph session. The Rockies won, 12–7, in a fairy-tale game that concluded a storybook home season. They had finished with a 39-42 home record, not bad after their horrendous 7-20 start. They had avoided 100 losses. They had broken the all-time attendance record, a mark that would probably never be broken. And Galarraga was on the threshold of history, close to becoming the first expansion player ever to win a batting title.

After the game, the fans stayed and the players stayed, for presentations and thank-yous and a final confirmation that this had, indeed, been something very special and unusual. The fans didn't want it to end, and there was the sense that the players didn't want it to end, either. There had been a unique symbiosis between the region and this team, a thoroughly mutual love affair. The players, most of them baseball nomads, hadn't really known what to expect when they arrived in Denver to find people attending their first-ever Mile High batting practice. But as Baylor tearfully thanked the fans after the game . . . as Young, his eyes moist, led a victory lap around the stadium, high-fiving hands being extended through the mesh-wire fence in left . . . as Girardi spoke eloquently to the power of support . . . as Jerald Clark beat both fists to his heart and gestured to the crowd before disappearing into the clubhouse, it was clear that the joy in the stands had been shared by these athletes. Players tend to sublimate their emotions, but you didn't have to look too deeply for genuine gratitude and even admiration.

"I've never seen anything like it," Baylor said later. "The boos are minimal, and they don't last until the next at-bat. In some cities, they last for a month. Playing here brought out the best in our players."

The Rockies players fed off the energy and the love they found in those stands. There were long losing streaks and stretches of terrible baseball, but the people kept showing up, and the players kept competing, and by this time the Rockies were playing some of the best ball in the league. Some teams, like the Reds, had fallen from contention and lost their edge, their desire. But four and a half million souls refused to let this ragtag team fall into the abyss. The Rocky Mountain region had received baseball due to the sheer force of civic will. The late success of this team was no less attributable to their devotion and passion.

They had waited 30 years, dealt with dashed hopes and monstrous disappointments. But it had been worth it. Hell yeah, they said in a joyful cacophony, it had been worth it.

19

Unfinished Business

THE ROCKIES' long, strange trip began with a parade and ended with a pennant race. While the club still bathed in the afterglow of their triumphant final home stand, there remained five road games with the two teams that just happened to be in the throes of the most epic divisional race in all of baseball—the San Francisco Giants and the Atlanta Braves. The Rockies would play the Giants twice at Candlestick, then finish out the year with three in Atlanta, knowing that they, incredibly, held the key to the pennant chase in their hands.

"For 10 days now, guys have been saying, 'I hope when we get to San Francisco, it counts for something,' " said Don Zimmer as he stood behind the batting cage before the first game of the trip on September 28. "Let's be honest. Guys are going to be more excited to play in this playoff atmosphere with all these fans and all the national exposure than they would be playing out the string in Pittsburgh or San Diego."

As evening fell on the unseasonably warm Stick—usually, by 6:30, the winds come howling in off the bay—Zimmer found himself glancing at the JumboTron above the left-center-field wall, watching the Braves lose to the Astros, and remembering his own team, the 1978 Red Sox. The parallels between that team and these Giants were too obvious to miss. The Giants had grabbed a huge late-season lead over their competitors just as the Red Sox had pulled away from the Yankees. But both leads dissipated in the heat of August and September, and both teams were branded as chokers, only to see the Giants of 1993 and Red Sox of 1978 stage gallant, late-season runs to reclaim their spot atop the division. "People talked about how we choked, right?" Zimmer asked. "How come nobody remembers that we won nine in a row at the end of the year to be in a position to get into the one-game playoff?"

The day began with the Giants one game behind, but just seconds before the first pitch of the Giants-Rockies game, the JumboTron showed Houston's Doug Jones sneaking a fastball past Atlanta's Jeff Blauser, and the Giants were a half-game out. Three hours later, it was all tied again as Steve Scarsone hit a three-run homer in a 6–4 Giants victory.

But the Rockies were not content to roll over. They were taking the responsibility of a pennant race seriously. Baylor continued to play his best team, continued to manage like it was the seventh game of the World Series. His team's 66 victories already guaranteed them the mantle as the best National League expansion team ever, but Baylor was still hoping his team could make some noise, show people the Rockies story wasn't all about crowd support. The Marlins had faded, having fallen three back, and the Rockies were hoping to put them out of their misery. And, of course, there was still the outside shot at winning four straight and reaching 70, tying the all-time expansion record.

"Look, we have absolutely nothing to lose," Baylor was saying before the second and final game of the Giants series. "We can use this as a building block and we still have goals to shoot for. But all the pressure is on them."

The Rockies looked like a team enjoying a sunny day at the park, driving a stake into the heart of the Giants' pennant hopes with an unlikely 5–3 victory. Daryl Boston hit two home runs and Nelson Liriano, who had joined the club late in the season and grabbed the starting-shortstop job, hit one. The Braves beat the Astros, and it was all even.

In the Giants' clubhouse, manager Dusty Baker gracefully handled wave after wave of media as they wedged their way into his small office. It was seven months ago that Baker and Baylor, the old friends, had met on the field in Tucson for the Rockies' first exhibition game. Now Baylor and his team were doing everything in their power to make a mess out of the race. "I've known that man for 25 years, and he's not going to give in," said Baker of Baylor. "Really, this is their World Series and playoffs. They can get their final satisfaction of the season by beating us or Atlanta. That team's got a lot of pride. And they're a lot better team than the one we saw earlier in the year. They have a more set lineup, their starters are getting them deeper into the game and they have more defined roles for their bullpen.

"I just hope they play Atlanta as tough as they played us."

Ohhh, Atlanta . . . The number kept flashing in front of the Rockies' faces, like a neon presence—0-10. They were 0-10 against the Braves this inaugural season; and a truly ugly 0-10, including a game on May 8 at Mile High when they blew a 6–0 lead in the eighth inning and managed to lose, 8–7, on Sid Bream's pinch-hit, opposite-field, altitude-aided, pop-fly grand-slam home run. This time, the Rockies said, it would be different. This time, they brought a competitive team into Atlanta's Fulton County Stadium. The Giants and Braves were now tied on October 1, after 159 games, and the Rockies would finish their exultant first season in the lion's mouth.

True to form, they were devoured.

Three games, three Atlanta victories, all with varying degrees of difficulty. The Braves won the first game, 7–4, as Greg Harris continued to look like a fellow who had pitched too many innings. He was gone after four innings of six-run baseball, leaving the Rockies' brass wondering whether they hadn't worked a questionable deal after all. Saturday's game was a blowout, 10–1 Braves, as pitcher Greg Maddux shackled the Rockies and limited them to four hits.

The lone bright spot came when The Big Cat came to the plate for plate appearance 502, thus qualifying him for—and, by this point, guaranteeing him—his first batting title, the first batting title for a Venezuelan and the first title for an expansion player. Fittingly, he lined a single. Afterward, he was surrounded by Venezuelan media who had come up from Caracas to chronicle the event. He donned a T-shirt with the Venezuelan flag and the words "Gloria al Bravo Pueblo," meaning "Glory to the brave." His smile was incandescent. He had traveled the long, hard road back.

But there was still baseball: 161 games, and it was still tied. This was just the 10th time in baseball history that two teams had gone into the final game of the season in a dead heat. It happened in 1908 (Chicago Cubs and New York Giants), 1944 (St. Louis Browns and Detroit Tigers), 1946 (St. Louis Cardinals and Brooklyn Dodgers), 1949 (New York Yankees and Boston Red Sox), 1951 (New York Giants and Brooklyn Dodgers), 1959 (Los Angeles Dodgers and Milwaukee Braves), 1964 (St. Louis Cardinals and Cincinnati Reds), 1967 (Boston Red Sox and Minnesota Twins) and 1982 (Milwaukee Brewers and Baltimore Orioles). "If you're a fan, you're rooting for a playoff," said Baylor. "As well as these two teams have played, they really deserve a chance to play one another to decide the thing." Zimmer had a slightly different view: "I can't stand those goddamn one-game playoffs," he said, visions of Bucky Dent's homer dancing in his head. "If you're going to do it, make it two-of-three. The game is played over such a long haul, it's ridiculous to have one game decide it."

The playoff would prove not to be necessary. In the afternoon, lefty Tom Glavine outpitched Colorado's David Nied for a 5−3 Braves victory—their 13th straight against the Rockies and their 104th of the season. Now all they could do was sit in the clubhouse, chow down on sandwiches and beer, watch television and wait. Meanwhile, out in the stadium, tens of thousands of fans stayed behind to share the moment, to watch the Dodgers spank the Giants on the JumboTron in the final game of the year, giving the Braves their third-straight divisional title.

"Remarkable," said Braves general manager John Schuerholz. "It's been a remarkable run for both teams. You hate to see anybody lose. Imagine winning 103 games and finishing second. Incredible."

The Rockies players and staff knew something else, though: *Their* season had been incredible. It had been an inaugural ball. It had been a crazy, wondrous romp, and as the team dressed and wandered around the clubhouse, waiting for the bus to take them to the airport, there was a palpable sense of satisfaction. They had been more than a simple part of history; they had also made their own history. The story of the Rockies' first year would not be written entirely in the Mile High stands, after all. It took almost 100 games, but the nomads and the might-have-beens and the castoffs metamorphosed into a pretty damn competitive baseball team.

"You know, we've been through so many battles, and when you're in those battles, you get to know one another," Steve Reed said. "What we learned is this team has a lot of guys with pride who won't give up. We had the bad start and that 13-game losing streak, but to see the way we turned it around is really inspiring."

What a joyride: They won 67 games, the most ever for a National League expansion team. They boasted the National League batting champion. They broke every attendance record known to American professional sports. They finished three games ahead of the Florida Marlins, who most had conceded at mid-season to be the far superior team, only to watch the Fish go 18-35 down the stretch. And they forged as good an in-season comeback story as any in the game.

When the Rockies dropped a ridiculously sloppy double-header to the Padres in San Diego on August 6, their losing streak reached 13, their record fell to 36-74 and the prospect of 110 losses seemed painfully inevitable. But something happened. Maybe it was Cat's continued brilliance. Maybe it was the sudden resilience and steadiness of the bullpen, which finished the season by going 14-3 with 14 saves over the last 42 games. Maybe it was the starting pitching, which, while not overwhelming, gave the team more six-inning efforts than ever before. Maybe it was the fans, an amazing total of 4,483,350, who kept coming by the hundreds of thousands despite the defeats. Maybe it was all of that. But from August 8 until the end of the season, the Rockies went an incredible 31-21, nearly a .600 winning percentage. They won 14 games in August and 17 in September, the first expansion team ever to have a winning record in that month.

As the team waited for the bus, phone numbers and insults were traded. Reed jabbed Charlie Hayes, telling him how he'd have Hayes falling into the third-base dugout with his delivery. Hayes insisted he could coax a walk from Reed in his first at-bat, then take him deep the next. Gary Wayne shook Galarraga's hand and congratulated him on his dream season. This was the happiest sixth-place team in baseball history.

On the charter flight home that evening, the attendant walked through the aisle with glasses of champagne. "These are on Cat," she said. A nice gesture. Within a half hour, Galarraga would be back in his seat, fast asleep. The coming weeks would be no less hectic; there would be a press conference the next day in Denver, a few days' respite in his Florida home, and then a triumphant return to Caracas, where he was to get a hero's welcome. Now the question was whether Galarraga, a free agent, would return to Denver. In the middle of the plane, Joe Girardi was sounding like a cantankerous radio talk-show host, arguing with Willie Blair about the coaching acumen of Kentucky basketball coach Rick Pitino. Greg Harris wondered aloud about his contract status and his inability to get umpires' strike calls before joining the talk-show fray. Amos Otis and Jerry Royster, the two coaches, sat near each other and quietly contemplated their futures. Both of them knew they were gone; it was just a matter of when. Of course, Royster had more compelling things to consider; the man who had missed part of Denver's Opening Day while attending his mother-in-law's funeral would return home to his very pregnant wife. "They're inducing labor tomorrow," he said. Jayhawk Owens joked about how all the other players would be returning to Denver to girlfriends or wives. "I need a life," he said. "I don't even have a pet."

Some would be returning home to warmer Southern climes. Some would be staying in Denver. Others would take time off, then go to either instructional ball or winter ball to refine their games. For a lot of them, the grim realization was at hand: They would not be coming back together as teammates. There were free agents and guys who disappointed and other business considerations. Many of these baseball nomads would continue their wandering. But they could always say they once had Denver, and 1993, and that magical and sometimes mysterious expansion year.

As the plane descended, the long season finally, officially finished, the Rockies players marked the moment with grim solemnity and proper reverence.

They had a pillow fight.

Colorado Rockies Team Statistics

Batter	AVG	G	AB	R	H	2B	3B	HR	RBI	SH	SF	HP	BB	SO	SB	CS	GI DP	E
Benavides, Freddie	.286	74	213	20	61	10	3	3	26	3	1	0	6	27	3	2	4	13
Bichette, Dante	.310	141	538	93	167	43	5	21	89	0	8	7	28	99	14	8	7	9
Boston, Daryl	.261	124	291	46	76	15	1	14	40	0	1	2	26	57	1	6	5	2
Castellano, Pedro	.183	34	71	12	13	2	0	3	7	0	0	0	8	16	1	1	1	4
Castilla, Vinny	.255	105	337	36	86	9	7	9	30	0	5	2	13	45	2	5	10	11
Clark, Jerald	.282	140	478	65	135	26	6	13	67	3	1	10	20	60	9	6	12	12
Cole, Jr., Alex	.256	126	348	50	89	9	4	0	24	1	2	2	43	58	30	13	6	4
Gainer, Jay	.171	23	41	4	7	0	0	3	6	0	0	0	4	12	1	1	0	1
Galarraga, Andres	.370	120	470	71	174	35	4	22	98	0	6	6	24	73	2	4	9	11
Girardi, Joe	.290	86	310	35	90	14	5	3	31	12	1	3	24	41	5	6	6	6
Hayes, Charlie	.305	157	573	89	175	45	2	25	98	1	8	5	43	82	11	6	25	20
Jones, Calvin	.273	86	209	29	57	11	4	5	31	5	1	0	10	48	9	4	6	2
Liriano, Nelson	.305	48	151	28	46	6	3	2	15	5	1	0	18	22	5	4	6	6
Mejia, Roberto	.231	65	229	31	53	14	5	5	20	4	1	1	13	63	4	1	2	12
Murphy, Dale	.143	26	42	1	6	1	0	0	7	0	2	0	5	15	0	0	5	0
Owens, J.	.209	13	86	12	18	5	0	3	6	0	0	2	6	30	1	0	1	7
Sheaffer, Danny	.278	82	216	26	60	9	1	4	32	2	6	1	8	15	2	3	9	2
Tatum, Jim	.204	92	98	7	20	5	0	1	12	0	2	1	5	27	0	0	0	2
Wedge, Eric	.182	9	11	2	2	0	0	0	1	0	0	0	0	4	0	0	0	0
Young, Eric	.269	144	490	82	132	16	8	3	42	4	4	4	63	41	42	19	9	18
Young, Gerald	.053	19	19	5	1	0	0	0	1	0	0	0	4	1	0	1	2	2
PITCHERS	.132	162	296	14	39	3	1	2	21	27	1	0	17	108	2	0	0	23
TOTALS	.273	162	5517	758	1507	278	59	142	704	70	52	46	388	944	145	90	125	167

Pitcher	ERA	W	L	G	GS	CG	SHO	SV	IP	AB	H	R	ER	HR	HB	BB	SO	WP	OPP AVG
Aldred, Scott	10.80	0	0	5	0	0	0	0	6.2	28	10	10	8	1	1	9	5	1	.157
Ashby, Andy	8.50	0	4	20	9	0	0	1	54.0	236	89	54	51	5	3	32	33	2	.177
Blair, Willie	4.75	6	10	46	18	1	0	0	146.0	601	184	90	77	20	3	42	84	6	.106
Bottenfield, Kent	6.10	3	5	14	14	1	0	0	76.2	285	86	53	52	13	1	38	10	0	.102
Fredrickson, Scott	6.21	0	1	25	0	0	0	0	29.0	115	33	25	20	3	1	17	20	4	.287
Grant, Mark	12.56	0	1	14	0	0	0	1	14.1	61	23	20	20	4	0	6	8	2	.177
Harris, Greg	6.50	1	8	13	13	0	0	0	70.1	294	88	62	53	15	4	30	40	4	.299
Henry, Butch	6.59	2	8	20	15	1	0	0	84.2	354	117	66	62	14	1	24	39	1	.331
Holmes, Darren	4.05	3	3	62	0	0	0	25	66.2	252	56	31	30	6	2	20	60	2	.222
Hurst, Bruce	5.19	0	1	3	3	0	0	0	8.2	31	6	5	5	1	0	3	6	1	.194
Knudson, Mark	22.24	0	0	4	0	0	0	0	5.2	34	16	14	14	4	0	5	3	2	.471
Leskanic, Curt	5.37	1	5	18	8	0	0	0	57.0	222	59	10	34	7	2	27	10	8	.266
Moore, Marcus	6.84	3	1	27	0	0	0	0	26.1	103	30	25	20	4	1	20	13	4	.291
Munoz, Mike	4.50	2	1	21	0	0	0	0	18.0	68	21	12	9	1	0	9	16	2	.309
Nied, David	5.17	5	9	16	16	1	0	0	87.0	335	99	53	50	8	1	42	46	1	.296
Painter, Lance	6.00	2	2	10	6	1	0	0	39.0	156	52	26	26	5	0	9	16	2	.333
Parrett, Jeff	5.38	3	3	40	6	0	0	1	73.2	285	78	47	44	6	2	45	66	11	.274
Reed, Steve	4.48	9	5	64	0	0	0	3	84.1	309	80	47	42	13	3	30	51	1	.259
Reynoso, Armando	4.00	12	11	30	30	4	0	0	189.0	745	206	101	84	22	9	63	117	7	.277
Raffin, Bruce	3.87	6	5	59	12	0	0	2	139.2	539	145	71	60	10	1	69	116	8	.269
Sanford, Mo	5.30	1	2	11	6	0	0	0	35.2	133	37	25	21	4	0	27	36	2	.278
Service, Scott	9.64	0	0	3	0	0	0	0	4.2	20	8	5	5	1	1	1	3	0	.400
Shepherd, Keith	6.98	1	3	14	1	0	0	1	19.1	78	26	16	15	4	1	4	7	1	.333
Smith, Bryn	8.49	2	4	11	5	0	0	0	29.2	130	47	29	28	2	3	11	9	1	.362
Wayne, Gary	5.05	5	3	65	0	0	0	1	62.1	246	68	10	35	8	1	26	49	9	.276
TOTALS	5.41	67	95	162	162	9	0	35	1431.1	5660	1664	967	860	181	41	609	913	82	.294

The 1993 Colorado Rockies, Game by Game

Date	Location	Score	Won/Lost Record
April 5	New York	Mets 3, Rockies 0	0-1, .000
April 7	New York	Mets 6, Rockies 1	0-2, .000
April 9	Denver	Rockies 11, Expos 4	1-2, .333
April 10	Denver	Rockies 10, Expos 5	2-2, .500
April 11	Denver	Expos 19, Rockies 9	2-3, .400
April 13	Denver	Mets 8, Rockies 4	2-4, .333
April 14	Denver	Mets 6, Rockies 3	2-5, .286
April 15	Denver	Rockies 5, Mets 3	3-5, .375
April 16	Montreal	Expos 3, Rockies 2	3-6, .333
April 17	Montreal	Rockies 9, Expos 1	4-6, .400
April 18	Montreal	Expos 4, Rockies 2	4-7, .364
April 20	St. Louis	Cardinals 5, Rockies 0	4-8, .333
April 21	St. Louis	Rockies 11, Cardinals 2	5-8, .385
April 22	St. Louis	Cardinals 5, Rockies 2	5-9, .357
April 23	Denver	Rockies 5, Marlins 4	6-9, .400
April 24	Denver	Marlins 2, Rockies 1	6-10, .375
April 25	Denver	Marlins 11, Rockies 1	6-11, .353
April 26	Denver	Cubs 6, Rockies 3	6-12, .333
April 27	Denver	Rockies 11, Cubs 2	7-12, .368
April 28	Denver	Cardinals 7, Rockies 6	7-13, .350
April 29	Denver	Cardinals 5, Rockies 2	7-14, .333
April 30	Miami	Rockies 6, Marlins 2	8-14, .364
May 1	Miami	Marlins 7, Rockies 6	8-15, .348
May 2	Miami	Rockies 2, Marlins 1	9-15, .375
May 4	Chicago	Rockies 14, Cubs 13	10-15, .400
May 5	Chicago	Cubs 3, Rockies 2	10-16, .385
May 6	Denver	Braves 13, Rockies 3	10-17, .370
May 7	Denver	Braves 13, Rockies 5	10-18, .357
May 8	Denver	Braves 8, Rockies 7	10-19, .345
May 9	Denver	Braves 12, Rockies 8	10-20, .333
May 10	Denver	Rockies 7, Giants 4	11-20, .355

Date	Location	Score	Won/Lost Record
May 11	Denver	Giants 5, Rockies 3	11-21, .344
May 12	Denver	Giants 8, Rockies 2	11-22, .333
May 13	Denver	Giants 13, Rockies 8	11-23, .324
May 14	Cincinnati	Reds 13, Rockies 5	11-24, .314
May 15	Cincinnati	Reds 5, Rockies 3	11-25, .306
May 16	Cincinnati	Reds 14, Rockies 2	11-26, .297
May 17	San Diego	Padres 4, Rockies 0	11-27, .289
May 18	San Diego	Rockies 2, Padres 1	12-27, .308
May 19	San Diego	Padres 7, Rockies 3	12-28, .300
May 20	San Diego	Padres 5, Rockies 4	12-29, .293
May 21	Los Angeles	Dodgers 8, Rockies 0	12-30, .286
May 22	Los Angeles	Dodgers 4, Rockies 3	12-31, .279
May 23	Los Angeles	Dodgers 4, Rockies 0	12-32, .273
May 25	Houston	Rockies 7, Astros 5	13-32, .289
May 26	Houston	Rockies 3, Astros 2	14-32, .304
May 27	Houston	Astros 8, Rockies 0	14-33, .298
May 28	Denver	Phillies 15, Rockies 9	14-34, .292
May 29	Denver	Phillies 6, Rockies 0	14-35, .286
May 30	Denver	Phillies 18, Rockies 1	14-36, .280
May 31	Denver	Rockies 6, Pirates 2	15-36, .294
June 1	Denver	Pirates 8, Rockies 6	15-37, .288
June 2	Denver	Pirates 5, Rockies 3	15-38, .283
June 4	Philadelphia	Rockies 2, Phillies 1	16-38, .296
June 5	Philadelphia	Phillies 6, Rockies 2	16-39, .291
June 6	Philadelphia	Phillies 11, Rockies 7	16-40, .286
June 8	Pittsburgh	Rockies 4, Pirates 1	17-40, .298
June 9	Pittsburgh	Pirates 4, Rockies 1	17-41, .293
June 11	Denver	Rockies 5, Astros 4	18-41, .305
June 12	Denver	Rockies 14, Astros 11	19-41, .317
June 13	Denver	Rockies 9, Astros 1	20-41, .328
June 14	Denver	Dodgers 9, Rockies 4	20-42, .323
June 15	Denver	Dodgers 12, Rockies 4	20-43, .317
June 16	Denver	Rockies 7, Dodgers 6	21-43, .328
June 18	Denver	Padres 11, Rockies 1	21-44, .323

Date	Location	Score	Won/Lost Record
June 19	Denver	Rockies 17, Padres 3	22-44, .333
June 20	Denver	Rockies 3, Padres 1	23-44, .343
June 21	Denver	Rockies 5, Reds 4	24-44, .353
June 22	Denver	Reds 16, Rockies 13	24-45, .348
June 23	Denver	Rockies 15, Reds 5	25-45, .357
June 24	San Francisco	Giants 17, Rockies 2	25-46, .352
June 25	San Francisco	Giants 7, Rockies 2	25-47, .347
June 26	San Francisco	Rockies 5, Giants 1	26-47, .356
June 27	San Francisco	Giants 5, Rockies 0	26-48, .351
June 29	Atlanta	Braves 6, Rockies 4	26-49, .347
June 30	Atlanta	Braves 3, Rockies 2	26-50, .342
July 1	Atlanta	Braves 4, Rockies 0	26-51, .338
July 2	Denver	Cubs 11, Rockies 8	26-52, .333
July 3	Denver	Rockies 5, Cubs 4	27-52, .342
July 4	Denver	Rockies 3, Cubs 1	28-52, .350
July 5	Denver	Cubs 10, Rockies 1	28-53, .346
July 6	Denver	Rockies 8, Marlins 3	29-53, .354
July 7	Denver	Rockies 6, Marlins 5	30-53, .361
July 8	Denver	Rockies 3, Marlins 2	31-53, .369
July 9	St. Louis	Rockies 5, Cardinals 4	32-53, .376
July 10	St. Louis	Cardinals 9, Rockies 3	32-54, .372
July 11	St. Louis	Rockies 4, Cardinals 1	33-54, .379

All-Star Break

July 15	Chicago	Cubs 1, Rockies 0	33-55, .375
July 16	Chicago	Cubs 8, Rockies 2	33-56, .371
July 17	Chicago	Cubs 5, Rockies 1	33-57, .367
July 18	Chicago	Cubs 12, Rockies 2	33-58, .363
July 19	Miami	Marlins 3, Rockies 1	33-59, .359
July 20	Miami	Rockies 6, Marlins 3	34-59, .366
July 21	Miami	Marlins 6, Rockies 4	34-60, .362
July 22	Denver	Rockies 7, Cardinals 6	35-60, .368
July 23	Denver	Cardinals 13, Rockies 11	35-61, .365

Date	Location	Score	Won/Lost Record
July 24	Denver	Rockies 9, Cardinals 8	36-61, .371
July 25	Denver	Cardinals 5, Rockies 4	36-62, .367
July 26	Denver	Braves 12, Rockies 7	36-63, .364
July 27	Denver	Braves 10, Rockies 5	36-64, .360
July 28	Denver	Braves 3, Rockies 2	36-65, .356
July 30	Denver	Giants 10, Rockies 4	36-66, .353
July 31	Denver	Giants 4, Rockies 3	36-67, .350
August 1	Denver	Giants 6, Rockies 5	36-68, .346
August 2	Cincinnati	Reds 6, Rockies 2	36-69, .343
August 3	Cincinnati	Reds 5, Rockies 4	36-70, .340
August 4	Cincinnati	Reds 9, Rockies 3	36-71, .336
August 5	Cincinnati	Reds 11, Rockies 4	36-72, .333
August 6	San Diego	Padres 6, Rockies 3 (1st)	
		Padres 6, Rockies 2 (2nd)	36-74, .327
August 8	San Diego	Rockies 5, Padres 2	37-74, .333
August 9	Los Angeles	Rockies 3, Dodgers 2	38-74, .339
August 10	Los Angeles	Rockies 4, Dodgers 2	39-74, .345
August 11	Los Angeles	Rockies 3, Dodgers 2	40-74, .351
August 12	Los Angeles	Rockies 4, Dodgers 1	41-74, .357
August 13	Houston	Rockies 5, Astros 3	42-74, .362
August 14	Houston	Astros 9, Rockies 0	42-75, .359
August 15	Houston	Rockies 4, Astros 3	43-75, .364
August 17	Denver	Phillies 10, Rockies 7	43-76, .361
August 18	Denver	Phillies 7, Rockies 6	43-77, .358
August 19	Denver	Rockies 6, Phillies 5	44-77, .364
August 21	Denver	Rockies 4, Mets 3 (1st)	
		Rockies 8, Mets 6 (2nd)	46-77, .376
August 22	Denver	Rockies 4, Mets 3	47-77, .380
August 23	Philadelphia	Rockies 3, Phillies 2	48-77, .384
August 24	Philadelphia	Phillies 4, Rockies 2	48-78, .381
August 25	Philadelphia	Phillies 8, Rockies 5	48-79, .379
August 26	New York	Mets 7, Rockies 1	48-80, .375
August 27	New York	Mets 3, Rockies 2	48-81, .372
August 28	New York	Rockies 7, Mets 5	49-81, .377

Date	Location	Score	Won/Lost Record
August 29	New York	Rockies 6, Mets 1	50-81, .382
August 30	Denver	Expos 6, Rockies 1	50-82, .379
August 31	Denver	Expos 14, Rockies 3	50-83, .376
September 1	Denver	Expos 11, Rockies 3	50-84, .373
September 3	Denver	Rockies 7, Pirates 6	51-84, .378
September 4	Denver	Rockies 10, Pirates 4	52-84, .382
September 5	Denver	Rockies 4, Pirates 1	53-84, .387
September 6	Montreal	Expos 4, Rockies 3	53-85, .384
September 7	Montreal	Expos 4, Rockies 3	53-86, .381
September 8	Montreal	Expos 6, Rockies 1	53-87, .379
September 9	Pittsburgh	Rockies 10, Pirates 5	54-87, .383
September 10	Pittsburgh	Rockies 9, Pirates 8	55-87, .387
September 11	Pittsburgh	Rockies 3, Pirates 2	56-87, .392
September 12	Pittsburgh	Pirates 4, Rockies 3	56-88, .389
September 14	Denver	Rockies 9, Astros 4 (1st)	
		Rockies 6, Astros 5 (2nd)	58-88, .397
September 15	Denver	Rockies 6, Astros 4	59-88, .401
September 16	Denver	Rockies 6, Astros 3	60-88, .405
September 17	Denver	Rockies 12, Dodgers 3	61-88, .409
September 18	Denver	Dodgers 9, Rockies 0	61-89, .407
September 19	Denver	Rockies 8, Dodgers 5	62-89, .411
September 20	Denver	Padres 11, Rockies 7	62-90, .408
September 21	Denver	Rockies 15, Padres 4	63-90, .412
September 22	Denver	Rockies 11, Padres 4	64-90, .416
September 24	Denver	Rockies 9, Reds 2	65-90, .419
September 25	Denver	Reds 6, Rockies 0	65-91, .417
September 26	Denver	Rockies 12, Reds 7	66-91, .420
September 28	San Francisco	Giants 6, Rockies 4	66-92, .418
September 29	San Francisco	Rockies 5, Giants 3	67-92, .421
October 1	Atlanta	Braves 7, Rockies 4	67-93, .419
October 2	Atlanta	Braves 10, Rockies 1	67-94, .416
October 3	Atlanta	Braves 5, Rockies 3	67-95, .414

ABOUT THE AUTHOR

BOB KRAVITZ is a sports columnist for the *Rocky Mountain News*, where he has worked since 1990. He was previously a columnist for the Cleveland *Plain Dealer* and has written for *The* (Bergen) *Record*, *The San Diego Union*, *The Pittsburgh Press*, and *Sports Illustrated*. He and his family live in Littleton, Colorado.